D0705338

Freedom of Choice

FREEDOM OF CHOICE

Vouchers in American Education

Jim Carl

Praeger Series on American Political Culture
Jon L. Wakelyn and Michael J. Connolly, Series Editors

 PRAEGER

AN IMPRINT OF ABC-CLIO, LLC
Santa Barbara, California • Denver, Colorado • Oxford, England

Library of Congress Cataloging-in-Publication Data

Carl, Jim.
 Freedom of choice : vouchers in American education / Jim Carl.
  p. cm. — (Praeger series on American political culture)
 Includes bibliographical references and index.
  ISBN 978-0-313-39327-3 (hardcopy : alk. paper) — ISBN 978-0-313-39328-0 (ebook)
 1. Educational vouchers—United States. 2. School choice—United States. 3. Federal
aid to education—United States. I. Title.
 LB2828.8.C37 2011
 379.1'110973—dc23   2011017335

ISBN: 978-0-313-39327-3
EISBN: 978-0-313-39328-0

15   14   13   12   11   1   2   3   4   5

This book is also available on the World Wide Web as an eBook.
Visit www.abc-clio.com for details.

Praeger
An Imprint of ABC-CLIO, LLC

ABC-CLIO, LLC
130 Cremona Drive, P.O. Box 1911
Santa Barbara, California 93116-1911

This book is printed on acid-free paper ∞

Manufactured in the United States of America

To Barbara

CONTENTS

LIST OF TABLES

LIST OF FIGURES

LIST OF MAPS

SERIES FOREWORD

In describing the development of American literature from colonial settlement to the early 20th century, Harvard professor Barrett Wendell noted that Britain and America began as one, particularly in shared language. "A common language, one grows to feel, is a closer bond than common blood," he wrote in *The Temper of the Seventeenth Century in English Literature* from 1904. "For at heart the truest community which men can know is community of ideals; and inextricably interwoven with the structure of any language—with its words, with its idioms, with its syntax, and nowadays even with its very orthography—are ideals which, recognized or not, have animated and shall animate to the end those who instinctively phrase their earthly experience in its terms." But after initial 17th-century settlement, the two diverged, leading ultimately to the 18th-century American Revolution. That divergence came from a lack of shared experience. While Britain rolled through the turbulence of urban growth, economic distress, and political revolution, America experienced "a period of almost stationary national temper" and retained its 17th-century idealism (what Wendell termed a delicate balance of common law rights with a sense of Biblical Right) long after Britain's had passed. Thus one common language came to be spoken in two entirely different nations. This divergence marked the creation not only of American literature, which emerged in full flower in the 19th century, but also a uniquely American political culture, a culture that Wendell could still see operating in the United States of William McKinley, Theodore Roosevelt, and Woodrow Wilson. This task, of understanding just what constitutes American political culture, what makes it unique from other nations as well as similar, and how that impacts our current understanding of national development continues to fascinate American historians.

American political culture itself is a diverse concept, but at its base marks the boundaries, constructed over 400 years, of our political discourse and understanding. We understand political change through a particular, historically developed, American lens, unique from other nations and their collective experience. How we learn political culture is also multifaceted: from friends and family, schools and universities, media sources, religious leaders and texts, or the community institutions that shape our daily experiences of life. Daniel Walker Howe, in his seminal *Political Culture of the American Whigs* (1979) defined political culture as "an evolving system of beliefs, attitudes, and techniques for solving problems, transmitted from generation to generation and finding expression in the innumerable activities that people learn; religion, child-rearing customs, the arts and professions, and, of course, politics." Jean Baker in her *Affairs of Party: The Political Culture of Northern Democrats in the Mid-Nineteenth Century* (1983) likewise noted that "Political Culture assumes that the attitudes, sentiments, and cognitions that inform and govern politics are not random arrangements, but represent (if only we could see them as an anthropologist does the tribal rites of Tikopia) coherent patterns that together form a meaningful whole." This collection of impressions and attitudes we call "American political culture," distinct from other national traditions, is framed by the intellectual debates, party clashes, partisan disputes, religious difficulties, and economic stresses experienced since the 18th century and earlier. Put differently, Alexander Hamilton and Thomas Jefferson have been dead since the early 19th century yet we still maneuver in the intellectual arena of political culture they constructed. American political culture, worthy of study in its own right, also helps frame contemporary policy disputes that rankle us in the 21st century. No debate over health care, environmental issues, foreign affairs, or economic policy occurs in a vacuum divorced from precedent, but is framed by developed and developing structures of political culture with roots stretching back hundreds of years.

The guiding theme of the Praeger Series in American Political Culture is explaining how cultural factors (education, family, community, etc.) and economic change (technological innovation, depression, prosperity, market alterations, etc.) intersect with political methods (elections, strategies, laws, policies, institutions, etc.) to shape human actions throughout American history. While the series exhibits a theme, it is understood broadly to encourage a wide array of new projects and scholars from many disciplines—history, politics, law, and philosophy, for example. We welcome diversity in approach to historical topics, like biography, institutional history, history of ideas, policy history, and the development of political structures, among others, but this series works within the discipline of history, not political science. We deal with political culture from a strictly historical perspective.

Jim Carl's work on the history of school voucher programs in the United States, *Freedom of Choice: Vouchers in American Education, 1954–2002*, helps us understand politics and political decision-making, and leads to the heart of American cultural values (and the "culture wars") of the past 60 years. By spotlighting the transformation of education policy, he aims at the heart of contemporary American political culture and the changes it underwent since the 1950s. Indeed, Carl turns the controversial issue of school vouchers into a narrative of American cultural values within its post–World War II political context. Instead of portraying them as an outgrowth of 1980s Reagan-era free market reforms as applied to public education, he skillfully illustrates how the voucher issue reaches back into the 1950s and the battles over racial segregation. Offended by forced public school integration after the 1954 Supreme Court's *Brown v. Topeka Board of Education* case, many southern communities grasped voucher programs as a method to maintain whites-only schools. Vouchers remained a remarkably versatile policy instrument, used for radically different purposes at different times: segregated southern schools in the 1950s and 1960s, parochial school funding in the 1960s, free market educational experiments as an antidote to bureaucracy in the 1970s, and urban school failings in the 1980s and 1990s. Different spokesmen for vouchers also emerged, from widely divergent ideological backgrounds, political cultures, and locales: the Louisiana segregationist Leander Perez, the Jesuit priest Father Virgil Blum in Milwaukee, the quixotic New Hampshire conservative Meldrim Thomson, and the Midwestern Republican governor Tommy Thompson. In postwar America, school vouchers became an education policy for all seasons.

A certain irony also presents itself in school vouchers, one that exposes a tension at the heart of American political culture. With voucher programs, governments spend money to promote and protect citizens' freedom of educational choice. Put differently, "big government" finances educational initiatives that, in their intent, are inherently hostile to government-directed educational initiatives. Statism funds anti-statism; Hamilton bankrolls Jefferson. Reform of public education remains a heated political issue today—witness the continued interest in vouchers, but also charter schools—and Carl's historical contextualization of educational battles is effective and timely.

—Jon L. Wakelyn and Michael J. Connolly, Series Editors

PREFACE

When the U.S. Supreme Court ruled in favor of publicly funded vouchers to religious schools in 2002, observers predicted their rapid expansion to other cities and states. While that has not happened at the rate observers envisaged, voucher advocates remain on the wings to remake American education into a system characterized by public funding and private delivery of services. School vouchers remain the most radical of a basket of reforms that have been labeled, since the 1980s, as "school choice." Voucher proponents blazed the trail for other forms of school choice that have become commonplace—public school open enrollment, tuition tax credits, and, especially, charter schools. Yet, the origins of school vouchers have not been widely studied.

In the United States, school vouchers began as tuition grants in southern states—a strategy with roots in massive resistance to the civil rights movement. While southern tuition grants were the only functioning voucher programs in the 1950s and 1960s, vouchers also had appeal for parochial school supporters seeking a share of federal support, and, at a more abstract level, for neo-classical economists uncomfortable with the New Deal. In the early 1970s the federal government sought to interest cities and states in free-market voucher plans, while Catholic and other religious leaders continued to lobby for public funds, some of them warming to the idea of vouchers. By the 1980s and 1990s, proponents of school vouchers added a new purpose—a means of counteracting real and perceived shortcomings of urban public schools. To date, there has been very little historical study of school vouchers that ties together their origins in the 1950s as a means

to maintain racial segregation, with their contemporary role as a mechanism to improve big city public schools. This book fills some of that gap.

One of the fascinating aspects to school vouchers is the wide array of
supporters they attracted since the Supreme Court's 1954 *Brown v. Board
of Education* decision: white supremacists, black nationalists, Catholic
and other religious leaders, free-market economists, free-schoolers, private school advocates, linguistic minorities, and left-leaning social scientists. The public schools have always had their critics; beginning in the
1950s disillusionment with and resistance to changes in the public schools
motivated parents and others to consider vouchers. Sometimes, efforts
to enact school vouchers led to strange bedfellows, with proponents of
various political stripes favoring the same public policy. But in spite of
such political and cultural diversity, the movements' most powerful advocates were almost always political conservatives. A history of school
vouchers provides a window with which to understand the evolution of
American conservatism. The conservatism that emerged from the World
War II years was in disrepute. It was also shot through with sectional and
religious divisions. But conservative ideology and activism, pitted against
the backdrop of a resilient welfare state, began to attract widened popular
support. Since the 1980s especially, American conservatism has shifted
the nation's entire political culture to the right. The rise of school vouchers, a policy that helped unify a variety of outlooks and sensibilities under
a consumerist banner, contributed to the rebirth of the conservative
movement.

In this history of school vouchers in the United States, I narrate their
checkered past in four states—Louisiana, New Hampshire, Wisconsin, and
Ohio. In the first two states, school vouchers had brief trajectories; in the
latter two, they gained permanence, becoming a part of the educational
landscape. While this work focuses on the development of school vouchers in these four states, I endeavor to make it more than a running account
of voucher "cases." Rather, I wanted to write a history of school vouchers
against the backdrop of political, religious, and cultural changes that influenced men and women to look to vouchers as a means of restoring educational freedoms—real or imagined—that their parents took for granted.
Most important to voucher supporters were what they perceived to be their
rights to freedom of association (parents, not the public schools, should
determine with whom their children associate and how their children are
educated), freedom of religion (parents' rights to educate their children in
religious settings to avoid public school secularism) and freedom of markets (choices of parents and entrepreneurs produce better schools than
public education monopolies).

My interest in school vouchers began in graduate school, where I studied comparative history in preparation for a Ph.D. in educational policy studies. At the time, school voucher controversies were unfolding before my eyes, first in Wisconsin with the 1990 Milwaukee Parental Choice Program and then in Ohio with the 1995 Cleveland Scholarship and Tutoring Program. School voucher debates, in the 1990s, helped lay bare for me that my personal position on school politics was, to a large degree, derived from my educational experiences as well as my class background and trajectory. To me the answer came easily—the best way to improve education was by ensuring every student a place in a well-funded, expertly staffed, and racially integrated public school. "Why turn to vouchers?" I asked myself. "We should all be working for better public schools." Meanwhile, I lived in public school districts where the schools my children attended, by nearly any measure, were of high quality—Madison, Wisconsin, and Shaker Heights, Ohio. In my relocation to Ohio, however, I did not consider moving to Cleveland, the city abutting Shaker Heights, because of my perceptions of what big city schools would mean for the education of my children.

As implemented in Milwaukee, Cleveland, and elsewhere in the 1990s, school vouchers provided options to parents who lacked the private resources to move to school districts with good educational reputations. "We too would like to see improved public schools," parents who were voucher proponents seemed to be telling me. "But our children need good schools now." A compelling argument. And, from the perspective of family self-interest in an era in which supporters of public-private hybrid forms of schools seem to set the parameters of school reform debates, it's an argument that seems irrefutable. But in the long run, it's also an argument in need of historical perspective—as I hope these pages will demonstrate—because schools vouchers served economic and social agendas that took priority over crafting high-quality schools open to all. This book does not seek answers on whether vouchers "work" in the sense of raising academic achievement beyond what students could achieve if they remained in public schools (I have no doubts that, for some students, in some schools, they do). Rather, it sets out to identify, over a 50-year period, the political actors behind vouchers, the interests they served, and the aims they had for the students. As is often the case in educational policy debates, in the controversies over school vouchers the goal of creating and preserving quality schools served as a tried and true rhetorical device. In the series of movements that established voucher programs, however, the more important goals were less universal and more parochial—preserving racially segregated schools that local authorities could control, securing public funding for religious schools, winning private school places for students from low-income families, and opening up school districts to compete with private schools for the same public dollars.

The Milwaukee program figured prominently in my 1995 dissertation, "The Politics of Education in a New Key." I sought to explain why school reform in two nearby cities—Chicago and Milwaukee—could embrace such different kinds of school policy: the 1988 Chicago School Reform Act provided parents and local residents greater authority in the governance of their local schools, whereas the 1990 Milwaukee Parental Choice Program provided funds that enabled parents to enroll their children in private schools. In Milwaukee and Chicago, different political alignments led to different school reforms. More recently, I set out to understand the political alignments that generated voucher programs in other cities and states. In Ohio, I followed closely the statehouse and Cleveland debates surrounding the voucher program that emerged there. During a sabbatical semester, I assembled sources on the origins of the Cleveland program and traveled to New Hampshire as a means of understanding a short-lived voucher program from the 1970s that federal and state authorities wanted implemented. In the course of my interviews and archival research, I noted that vouchers advocates in New Hampshire and Wisconsin distanced their proposed programs from earlier tuition grant programs that were in operation in several southern states from the late 1950s to the late 1960s. Hence I consulted sources that shed light on southern grants-in-aid programs. Since Louisiana had a large Catholic population in its major city, much like New Hampshire, Wisconsin, and Ohio had in theirs, I focused my efforts on Louisiana. Looking at these four states contributes to our understanding of the ebbs and flows of school vouchers as national phenomena.

I have come to realize that writing a book is a joint effort—not only did I rely on the work historians, social scientists, and educators from my past, those who were formative in my own education, but I also depended on relationships I have cultivated over the years with colleagues, professionals, friends, and family. I could not have written this book without them, though any mistakes herein are entirely my own. Several professors at the University of Wisconsin and elsewhere have helped me to sharpen my thinking about U.S. culture and politics, as well as educational privatization in general and school vouchers in particular. They are Michael Apple, Nancy Beadie, Sigal Ben-Porath, Randall Curren, Adam Fairclough, Michael Fultz, Bob Hampel, Andreas Kazamias, Bob Koehl, David Labaree, Henry Levin, Nancy MacLean, Maggie Nash, Chris Ogren, Dan Pekarsky, Bill Reese, John Rury, Argun Saatcioglu, Fran Schrag, Kim Tolley, and Jon Zimmerman.

Many of the people closest to the debates over school vouchers granted interviews. I thank Dismas Becker, George Boas, David Brennan, Barbara Byrd-Bennett, Leslie Darnieder, Steve Dold, Denis Doyle, Mae Duggan,

Patrick Flood, Tom Fonfara, Michael Fox, Milton Friedman, Howard Fuller, Wanda Jean Green, Herbert Grover, Larry Harwell, Douglas Haselow, Mikel Holt, Christopher Jencks, Fannie Lewis, Sara Morales, Martha Owen, Howard Phillips, Callista Robinson, Patrick Sweeney, Michael White, Julie Underwood, and Susan Wing.

Cleveland State University, its College of Education and Human Services, its Department of Curriculum and Foundations, and its Center for Urban Education generously supported my research for this book by providing a one-semester leave, funds to consult archives in several states, and a warm and congenial climate in which to share my work. My friend and colleague at Cleveland State, David Adams, provided wise guidance over the years as well as commenting on chapter drafts. Other faculty and staff at Cleveland State have also been helpful, especially William Barrow, Cliff Bennett, Kathy Dobda, Anne Galletta, Rodger Govea, Sharon Jefferson, Wenqing Kang, Eileen Logan, Joyce Mastboom, Ralph Mawdsley, Jay McLoughlin, R.D. Nordgren, Justin Perry, Fran Peterman, Michael Schwartz, Mark Tebeau, and Brian Yusko. I would also like to thank my graduate assistants at Cleveland State University who tracked down sources, made phone calls, read through drafts of chapters, and helped sharpen my thinking on the origins of school vouchers. They are Tamea Caver, Ellon Dedo, Kif Francis Deepak Garg, Jim Gutowski, Saygin Koc, Lovleen Singh, and Yasmine Suliman. Finally, the thoughtful exchanges I have had over the years with students in my classes on urban education policy and the history of American education have provided me with clarity and even joy.

Archivists and librarians welcomed me and provided expert assistance. They guided me through the sources, helped me formulate better questions, and suggested fresh ways to look at historical actors whom I thought I had figured out. I would like to thank Rachel Bauer, Margaret Burzynski-Bays, William Fliss, Allen Fisher, Donna Gilbreth, Christopher Harter, Sarah Hartwell, James Lien, Mary Mayo, Doug McCabe, Laura McLemore, Benoit Shoja, Ann Sindelar, Brenda Billips Square, Jane Stoeffler, Irene Wainwright, and Lisa Werling.

I am especially grateful to series editors Michael Connolly and John Wakelyn for their kind advice and encouragement, as well as for their understanding, from the first, that education politics is as fine a vantage point as any from which to view American social history. A special thanks is due, also, to Michael Millman at Praeger—his professionalism and care made writing this book a pleasure. The team at ABC-CLIO also put me at ease. I thank Vicki Moran, Erin Ryan, Drew Tillman, and Valentina Tursini. Thanks also to L. Martindale for the copyediting assistance.

Portions of this work have been published elsewhere. For New Hampshire I extend a discussion from 2008 in the *Harvard Educational Review* called "Free Marketeers, Policy Wonks, and Yankee Democracy: School Vouchers in New Hampshire 1973–1976." The chapter on Wisconsin revises relevant sections of my 1995 dissertation, "The Politics of Education in a New Key: The 1988 Chicago School Reform Act and the 1990 Milwaukee Parental Choice Program." It also draws from a 1996 *Teachers College Record* article titled "Unusual Allies: Elite and Grass Roots Origins of Parental Choice in Milwaukee." I thank the *Harvard Educational Review* and *Teachers College Record* for permitting me to use these works.

I am grateful to all my good friends who have helped me professionally and personally during the research and writing of this book. Some lent me guest bedrooms on my travels, some offered creative suggestions on the book's organization, some made improvements to drafts of chapters, and all helped lift my spirits. I thank, especially, Michael Bemis and Duane Hansen, Chris Boehm, Michael Charney, Susan Flood, Nick Glass and M. J. Bauman, Terrance and Holly Humphrey, Tom Karoff, David Levine, Bill O'Conner, Larry Schulman, Mike Shaut and Terrese Tuchscher, and Guy Williams.

My family provided invaluable support and encouragement—my children Jenna, Luke, Michael and Trevor Carl; my son-in-law Dave Soskin; my parents Charles and Julianne Carl; my brothers and sisters John Carl, Helen Aouad, William Carl, Anne Carl, and Mary Benedetto; and my cousins Nanette and Paul Bracken, Walter and Meredith Carl, and Kathy Riopelle. Words are not enough to express my gratitude for the love and kindness given me by my wife, Barbara Carl. This book is dedicated to her.

Chapter 1

FREEDOM

On August 29, 2005, Hurricane Katrina churned through the Gulf Coast with 150-mile-per-hour winds and storm surges 25 feet high. The hurricane leveled buildings in coastal Louisiana and Mississippi counties and breached levees protecting New Orleans, putting some 80 percent of the city underwater. Among the 1,815 fatalities in southern Louisiana and Mississippi, which disproportionately struck residents who were older and poorer, at least 62 were under the age of 18.[1] Damage to school infrastructure was extensive. In the New Orleans public schools alone, 118 of the district's 126 school buildings sustained major damage, and the school system closed for the year. The parochial schools did not fare much better—in the eight civil parishes of the Archdiocese of New Orleans, hurricanes Katrina and Rita damaged 1,100 of the more than 1,200 properties that it owned. The destruction and dislocations of the storm and its aftermath overwhelmed state and local authorities as they scrambled to resume the education of some 372,000 students that the hurricane displaced.[2]

Education vouchers figured prominently in the federal relief efforts. Noting that the four Louisiana counties in and around New Orleans had higher private school attendance rates than the national average, on September 15, 2005, U.S. Secretary of Education Margaret Spellings earmarked $488 million for payments of up to $7,500 per student "to compensate families for the costs associated with attending these private schools." This aid to private school families represented more than 25 percent of the $1.9 billion in proposed hurricane relief for elementary and secondary education in the two states. Responses to Secretary Spellings's decision were predictable. Voucher proponents observed that the storm destroyed private schools along with public ones, so federal aid ought to include all the schools. Clint Bolick, president of the Alliance for School Choice and a long-time veteran of the "voucher wars" in the courts, added that the "abysmal condition of the New Orleans public schools" contributed to the high private school enrollment rate. On the other side of the voucher aisle, opponents argued that the Bush administration was using the hurricane opportunistically to widen federal aid to private schools. "Vouchers do nothing to solve the problems of Hurricane Katrina," declared National Education Association President Reg Weaver. "It is just simply not the time to open up a policy debate on vouchers."[3]

But the ground for a policy debate had already been tilled, and in a sense Hurricane Katrina brought vouchers full circle, back to the South where the first efforts to apply them as an alternative to the public schools began. In 1958, the Louisiana legislature established publicly funded tuition grants for children attending private schools. Supporters passed this law to circumvent federally sanctioned racial desegregation and limited the tuition grants to districts under federal court orders. In this earlier "massive resistance" incantation of school vouchers, which the federal court struck down in 1967 and 1968, the state of Louisiana spearheaded a tuition grants program that the federal government opposed, and the plan excluded the participation of parochial schools. In the Hurricane Katrina version, the federal government spearheaded a vouchers initiative that included parochial schools, and this time the largest school district targeted, New Orleans, was officially desegregated, albeit with a student enrollment that was overwhelmingly black. Nevertheless, in both the 1958 and the 2005 versions, taxpayer dollars favored white students. In the earlier tuition grants program that dated to the reaction to the Supreme Court's 1954 *Brown v. Board* ruling, the state of Louisiana favored the creation of an extensive network of schools for whites only, many housed in erstwhile public school buildings. In the 2005 program, white students already attended private and parochial schools in greater proportions than black students.[4]

From a policy that most Americans in the 1950s associated with southern segregationists, however, vouchers in the first decade of the 21st century were often perceived as an urban school reform that was most helpful to racial and linguistic minority students. Vouchers became a part of the mainstream in educational policy, embraced as cutting edge not only by President George W. Bush and in several state legislatures around the nation but also among wide swaths of the population North and South, including some support within demographic cross-sections that, prior to the 1950s, were not typically associated with private school attendance—European American and African American families whose identities were working class and Protestant. What explains the increasing popularity of school vouchers? How did they become a respectable solution to the perennial tensions inherent to mass schooling in a democracy?

SETTING THE PARAMETERS

In essence, an education voucher is a mechanism for the public funding of education. Tax dollars follow the student and help pay the costs of education at whatever school the student attends—a pre-existing public school, a pre-existing private school, or a new school established to educate students with vouchers. A combination of parental decisions and school decisions determine admissions and enrollments, and for this reason voucher observers, at least since the 1980s, considered such programs as examples of school reforms under the monikers of "parental choice" or "school choice." The education voucher offers a stark contrast to the traditional way that public dollars are spent for elementary and secondary education in the United States. At the risk of oversimplifying, in the traditional form local school boards levy taxes and assign students to schools, with the proviso that district authorities will educate any school-age student who resides within the district, but that any such student may attend a private school instead, albeit without tax support. Vouchers, by contrast, break traditional public education in two—the state continues to fund students and regulate the schools, but public funding follows the student to whatever school the student attends, be it a pre-existing private school (sectarian or secular), a new private school established to enroll students with vouchers, or a public school funded through vouchers but governed through traditional means.

This book takes both a long view and a short view of educational vouchers. In the long view, advocates first enacted school vouchers in the 1950s, not in the 1990s as is often supposed. Southern state legislatures established tuition grants programs to maintain racially separate and unequal schools in the face of a series of movements and lawsuits that challenged customary Jim Crow education policies. Riding on a crest of white resistance to the civil rights movement, educational vouchers were first proposed in Georgia in 1951 and then in several other states of the former Confederacy by the end of the decade. The rhetoric of most of the early advocates of tuition grants for elementary and secondary students was not only Jim Crow, it was also Cold War: freedom of choice was a patriotic alternative to a civil rights movement tinged by communism and it was a way out of the growing collectivism of public schools regulated by distant federal bureaucrats, according to advocates. The efficiencies generated by competition in an educational marketplace governed by the invisible hand of parental choices—this was the script that germinated amid the reactions to *Brown*, but it took at least a generation before free-market justifications lost their regional association with the preservation of white supremacy and became viable on the national stage.

By the late 1960s the perception and, to an extent, the reality of urban schooling in free-fall, both public and private, brought new voucher supporters to the fold, who took their places alongside the free marketeers, but even though the new battlegrounds moved outside of the South, racial politics were never far behind. Shaky coalitions of new and old voucher proponents sought, in the late 1960s, to revitalize northern urban schools and protect the students who attended them—usually students of color— from the bureaucratic slights of big-city public school systems. However, their efforts to tie vouchers to identity politics, usually in the guise of "community schools" and "community control," did not result in any lasting voucher programs. Proponents of Catholic education also took a closer look at voucher programs in this period, as Catholic enrollments in urban parish schools began to fall. In the early 1970s the federal government, under the auspices of the Office of Economic Opportunity, sought to sponsor a series of voucher programs in various states, partly as an alternative to mandatory school desegregation, partly as a strategy to open public schools to competition and innovation. School boards, school administrators, and especially teachers unions opposed the federal initiatives; this coalition of public school supporters prevented private schools from participating. Office of Economic Opportunity–sponsored plans resulted in a single program in Alum Rock, a school district in San Jose, California. It was essentially an open enrollment plan that excluded private schools. The most ambitious federal voucher plan—the one with the most free-market overtones—was formulated for New Hampshire, in which a handful of school districts considered a voucher program that included private schools. In 1976, however, New Hampshire voters declined to implement the plans.

In the 1980s state lawmakers began to formulate voucher plans for their states, this time without active federal support. While legislatures rejected all proposed voucher programs that were statewide, proposals that gained support were targeted to cities and billed as experimental programs that could help improve the urban schools. This new purpose trumped constitutional concerns that religious schools would rely increasingly on public funding. The Milwaukee Parental Choice Program began in 1990, for students attending non-sectarian private schools, and the Cleveland Scholarship and Tutoring Program followed in 1995, for students attending religious and secular private schools. The Wisconsin legislature expanded the Milwaukee program to include religious schools in 1995. Although lawsuits challenged the experimental urban programs as unconstitutional state promotion of religious schools, the U.S. Supreme Court, in its *Zelman v. Simmons-Harris* decision, upheld the Cleveland program in 2002. This triumph for school vouchers proved fleeting, however, not because of a groundswell of opposition to expanded voucher plans, but rather because the center of gravity in educational privatization already shifted to a competing public-private hybrid form—the charter school.

That's the long of it. The short view is that this study confines itself to voucher movements in the post–World War II era. There are 19th- and even 18th-century antecedents to educational vouchers in the United States that are not addressed here. To take a well-known example, in 1792 Anglo-American revolutionary Thomas Paine proposed a vouchers-like scheme for the education of children from poor families in England. In another famous instance, in 1840 New York State governor William Seward floated a proposal whereby public school funds were to be directed to public and parochial schools based on attendance, in a sense resurrecting a mechanism, abolished in New York City in the 1820s, whereby state funds were distributed to sectarian schools on a per pupil basis.[5] The struggle to win public funding for Catholic education achieved a crescendo of sorts in the 1870s, even reaching into the fractious presidential election of 1876 that marked Reconstruction's end.[6] The late 19th century also marked the religious limits of public education in the United States—sectarian religion, for the most part, was hereafter outside the bounds of the public school. In a final example, academies were in widespread existence for much of the 19th century. These secondary schools, which were funded something like late 20th-century voucher programs, received public funding on a per pupil basis, which supplemented the tuition that the academies also charged. Indeed, historians of 19th-century education are beginning to reappraise the growth of modern schooling as both a trigger of the market revolution and a consequence of a growing education marketplace.[7]

More recently, in the late 20th century, efforts to privatize public education have encompassed tools other than vouchers. Education management companies, tuition tax credits, and charter schools are some of the newer entities to join the older constellation of private vendors that continue to market textbooks, school construction, transportation services, and the like to the public schools. But such forms of privatization are not the same as vouchers, and while I will touch on some of them as they interact with vouchers movements, this study is not intended to address all of the examples of public-private funding in American education. Nor does it cover the many state referenda on vouchers that emerged beginning in the 1970s, not because voters turned down all such proposals for statewide voucher programs (they did), but because of the confines of space. The parameters here are limited to school vouchers in postwar America, with the Supreme

Court's 1954 *Brown* decision marking the start and its 2002 *Zelman v. Simmons-Harris* decision marking the finish.[8]

As a work of contemporary political history, there were myriad actors who circulated in and around the movements for school vouchers, each representing specific interests and, in turn, shaped by distinctive social contexts. Such an array of participants active simultaneously in several regions of the country does not readily lend itself to a neat, coherent narrative. If what happened was that vouchers, after an initial phase as a weapon in the arsenal of white resistance to racial desegregation, had an apotheosis as a color-blind policy of urban school reform grounded in the sanctity of market and family, "the facts are considerably messier than that simple tale," to borrow a phrase from historian Noel Ignatiev.[9] As I hope to demonstrate in these pages, this is, nevertheless, the essential story and the most judicious narrative to erect over the complicated evidence on school vouchers in the United States. Although vouchers attracted a variety of advocates who supported them for various reasons, there were nevertheless differences in the amounts of power they wielded. And whereas a smattering of left-leaning liberals and civil rights advocates looked to vouchers to redistribute educational opportunities on a more equal basis, they did not lead the charge. As vouchers movements shifted out of the South, social and economic conservatives provided their driving force, and together with supporters of religious schooling and educational entrepreneurship they eclipsed the efforts of those who supported them as a means for racial and economic equality in American education.

There is at least one other way to tell the story. In this alternative, we can consider vouchers as a "policy tool," one that is neutral in and of itself. In this version, vouchers as a mechanism of organizational and fiduciary control are separate from the politics. Money flows from governments to parents to be used for tuition at schools that meet state standards. At root the voucher is a neutral mechanism, but policy makers politicize it; they call upon the voucher to meet various aims in a pluralistic society.[10]

In this framework, voucher proponents can be placed in single categories. White supremacists look to them to maintain single-race schools. Private and parochial school supporters favor them as a means to defray the costs of tuition for parents who already pay taxes that support public schools. Free market advocates use them to bring competition among schools in which parents select schools for their children in an education market characterized by variations in quality and philosophy. Advocates of educational equality support vouchers as a pragmatic strategy, in which policy makers index vouchers progressively so children from poor families can make up for their modest cultural capital with larger vouchers attractive to schools. Working-class parents view them as an equalizer to the educational options that middle-class families already enjoy. Urban school reformers see them as a promising experiment. Advocates of homogeneous educational settings, whether racial, religious, cultural, linguistic, or single-sex, look to vouchers as a means to stay viable. Educational entrepreneurs view them as a means to enter the education market. Educators in schools with declining enrollments look to them as a means to reverse the trend. The list could go on, but the point here is that the various constituencies do not necessarily have anything in common as they reach for vouchers in the educational policy toolkit. There is much truth to this perspective. Not only is it is far-fetched to cast all advocates of vouchers as fellow-travelers, but many were outright hostile to each other. Moreover, vouchers systems can be engineered for contradictory purposes. Whether individual liberty or educational equality, curricular uniformity or innovation, sectarianism or secularism—vouchers systems can be designed to achieve various goals.[11]

Nonetheless, the evidence marshaled here indicates that social and political conservatives had the upper hand in generating school vouchers programs in postwar America. Defenders of traditions—the southern social order, the free market, religious values, ethnic solidarity, parental authority—created school voucher programs to defend children from threats real or perceived, such as civil rights and Black Power, secularism, permissiveness, bureaucratic indifference, and—above all—public schools that no longer met their needs.

FREEDOM TO CHOOSE

Vouchers emerged within an historical context that began with the advocates' justifications amid a postwar scene that was undergoing significant change—geographic, economic, political, and ideological. It was on the terrain of ideology that unlikely coalitions of vouchers supporters came together, and the predominant ideology of school vouchers can be distilled down to one word: freedom. School vouchers, in the view of most advocates, are at heart an expression of freedom, something that has always been a defining principle of what it means to be an American. Freedom is a concept that many observers of education shy away from, whether historians, social scientists, or educators. For them, questions of equality and access have had more resonance than freedom and liberty, at least in the postwar era. But it is freedom—a plastic concept—that was the ideological spark for voucher movements, whether that has meant freedom for races, religions, markets, parents, or individuals. More than any other ideological trope, freedom is what gave education vouchers their populist appeal.

Freedom encompassed a large dose of liberalism, both as a political philosophy and as a political reality. Philosophically, liberalism takes the freedom of the individual as the basis of a good society; the state exists to prevent one individual's freedom from impinging on another's. As a philosophy, liberals divided over the size and the purpose of the state that is necessary to ensure liberty. As a political reality, liberalism arose in the Enlightenment to counter the feudal practice of social orders fixed at birth.[12]

According to historian Alan Brinkley, 20th-century American liberalism had three strands. The first was "laissez-faire liberalism," whereby the state encouraged economic and social marketplaces so that "individuals could pursue their goals freely and advance according to their own merits and achievements." The second strand, which he calls "reform liberalism" had origins in the Progressive era movements and had as its distinguishing characteristic "the need to protect individuals, communities, and the government itself from excessive corporate power" and "ensure the citizenry a basic level of human subsistence and dignity." In this guise capitalism replaced feudalism as the most significant threat to individual freedom. In the third strand, capitalist reform traded center stage with identity politics, whereby individuals organized into social groups asserted power in a "rights-based liberalism." In Brinkley's view, this third stage emerged, in part, as a consequence of the blunting of reform liberalism. It is the second two strands that most Americans think of when they hear the word "liberal," but the stand of liberalism that has had the most import for education vouchers has been the first, laissez-faire variety which, to a large degree, eclipsed the reform and rights-based liberalisms that were in ascendance until the 1960s.[13]

"Freedom is a rare and delicate plant," remarked Milton Friedman in 1962. He was the public intellectual perhaps most associated with laissez-faire liberalism and school vouchers. His writings on vouchers spanned 50 years, 1955–2005. "Government is necessary to preserve our freedom," continued Friedman. "It is an instrument through which we can exercise our freedom; yet by concentrating power in political hands, it is also a threat to freedom." Writing during the Cold War, Friedman stated that "competitive capitalism" was freedom's bulwark, a far superior alternative to communism. Not only did capitalism serve to check the concentrated power of the state, but the ideal state, according to Friedman, was one whose power was "dispersed" and whose primary missions were to "preserve law and order, to enforce private contracts, [and] to foster competitive markets." The government, then, was to serve as referee for competitive capitalism, and, wherever possible, its role was to extend markets rather than concentrate its own power. Government had good reason to educate its citizenry, according to Friedman, but this could be best accomplished by using public funds to foster a competitive marketplace in education. Ergo, the education voucher.[14]

"Rights-based" liberals also used freedom to justify school vouchers. In the 1950s South, for example, resistors to the civil rights movement, whites who sought to preserve a Jim Crow social order embraced "freedom of association" as the value they sought to protect. Desegregation prevented people from associating with whom they wished. More to the point, school desegregation interfered with the "rights" of parents to have their children attend school with those of the same race. According to historian Kevin Kruse, white resistance was not only a question of segregationists "fighting *against* the rights of others." They were also defending their own individual freedoms—"the 'right' to select their neighbors, their employees, and their children's classmates, the 'right' to do what they pleased with their private property and personal businesses, and, perhaps most important, the 'right' to remain free from what they saw as dangerous encroachments by the federal government." Identity politics in education, spurred on by the civil rights movement, encompassed minority racial and linguistic groups as well. For example, sociologist Kenneth B. Clark, writing in 1967, noted that "the goal of democratic education must be to free Americans of the blinding and atrophying shackles of racism." Clark was the author of the famous doll studies cited in the *Brown* decision, but now he had grown skeptical that desegregation within the public school system would have robust positive results for black children. Alternatives to the public schools were needed. Several school reformers in the late 1960s, such as Theodore Sizer, echoed Clark's views, and advocated for "publicly financed black private schools," in part as an alternative to the public system's "total monopoly over ghetto education."[15]

Those seeking to bring "community control" to black schools often looked to the Catholic schools for inspiration. Catholics had created, several generations before, a school system that was independent of the public schools. The American Catholic Church in the post–World War II era had undergone its own transformation in its position on freedom of religion. Always a minority religion in the United States, Catholics understandably looked favorably on the First Amendment separation of church and state. But such sentiment was often downplayed. In the 1930s, for example, American Catholic thought was supportive of authoritarian regimes of Europe. Secure in the belief that Catholicism was—in Protestant theologian Reinhold Niebuhr's words—the "one true church," Catholic theologians often endorsed the assistance that governments with established Catholic religion could provide. Indeed, Catholic churches were privileged and instrumental to the power wielded in fascist states such as Spain, Portugal, and Austria.

World War II changed all that: American theologians began to view the separation of church and state not as a promoter of secularism, but, rather, as a means for religious liberty. This ethos of the freedom of individual human conscience in religious matters helped open the doors for some Catholic educators to turn to education vouchers as a means to shore up Catholic education, rather than lobbying only for direct forms of state support in areas such as auxiliary services and transportation.[16]

THE FEDERALIST STATE

Due to the decentralized structure of the American federal system, Friedman could be assured that government in the U.S. context was "dispersed," and as such, the Byzantine structure of American education provided spaces for reforms such as school vouchers. It was possible to create pockets of radical reforms rather than change the system whole cloth. Layers of governance enabled education reforms such as vouchers programs to coexist outside of the orbit of centralized national control. Moreover, overlapping jurisdictions provided foils that supporters used to their benefit. However, the same federalism also revealed limits to school vouchers. In the 1990s, for the first time, a majority of voters hailed from the suburbs. In many affluent, homogeneous suburbs the voters taxed themselves to maintain school districts of high quality. In such instances, there was less popular support for vouchers and greater support for "our" public schools. And in rural America, where revenue for high-quality public schools was often in short supply, it was nevertheless impractical to establish alternatives to traditional public schools because the low population density could only support a limited number of them. Schooling in districts with stable tax bases—arguably the bulk of public education in America—seemed immune to calls for opening the system to radical change. Local school districts organized within the federalist system have been vulnerable to school vouchers only to the extent that their local revenues have been insufficient to meet educational needs.

While federal, state, and local governments all exercised authority over the schools, the entities with the most responsibility were the 50 states. In other words state legislatures and constitutions, rather than the federal government or city charters, play the controlling role. Among the states there was nevertheless considerable variation, as the educational provisions of the following three states attest. According to Ohio's constitution, in force since 1851, "The General Assembly shall make such provisions, as...will secure a thorough and efficient system of common schools throughout the state." In Louisiana's 1974 constitution the wording is vaguer: "The legislature shall provide for the education of the people of the state and shall establish and maintain a public education system." And in perhaps the most opaque reference of all, New Hampshire's 1783 constitution states that "knowledge and learning, generally diffused through a community, being essential to the preservation of a free government... it shall be the duty of the legislators and magistrates... to cherish the interest of literature and the sciences, and all seminaries and public schools." Not only do state educational provisions vary, but so do their interpretations by legislatures, governors, and court systems.[17]

In the last half of the 20th century, state governments increased their authority over public and private schooling considerably. Many states, either individually or through the efforts of the National Governors' Association, raised graduation requirements and added proficiency tests and curriculum standards. Moreover, over the past 30 years there was an up-tick in the amount of state dollars earmarked to fund education, public and private. State courts initiated some of this increase by ruling that large district-to-district differences in school funding violated state constitutional provisions. For example, Ohio's Supreme Court ruled in 1997 that the provision of a "thorough and efficient" system of schools made the state's current system of educational funding unconstitutional. States responded in various ways (and rarely to equalize funding in the districts) but the net effect was rising state contributions to school districts coupled with more state control over curriculum and instruction. In this context of growing state centralization, school vouchers were, on the surface at least, something of an anomaly.[18]

Although the states played the primary role in organizing and providing for elementary and secondary education, they recognized local school districts as the governmental agencies with direct educational authority. Indeed, localism in public education is a tradition that stretches back to colonial times. Currently, there are some 15,000 school districts in the United States, most with elected school boards (Ohio has 602, Louisiana has 64, and New Hampshire has 246 districts). Although state authority in public education grew considerably in the postwar era, it was still in the local entities where the nuts and bolts of education funding and governing took place. On average, "local school districts raise almost half the money used to support schools" and it is the local revenue that generates most of the differences in school district funding.[19]

The federal government also played a role in shaping American education, but compared to other countries, the national role was a small one. In terms of funding, for example, on average less than 8 percent of public support came from federal sources since 1965. Since the federal constitution does not mention education, and since, according to the Tenth

Amendment, powers outside the province of the federal government are reserved for the states or the people, the federal role is largely one of ensuring that schools uphold the people's rights enumerated in the federal constitution. It has an advisory and hortatory role in educational leadership. Efforts that began in the 1950s to provide across-the-board federal funds for states to distribute to schools as their legislatures saw fit "foundered" on disputes over racial segregation, parochial schooling, and federal control. Even though educators desperately needed funds to build and refurbish schools and hire teachers to meet the challenges of the baby boom and internal migration, for example, federal leaders could not agree on sending along money to states that segregated students, to schools that had religious affiliations, and to the complaints of local authorities that the federal government would have too much power. Federal policy usually tied funding to specific programs, some of them experimental, rather than to open-ended grants to the states.[20]

Beginning in the 1970s and gaining momentum in the administrations of Ronald Reagan, George H. W. Bush, Bill Clinton, and George W. Bush, however, the federal government began to question the condition of the nation's public schools. In *A Nation at Risk* (1983) the federal Department of Education used a discourse of crisis—"a rising tide of mediocrity," "an act of war"—to argue that increased academic achievement could only come through a reassertion of traditional academic standards. With the federal No Child Left Behind Act of 2002, the national government went further than ever in setting such standards. Moreover, the federal government encouraged experimentation to achieve higher academic standards, providing a context favorable to pilot voucher programs.[21]

WELFARE STATE CONTRADICTION

Laissez-faire liberals and rights-based liberals often viewed the concentration of power in centralized governments as a threat to freedom—the postwar welfare state needed to be checked. Yet, there was a contradiction inherent in the postwar welfare state—it was a drain on the economy and it wielded power that threatened traditional organizational forms, therefore it had to be rolled back. But it was also essential for economic growth, financial security of families, and political liberties of individuals, and therefore it had to be extended. "The contradiction," according to political scientist Claus Offe, "is that while capitalism cannot coexist *with,* neither can it exist *without,* the welfare state." The welfare state grew as a political solution to an economic dilemma—the Great Depression indicated that the private sector was unable to insure capitalism's survival. In the industrialized bloc of economies led by the United States, businesses and organized labor reached an accord whereby government regulation and deficit spending for economic growth was welcomed, and in the immediate postwar era, the major U.S. political parties vied over which could better lead the expanding welfare state.[22]

State-supported schooling was characteristic of the American welfare state. In the education of human capital a degree of centralized, planned educational policy in the curriculum and in control of access was necessary to direct it where it was most needed for national prosperity, something that has been called the "social efficiency" purpose of schooling. Universal entry to formal education also helped insure that everyone had an equal educational starting point in the competition for jobs—differences in academic achievement were alleged to explain occupational hierarchies better than ascribed characteristics such as class, race, gender, religion, or region—at minimum, mass schooling made a "meritocracy" at least plausible. And finally, education played an important economic role even when discounting its role in training and directing human capital. "Almost one in four Americans work in schools either as students or staff," as the eminent historian of education David Tyack notes.[23]

As long as prosperity continued, as it did for much of the U.S. economy in the postwar boom, opposition to the welfare state was weak. By the late 1960s, however, worldwide economic restructuring, rising rates of inequality, and shifting political alignments exposed the welfare state's contradiction. There were a variety of stalemates in the attempts to limit the footprint of the welfare state and to roll back its regulative and social welfare provisions. While such rollbacks occurred in ways that either benefitted or harmed particular sectors of the population, they did not reduce the size of the state overall. Rather, political parties redeployed government services—reductions in taxes were coupled with increases in borrowing, reductions in social services were coupled with increases to the military and law enforcement, reductions in public provision of social benefits for the poorest Americans were coupled with funding for their private delivery, and reductions at the federal level were coupled with expanded state and local services. Moreover, the welfare state contradiction was not limited to the federal government. State governments, too, had their welfare state contradictions, as symbolized with the residential property tax revolt that began in California in 1978 and swept eastward.[24]

Public education has long been in the cross-hairs of such revolts. But privatization, at least in the form of K–12 vouchers, only occurred around the edges. On the surface, education vouchers were a promising form of funding that had precedents elsewhere—housing and nutrition, for example, where public funding and private delivery is common, in the forms of housing vouchers and food stamps. Moreover, in education itself there are voucher-like mechanisms for the delivery of federal aid. In higher education, for example, government grants and loans follow individual students to universities that are both public and private. However, the continued presence of the public school as a well-entrenched American social institution highlighted the welfare state contradiction and limited the appeal of the education voucher. Due to the welfare state contradiction, elementary and secondary education—unlike preschool and higher education—has remained mostly outside the voucher orbit. In the 1980s Congress cut back funding to K–12 schools and folded manifold categorical aid programs into bloc grants to the states. The Reagan administration even threatened to abolish the federal Department of Education. However, by century's end the federal government returned its support for elementary and secondary education to early 1980s levels. The well-entrenched nature of the public school, backed by the lobbying muscle of school boards and teacher organizations, organized powerful support for maintaining traditional public schools.[25]

Vouchers movements illustrate the welfare state contradiction in other ways also. Even in their early, segregationist guise, vouchers advocates reacted to an education policy that had welfare state overtones, since the archetypical civil rights decision, *Brown v. Board,* sought in part to shore up U.S. political and economic hegemony in the Cold War. Although school vouchers represented struggles over control of public education, contrary to the rhetoric of some opponents, they did not represent an end to the state's role in education. Rather, what was at stake was the purposes that would be served once state funding of education was uncoupled from state delivery of education. Rather than asking, as Albert O. Hirschman's taxonomy implied, would public school districts or parents and individual schools control government expenditures for education, it is better to ask, what ends were met when funding was uncoupled with delivery? In whose interests did vouchers serve?[26]

CONSERVATISM

Since the 1960s, the most successful challenges to the welfare state were spearheaded by conservatives, and nowhere in the industrialized world was the conservative movement more potent than in the United States. American conservatism flowed in two strands, one economic, the other social. For economic conservatives, the goal was the extension of private markets unimpeded by government control, whereas for social conservatives, the sanctity of traditional values received greater emphasis. Milton

Friedman is best known as an economic conservative, but he was uncomfortable with the conservative label, preferring instead "the rightful and proper label of liberalism" (in Brinkley's nomenclature, "laissez-faire liberalism"). To Friedman the conservative label was second best because liberalism (in the 19th-century sense of the term) had a radical element; it did not merely seek to conserve. The two strands, economic and social, did not necessarily complement each other—the profit motive did not lead logically to support for a state that policed individual morality, nor did the extension of religiosity and tradition lead logically to laissez-faire capitalism. Opposition to the welfare state bound the two wings of conservative coalitions together. School vouchers resonated well with both: by opening up education to the market, the schools likely to benefit were those with strong discipline (private schools had options such as academic expulsions that public schools lacked) and religious authority (most private schools were sectarian). By creating markets that encouraged the growth of private schools, education vouchers transferred control from the welfare state back to the "people," which, to economic conservatives, meant individuals, and to social conservatives, meant parents.[27]

According to two British writers sympathetic to conservatism, John Micklethwait and Adrian Wooldridge, American postwar conservatism is suspicious of the large state, emphasizes freedom over equality and patriotism over transnational cosmopolitanism, celebrates social mobility, exudes optimism for the future, and embraces grass-roots populism. Micklethwait and Wooldridge believe that the latter three characteristics distinguish American conservatism from its European counterpart—in the United States conservative leaders were more likely to hail from humble origins, promoted social policies with a belief that they would unleash prosperity, and appealed to the proverbial everyman. Activism and innovation were necessary for conservatism's electoral viability; creative alternatives to big government attracted elite and popular adherents. Mobilizations that coalesced around policies that countered the welfare state took many years to develop, however. In the early postwar period there was nothing akin to a unified, national conservative movement, since conservatives were deeply divided by region and religion, and since the American welfare state possessed seemingly unstoppable momentum. Early postwar conservatives condemned the modern state but did not offer alternatives that matched Americans' grand expectations. From the economic conservative wing, Austrian economist Friedrich Hayek argued in *The Road to Serfdom* that leftist social policies in a growing welfare state led to fascism and catastrophe, but the postwar boom flew in the face of this dour assessment. On the social conservative side, Richard Weaver's *Ideas Have Consequences* proclaimed that bad ideas caused the moral decline of contemporary western civilization. Weaver's solution smacked of southern sectionalism, however, and his nostalgia for the asceticism of the Middle Ages rang hollow to a population that experienced postwar society as ascendant. With consensus on the benefits of the welfare state, dissenters such as Hayek, Weaver, and Friedman seemed out of step in the 1940s and 1950s.[28]

American conservatism gained intellectual traction as corporate leaders established foundations and sponsored think tanks whose speakers and publications grew in influence. After the backlash to the civil rights movement caused leaders of the southern wing of the Democratic Party to defect, the party that emerged with the most affinity with conservative purposes was the Republican Party. The New Deal consensus nearly ended in the Republican Party with the unsuccessful 1964 presidential candidacy of Barry Goldwater. Motivated by the social crucible of the 1960s and the economic doldrums of the 1970s, conservative activists with their suburban, rural, and southern constituencies recast the Republican Party as representative of an insurgent, conservative populism with national reach. It was bolstered with support from religious conservatives spurred on by the Supreme Court rulings that abolished prayer and bible reading in the schools. And it drew strength from the revulsion of Middle America to what they perceived as the social and political excesses of the civil rights movement, the anti–Vietnam War movement, and the growth of single-issue identity politics. Voters elected Richard Nixon to the presidency in 1968 and, after the Watergate interregnum, elected Ronald Reagan president in 1980, cementing a new conservative ascendency.[29]

By the 1970s justifications for education vouchers suited Micklethwait and Wooldridge's five characteristics of American conservatism. In its opposition to large states, conservatives could point to the radically decentralized nature of the voucher, something that could break up the public school "monopoly." In its emphasis on freedom over equality, vouchers' larger promise was choice rather than standards. Regarding social mobility, the voucher resonated with the ideal that the state would provide opportunities for deserving students hailing from families striving to use the welfare state to escape poverty rather than relying on the state to languish at the bottom of the social structure. The education voucher was an optimistic, innovative reform, in the conservative view, since it stood to solve the heretofore intractable problems of urban public schools. Finally, in voucher politics conservatives welcomed the activism of parents and educators who supported private schools.

Milton Friedman was the public figure most responsible for infusing school voucher policies with intellectual credibility. His advocacy began with an obscure 1955 book chapter that he wrote while on leave from the University of Chicago in Cambridge, England, and his thoughts on neoliberal policies reached a wide national audience over the next several decades via columns in popular magazines such as *Newsweek* and *Playboy* and through two notable books, *Capitalism and Freedom* (1962) and *Free to Choose* (1982, with spouse Rose Friedman). He distanced himself from tuition grants programs in the South, but their existence was not enough for him to reject vouchers in principle. Although Barry Goldwater did not make vouchers a campaign issue during his 1964 bid (Friedman served as a campaign advisor), Friedman popularized vouchers during the presidency of Richard M. Nixon, whose Office of Economic Opportunity actively encouraged them.[30]

In a 2005 opinion piece published in the *Wall Street Journal,* Friedman stated the neoliberal case for school vouchers in a way that remained remarkably consistent with his earlier pronouncements. According to Friedman, the government is justified in mandating compulsory schooling and in providing the funds to make this possible. Quoting from his 1962 chapter in *Capitalism and Freedom,* Friedman reiterated that the government is not justified, however, in its "nationalization" of the "education industry" whereby the bulk of education takes place in government schools. Instead, "governments could require a minimum level of education which they could finance by giving parents vouchers," and the administrative role of "government would be limited to assuring that the schools met certain minimum standards." In this way, "a wide variety of schools would spring up to meet the demand.... Here, as in other fields, competitive enterprise is likely to be far more efficient in meeting consumer demand." According to Friedman, there was one essential difference that increased the popularity of vouchers since his original 1955 proposal—the dismal quality of the public schools.[31]

THE COLOR OF AMERICAN POLITICS

Of the voucher programs in existence since the 1950s most were explicitly or implicitly tied to racial politics. Tuition grants programs that flourished in the South in the late 1950s and early 1960s continued a longstanding tradition of racial segregation in public education. Of the later voucher programs that received public funds—Alum Rock in San Jose; New Hampshire's voucher project in the 1970s; Milwaukee, Cleveland, and Washington, D.C., programs in the 1990s—racial politics provided a backdrop for most of them. Congress and state legislatures established vouchers as a means to improve the educational opportunities of urban children and youth—a population with higher percentages of students from racial minority groups than the national as a whole.

In his seminal study of race in the shaping of 20th-century American nationhood, historian Gary Gerstle argues that two traditions vied for political ascendency. The first was racial nationalism, whereby American identity
changed via adjustments to the boundaries of racial inclusion in terms of
who is, and who is not, an American. In the crucibles of the two world wars
in particular, the state extended the boundaries of national belonging to
the descendants of European immigrants. Racial nationalism collapsed—
or at least was put under severe strain—as an American creed in the postwar era, due to increasing demands for inclusion in the American polity
by descendants from Africa, Latin America, and Asia, along with Native
Americans. Within the 20th century, another political ideology competed
with racial nationalism. Also helping to cement American nationhood was
civic nationalism, which stressed "the fundamental equality of all human
beings" and promoted ideals such as "every individual's inalienable right
to life, liberty, and the pursuit of happiness, and in a democratic government that derives its legitimacy from the people's consent." When racial
minorities invoked civic nationalism in the aftermath of World War II, the
ensuing responses disunited the American polity that had held such as-
pirations in check by enforcing racial nationalism and soft-pedaling civic
nationalism.[32]

Gerstle and others, such as political scientist Michael Goldfield, make
convincing cases that maintenance of white racism and struggles for racial
inclusion "form the mainsprings of American politics." The material results
of this struggle, in the postwar era, have been ambiguous. For example,
blacks' civil rights have been transformed, and voting rights have led to
increased political gains. In addition, "blacks are included in the economic
mainstream today in ways unheard of fifty years ago." Incomes are higher,
"both in absolute terms and compared with those earned by whites." Yet,
"many blacks still live in poverty, in slums, and face a much greater threat
of physical violence than they did back in the 1940s in the rural South or
Harlem." Moreover, since the 1980s "gains in economic and social inclusion for blacks have all but come to an end."[33]

The centrality of racial politics in school vouchers has also yielded ambiguous results. On the one hand, voucher programs designed to evade
racial desegregation were prohibited—in 1968 the Supreme Court forced
states to abandon "freedom of choice" plans such as tuition grants and open
enrollment policies if they did little or nothing to integrate the schools.
On the other hand, racial desegregation in the nation's public schools was
"blunted" since the 1970s by four factors: "apparent white aversion to interracial contact, the multiplicity of means by which whites could sidestep the
effects of the policy, the willingness of state and local governments to accommodate white resistance, and the faltering resolve of the prime movers

of the policy." Black and other minority advocacy of voucher programs, then, grew within a context of retreat in school desegregation. With school desegregation off the table, especially in terms of transfers among school districts, voucher programs become a more appealing option for parents looking for the best education for their children. Paradoxically, these individual efforts have resulted in growing numbers of single-race schools, if the research on charter schools is any indication. Moreover, the Milwaukee and Cleveland voucher programs have segregated enrollment patterns.[34]

PLAN OF THE BOOK

While the chapters of this book proceed in rough chronological order, four themes tie them together: the backlash to school desegregation, liberal attempts to expand the education marketplace, efforts to bring public funding to Catholic schools, and responses of parents and others to changes in urban public schools.

Chapter 2 examines the rise and fall of tuition grants in Louisiana, with a special focus on the first school funded through tuition grants in the Pelican State, the Ninth Ward Elementary School. It describes four aspects of this movement. First it traces the reaction to *Brown* and how the state legislature responded to federal pressure by shifting from "interposition" to taking the public schools private through grants-in-aid. Second it focuses on the rise and fall of the Ninth Ward Elementary School, founded through the efforts of boycotting white parents at the two New Orleans desegregating public elementary schools, Frantz and McDonogh 19. The boycotters initially sought refuge across the city border in the segregated schools of St. Bernard Parish, but the next school year they began construction on a new elementary school in the Ninth Ward that received state tuition grants. The third focus is the efforts of the New Orleans NAACP and its lead attorney, A. P. Tureaud, to challenge the Louisiana grants-in-aid program. Tureaud targeted the segregated private schools such as the Ninth Ward Elementary School that the state had set up. The plaintiffs he represented ultimately prevailed in federal court; *Poindexter v. Louisiana Financial Assistance Commission* (1968) struck down Louisiana's school voucher program as an evasion of *Brown*. Finally, the chapter traces the growth of a system of segregated academies in Louisiana, which flourished in response to desegregation of all of the parishes in the state beginning with the 1968–1969 school year.

Chapter 3 looks at the federal government's growing comfort with school vouchers beginning in 1969, with attention to the federal effort to bring school vouchers to New Hampshire. In 1973, the New Hampshire Department of Education initiated an initiative, funded by the U.S. Office of Economic Opportunity, to institute vouchers in a handful of rural school districts. The voucher program was to include private school options and would be open to all students regardless of income. In spite of backing by free-market economists, federal officials, a libertarian governor, and prominent think tanks, the state's urban districts declined to participate, and in the handful of districts that agreed to the planning phase, voters rejected vouchers in 1976. Although supporters chalked up the reversal to voter apathy and opposition from the teachers union, deeper reasons for their rejection included the exclusion of sectarian schools, concerns about federal interference, and logistical difficulties of adopting vouchers to rural areas. Such obstacles overrode ideological support for the market and motivation among leaders of financially strapped school districts to use vouchers as a means of attracting federal dollars. The second impetus behind school vouchers was more intellectual than populist—that of liberal and conservative policy makers who were convinced of the efficacy of the free market in solving the problems of the bureaucratic public schools. After rejecting tuition grants as evasions of *Brown* in the 1960s, the executive branch of the federal government flirted with them in the early 1970s, as conservatives in both of the major political parties struggled to find affirming educational counterweights to their staunch opposition to school desegregation. The state that proved the most fertile ground for this new voucher initiative was New Hampshire, ironically a state that was by and large untouched by formal racial segregation (the population was overwhelmingly white).

The segregationist drive to preserve separate schools and the free market push to open competitive markets in public education were not the only roots of school vouchers. Chapter 4 begins with a third strand, the efforts of Catholic and other religious leaders to win for parochial schools a larger share of public funding as the federal government widened its aid to elementary and secondary schools in the 1950s and 1960s. Reverend Virgil C. Blum, a Jesuit priest and a political scientist at Marquette University in Milwaukee, authored one of the earliest treatises on school vouchers, *Freedom of Choice in Education* (1958), which, together with economist Milton Freedman's *Capitalism and Freedom* (1962), helped to break the association of school vouchers with Jim Crow. Blum also founded an advocacy group for school vouchers in 1959 called Citizens for Educational Freedom. While Citizens for Educational Freedom always had a predominantly Catholic membership, Blum spearheaded efforts to bring Protestant and Jewish educators into leadership positions, efforts that roughly paralleled the growth of Christian schools and Jewish day schools in the 1960s. Blum and his allies justified vouchers on the grounds of religious freedom, and although Blum brought increased state aid to Wisconsin's private schools through his efforts, he was not successful in bringing vouchers to the Badger State. In the 1980s, however, an alliance of neoliberal reformers who sought to bring competitive markets to public education and supporters of a handful of independent community schools located in Milwaukee's central city, generated a voucher program in 1990, when the Wisconsin legislature passed the Milwaukee Parental Choice Program, the first publicly funded voucher program since their demise in the South. Four factors drove this conditional alliance: dissatisfaction among black Milwaukeeans with the Milwaukee public schools, efforts of community school supporters who had been working since the late 1960s to bring public funding to their schools, the growth of black political power in Milwaukee during an era of rightward-tilting state politics, and the actions of conservative politicians and foundations to craft market-based social policy for the Badger State.

Chapter 5 narrates the interplay of political and ideological forces behind the creation of the Cleveland Scholarship and Tutoring Program. The Ohio legislature created school vouchers for Cleveland in 1995, as part of Ohio's biennial budget. Initially, the proposal had encompassed private schools statewide. As enacted, the law diverted $5 million yearly of the state's Disadvantaged Pupil Impact Aid from the Cleveland Public Schools to a new "Cleveland Scholarship and Tutoring Program." Its key provision awarded vouchers of up to $2,250 to students residing in Cleveland for attendance in private and religious schools. The program was the subject of intense public and judicial debate at local and national levels, culminating in the Supreme Court decision *Zelman v. Simmons-Harris* (2002). Efforts to bring state aid to Ohio's parochial schools through education vouchers dated to the Great Depression, as the state for the first time began to supplement local taxes in support of public school districts. Over the next two generations, public and parochial school supporters were quite successful in generating categorical support for their programming; Ohio led the nation in public support for schools in the private sector. In the early 1990s, spurred on by the example of the Milwaukee Parental Choice Program, support for school vouchers began to complement categorical aid, to enable disadvantaged urban students to attend Catholic schools. Whereas in Wisconsin parochial school supporters engaged in the voucher debate relatively late, after the Milwaukee Parental Choice Program was already enacted, in Ohio parochial school supporters were school vouchers' most valuable, albeit clandestine, asset. The Ohio story, then, is one of linking ongoing efforts by private school interests to earmark tax dollars for private and parochial schools to the rise of a new clarion-call—reversing the decline of urban public schools.

Chapter 6, which concludes the book, does three things. It follows Cleveland's voucher plan as it winds its way to a successful conclusion in the chambers of the U.S. Supreme Court, makes sense of the multiple roots of school vouchers within the context of the postwar United States, and considers the prospects of school vouchers in the first decades of the new century. The first section narrates the legal struggles that culminated on June 27, 2002, when a divided U.S. Supreme Court declared public vouchers to students at religious schools to be constitutional. The middle section takes stock of school vouchers in the 1954–2002 time frame. The final section considers vouchers' future. Borrowing from geographer David Harvey and sociologist Giovanni Arrighi's concept of the spatial-temporal fix, historical actors "fix" vouchers to spatial-temporal ends such as massive resistance to the civil rights movement, the survival of parochial schools in the midst of Catholic migrations from cities to suburbs, or maintenance of educational opportunities for racial and linguistic minorities in declining regions of large cities. Vouchers also fixed themselves to two important postwar trends that made them appealing to wider constituencies. They were an ideal policy in an era in which the New Deal consensus came unhinged even as the growth of the American welfare state continued. As a neoliberal public program, the education voucher extended state support to private schools but justified this expansion as freedom of choice. The chapter wraps up with remarks on vouchers' prospects for the future by continuing the metaphor of "fixing" school vouchers, this time in the "repair" sense of the word. Voucher advocates used them to fix what they viewed as the problem with public education, whether that problem was desegregation, social engineering, secularism, racism, or monopoly. But vouchers would provide bigger social benefits if they too, could be repaired.

Education vouchers served a variety of constituencies, but for ends that conserved idealized social orders based in racial identity, authoritative religions, open markets, and strong families. Early in the post–World War II era, vouchers were proposed, initially, not by free market ideologues, nor by parent groups, nor by innovative educators, nor by religious leaders. The education voucher served white supremacists seeking to preserve a social order that faced a potent challenge: the civil rights movement.

Chapter 2

TUITION GRANTS

Writing in the *Harvard Law Review* in January 1954, two professors at the University of Arkansas considered possible ways the Supreme Court might rule in the consolidated school segregation cases now before it. They speculated on how the justices might uphold *Plessy* (the 1896 ruling that provided the legal sanction for Jim Crow) and interpret its separate-but-equal doctrine, and on how the justices might overturn *Plessy*. Based on research conducted in 1953, the authors predicted that states and school districts would use several "tactics of resistance" should the justices rule against racial segregation. "Most well-to-do families would presumably send their children to private schools," they suggested. As a consequence, "the desegregated public schools would become badly financed institutions attended mostly by Negroes and poor whites." The authors also suggested that states might decide to end their state constitutional commitments to public education, should other devices fail. They added that this would be a tall order, however, given that "elementary education of the masses in America has become firmly established as a regular state function." While "grants from tax funds" would be the likely mechanism to square the circle of popular education and private schooling, this device would ultimately prove futile, according to the authors.[1]

The law professors' predictions were not idle chatter. In Georgia, the political strategist and kingmaker Roy Harris advocated the abolition of the public schools in 1950 in the *Augusta Courier*, the newspaper he published. "If the public school system is to mean the destruction of the pattern of segregation," he wrote, "then we ought to do away with the public school system and devise another to take its place." The next year his protégé, Governor Eugene Talmadge, and the General Assembly began contemplating proposals to end state funding of public schools, locate private schools in former public school buildings, and provide public grants to enable students to enroll in the new segregated schools. The Assembly passed a private school bill in 1953 and put it before the voters the following year.[2] In a similar vein, South Carolina voters approved an amendment in 1952 that gave its legislature authority to abolish the public schools and establish private schools instead. Legislatures in Mississippi and Alabama considered similar proposals in 1953. After the justices handed down their *Brown* ruling, calls to end the public schools intensified. In his July 1, 1954, address to the Greenwood chapter of the Sons of the American Revolution, Mississippi judge Tom P. Brady remarked "with considerable regret" that the end of the public schools was near. In their places "will be private schools, with small classes on every other corner." Parents could afford the new schools because of the money saved from abolished school taxes. And for the "small segment of the white people... not financially able to send their children to these private schools," Brady urged affluent whites to fulfill their "solemn duty" and "help carry the burden of those who are not able." State legislatures across the South considered measures to support private, segregated schools in the aftermath of *Brown*.[3]

Although Louisiana did not pass its first legislation to establish publicly funded tuition grants until 1958, its leaders nonetheless viewed the *Brown* decision as the threat that it was, and responded to the ruling in a hostile fashion, similar to legislatures in other southern states. When actual school desegregation came to the Pelican State in 1960, lawmakers were ready. The New Orleans School Crisis, involving token integration at two elementary schools in the Ninth Ward, generated iconic imagery of white hostility to school desegregation—mobs of angry working-class mothers who harassed first grader Ruby Bridges, her supporters, and the handful of white students who attempted to attend school with her. The new private school laws enabled whites to resist in more respectable ways, however. Government support enabled boycotters of desegregating public schools to move their children to segregated quasi-private schools, the first of which emerged in the Ninth Ward. From 1962 to 1968, the Louisiana Financial Assistance Commission distributed tuition grants to thousands of students attending whites-only schools. It also distributed a smaller number of grants to black students attending all-black schools.

It was no secret, of course, that Louisiana established tuition grants to circumvent federal court orders to desegregate the public schools. Hence, in 1967 and again in 1968, the federal courts struck them down. Louisiana's voucher program ended in 1968, and the civil rights juggernaut rolled on. No longer satisfied with voluntary "freedom of choice" policies that produced token instances of desegregation, the Supreme Court in its *Green v. School Board of New Kent County* ruling of 1968 insisted on desegregation that "promises realistically to work now." Public schools across Louisiana began to desegregate in earnest the following year. In response, segregationist politicians, business leaders, and parents created new networks of segregated private academies in this period, this time without the prop of publicly funded grants-in-aid. Supplemented with the growth of Christian elementary and secondary schools that arose with the rising popularity of conservative Christian evangelicalism in the 1970s, private school attendance rose in Louisiana and across the South, moving from slightly more than 5 percent of all students grades 1–12 in 1970 to slightly more than 9 percent in 2000, with most of the increase coming in the 1970s. While Protestant zeal explains the bulk of private school enrollment growth in the South, the initial upsurge in private school attendance was a white reaction to school desegregation as it became widespread in southern public school districts in the wake of *Green*.[4]

THE LEGISLATIVE BACKLASH TO BROWN

When the Supreme Court issued its *Brown* decision in May 1954, the reaction was mixed. Prominent New Orleans attorney Alexander P. Tureaud, who had filed an NAACP lawsuit some two years previously to desegregate the Orleans Parish schools, greeted it as a "momentous decision and one which will go down in the annals of our jurisprudence." At an NAACP conference in Atlanta five days later, Dr. E. A. Johnson, reporting on political conditions in Louisiana, optimistically "told the conclave that in Orleans and St. Helena Parishes...desegregation was an imminent possibility." Most of Louisiana did not see it that way, however. To white Louisianans the specter of integrated schools meant the end of a southern "way of life." Yet, while the Citizens' Councils and other white supremacist organizations from the grass roots viewed the "Black Monday" decision as a wake-up call to defend Jim Crow, to many rank-and-file white southerners the *Brown* decision remained "an abstraction" in 1954, something "decided in Washington" that had little bearing on their day-to-day lives.[5]

Nevertheless, official reaction to *Brown* in Louisiana was defiant and disapproving, more in accord with the fiery denunciations of the newly established Citizens' Councils than with the latent hostility of ordinary whites. The state legislature in Louisiana was the only one in session in the southern states when *Brown* was handed down on May 17. In a resolution introduced on May 20, the legislature declared *Brown* to be an "unwarranted and unprecedented abuse of power...which can only result in racial turmoil, strife, and confusion to the irreparable harm and injury of the people of the state." The Louisiana State Education Committee also weighed in: it "passed a resolution, by a vote of 83–3, in favor of maintaining school segregation."[6] One of the distraught lawmakers was William Rainach, a soft-spoken senator from Claiborne Parish in the northern part of the state. Something of a rags-to-riches story, Rainach spent time in an orphanage and grew up as an adopted child prior to his attraction to the business world. As a young man he worked for a year in Washington, D.C., and then established a cooperative in the late 1930s that brought rural electrification to his parish. His New Deal–inflected background did not soften his support for racial segregation, however. First elected as a state representative in 1940, Senator Rainach "had looked forward to taking a vacation from politics" at the completion of his 1952–1956 term. But *Brown*, in his words, "rudely shattered my plans."[7]

Rainach understood, like many Americans, that *Brown* in its essence was more than an education decision; it was an assault on Jim Crow in all of its forms. Together with like-minded allies inside and outside of the state legislature, he threw himself into segregation's defense. The legislature created a Joint Legislative Committee on segregation, with Rainach as its chair. The Committee's purpose was to respond to "problems arising from the Supreme Court decision" so that "segregation in all its phases" would be maintained. He also spearheaded the creation of Citizens' Councils in the Pelican State. The Councils were networks of segregationist businessmen, politicians, and professionals whose primary purpose was to undermine the civil rights movement in the wake of *Brown*, ostensibly through legal, respectable means. Rainach and his cronies readied a counterattack in which the Joint Legislative Committee worked in concert with local district attorneys, judges, and police to undermine black civil rights organizations.[8]

One of Rainach's most important allies was Leander Perez, a lawyer and former district judge whose territory encompassed two parishes at the mouth of the Mississippi River: Plaquemines, and St. Bernard. Judge Perez controlled a political machine in South Louisiana that reached upward to the state legislature and across the St. Bernard parish boundary into neighboring New Orleans. Famous for restricting African American voting and doling out patronage in his home turf, Perez had near-dictatorial control of his parishes, but lacked the spirit of discretion necessary for electoral success on the statewide stage. Nonetheless, Perez's energetic and flamboyant presence among the hard right of Louisiana segregationists helped to broaden the resistance. A Catholic who did more perhaps than any other layman to squelch New Orleans Archbishop Joseph Rummel's tentative plans to desegregate parochial schools in the mid-1950s, Perez provided a Catholic counterpoint to Rainach's Baptist roots. Because of Perez's legal training, Rainach relied on him to draft much of the anti-black legislation that characterized the Louisiana Capitol in the late 1950s. Perez also organized Citizens' Council chapters in his domains, including the influential Citizens' Council of Greater New Orleans. Like Rainach, Perez considered *Brown* anathema. It was, to the Boss of the Delta, confirmation of "pro-Communist penetration of the highest court in the land."[9]

The Joint Legislative Committee worked to get the state's two pending school segregation cases thrown out of court, but the bigger targets were black voters and black organizations that spearheaded the civil rights movement. In the St. Helena Parish school segregation case, the Joint Legislative Committee hired lawyers and investigators for the defense of school segregation. When the NAACP filed a lawsuit protesting the state's appropriation of funds to investigate and intimidate plaintiffs, this provided Rainach with the opening he needed. When Judge J. Coleman Lindsay threw out the NAACP's challenge to state funds in the St. Helena case (a ruling Rainach learned in advance), State Attorney General Fred LeBlanc labeled the Louisiana NAACP subversive. The Joint Legislative Committee and its network of Citizens' Council allies inside and outside of government criminalized the Louisiana NAACP, raided its offices, and seized its assets. The Joint Legislative Committee operated with devastating effectiveness from 1956 to 1960, purging some 100,000 African Americans from the voter rolls.[10]

Since Rainach and his allies upset the equilibrium in African American voting, it even seemed in this period that implacable segregationists such as Rainach could threaten the state's most popular politicians—New Orleans mayor Chep Morrison and (after 1956) the new governor, Earl Long—who were, in the Louisiana context, relatively less strident white supremacists and who cultivated and relied upon carefully managed lists of black voters. Even though the school desegregation cases in St. Helena and New Orleans did not proceed according to segregationist wishes (unlike Louisiana judges, federal judges did not always act according to script), and in spite of the fact that the most strident and one-dimensional of the segregationists—such as Attorney General Fred LeBlanc—proved vulnerable at the polls, in the late 1950s Rainach, Perez, and their segregationist forces seemed to have the civil rights insurgency well in hand. The principal threat to Jim Crow was increased black voting, but the combination of the Joint Legislative Committee and the Citizens' Councils rolled back African American access to the franchise and made it all but impossible for the NAACP to operate in Louisiana.[11]

Nor did the state legislature ignore the public schools. In the summer of 1954, Rainach led several counterstrikes to the Supreme Court's ruling in the state legislature, most of which Governor Robert F. Kennon signed into law. Rainach's preferred strategy was to legislate as if *Plessy* were still in force. In his view, additional funds for the Negro schools could re-inflate the separate-but-equal doctrine. That July, the state passed a law that permitted local school districts to raise additional funds "to help equalize the white and colored school facilities." School districts were not going to raise additional revenue on their own, however. The real money lay with the booming petroleum industry that the state ostensibly regulated. Rainach therefore redoubled his efforts to divert a portion of tideland revenue to education, something he had introduced before the *Brown* decision was handed down. "We who believe in education," claimed Rainach, must ensure that "minimum adequate facilities and operating costs are provided within the next few years for the education of every school child in our state." Perhaps because Rainach's plan involved the golden goose, the legislature stopped short of passing the school equalization bill. Moreover, Rainach had helped to engineer a "Right to Work" law just before *Brown*, something unpopular with downstate workers and those allied with the Long machine. Perhaps the rejection was payback.[12]

There were so many other weapons to fight desegregation at the state's disposal that most lawmakers deemed Rainach's equalization bill unnecessary. For instance, that summer the state made it a crime to operate desegregated schools. It also directed parish superintendents to assign pupils to public schools on an individual basis, assuming that superintendents would always assign students to segregated schools, using, as justification, that "the assignment of an inept colored child to a white school in which the children have greater aptitude" would be injurious "both to the colored child and to the white children." The penultimate act called for a constitutional amendment to be put to the vote in the November election. The amendment required all public schools to operate on a segregated basis, "not purely because of race," but "to protect the health, morals, better education, peace, and good order" of the state. In the run-up to the vote, Rainach wrote to every white principal in the state, exhorting them to "call a meeting of your faculty and get the message over to your teachers and bus drivers!" He added that they could also "send notes by the school children to their parents" urging them to go to the polls.[13] The amendment also gave Louisiana the option to amend its constitution at special elections rather than biennially, and it authorized the legislature to draw up "entrance requirements and qualifications for admission to public schools." Voters ratified the amendment by a five to one margin.[14]

One bill that did not reach the governor's desk in the summer of 1954 pertained to school vouchers—tuition grants were one of Leander Perez's pet projects. This bill would have "authorized financial assistance to pupils attending private schools and the disposal of public school properties."

Judge Perez believed that "the most effective answer to the Supreme Court's anti-segregation decision would be the abolition of the public school system and of compulsory school attendance." In its place, "the state could allocate the taxes so that each pupil could go to the private school accepting him at the cost of the state." But while Perez's initiative on tuition grants had precedent in the South, for a couple of reasons Rainach did not share Perez's enthusiasm, at least not in 1954. The Supreme Court delayed issuing guidelines on implementation, so none of the affected states knew exactly what they were fighting. Moreover, Rainach expressed private misgivings about putting an end to public education because he was not convinced majorities of whites would back such a strategy. As recounted by historian Adam Fairclough, the senator from Claiborne parish admitted that "Our whole cause would be lost if we are forced to abandon our public schools." Hence, the Joint Legislative Committee "did not recommend the adoption of Judge Perez's proposal because we did not feel it necessary at this time," Rainach said.[15]

In the year that followed *Brown*, the Joint Legislative Committee entertained a raft of education proposals, most of which could be categorized under the heading "Freedom of Choice." All were strategies to maintain public schooling on a segregated basis, but all were justified on grounds of individual liberty for parents and students to associate with whom they pleased. A proposal from Texas that was mailed to governors and attorneys general across the South called for each parent, upon registering children with school authorities, to choose between segregated or unsegregated school buildings. "In this manner the rights of the parents to determine the associates and companions of his child will be respected." According to this Texas advocate of segregated schooling, the key was making education "a matter of parental control and not a policy of the State." The Junior Statesmen of America had a different twist. "Adopt a 'Group Registration and Enrollment Law,'" they suggested. Parents "will be able to maintain segregated schools...by organizing their children into clubs and groups of our organization and presenting them for enrollment in the public schools." Since each privately segregated group of students would closely correspond to the rosters of the old, publicly segregated schools, "each club or group will fill its school reasonably close to capacity," so that children who are not members of the private club "will have to be assigned to another school."[16]

Private school tuition plans were the most prominent of the proposals that featured choices for parents. "In my opinion there is but one plan that will succeed," intoned Baton Rouge attorney P. G. Borron, one of Rainach's closest associates. "As a last resort, the Southern states will end the present public school system and rent to private school associations the public school buildings and parks and recreation centers." Only in this way could the "children of the South" be saved "from having to associate in school with Negroes and to have them taught by Negro teachers." Attorney W. Scott Wilkinson of Shreveport, another Rainach ally and one of the lawyers representing the school board in the New Orleans school segregation case, added, "Ample power should be vested in the Legislature to afford financial aid to students attending private schools." Rainach disagreed with the timing of these suggestions: "I do not believe... that the private school system can be put over in Louisiana until the people are actually faced with a court order directing the integrating of specific schools in our state." Rainach had good reason to make this appraisal. With little in the way of federal court orders to desegregate the public schools of Louisiana, the legislature viewed drastic measures like tuition grants with indifference. And his preferred solution, using oil revenues to upgrade facilities in the black schools, went down to defeat.[17]

The Little Rock crisis of 1957–1958 was the catalyst that spurred the legislature back to action. When, in September 1957, President Eisenhower federalized the Arkansas National Guard and sent paratroopers of the 101st Airborne Division to protect nine black students at Central High School, it tested the resolve of Louisiana segregationists and they responded by upping the ante. The crisis became a cause célèbre for the civil rights movement and for massive resistance to *Brown*. For his part, Senator Rainach traveled to Little Rock in October 1957 to deliver a speech at a states-rights rally sponsored by the local Citizens' Council. But the federal government had the upper hand in Little Rock in this first round—Central High School remained nominally integrated for the duration of the school year.[18]

Governor Orville Faubus and the state legislature, however, closed Little Rock's high schools for the 1958–1959 school year rather than allow token integration to proceed. Arkansas coupled this with a private school law and compelled the Little Rock School Board to lease four of its high school buildings to a private school corporation. Plans to privatize Little Rock's high schools reverberated to the U.S. Supreme Court. The justices deliberated in September 1958 on an earlier plan by the Little Rock School Board to postpone desegregation due to the violent resistance it engendered. The Supreme Court rejected this logic unanimously: "The constitutional rights of respondents are not to be sacrificed or yielded to the violence and disorder which have followed upon the actions of the Governor and Legislature." The justices also responded obliquely to Arkansas's legislation to privatize desegregating public schools. "State support of segregated schools through any arrangement, management, funds, or property," they ruled, "cannot be squared with the Amendment's command that no State shall deny to any person within its jurisdiction the equal protection of the laws."[19]

Arkansas Governor Orville Faubus displays an anti-federal desegregation cartoon from the New Hampshire, *Manchester Union Leader* in 1957. The Little Rock Crisis sparked proposals for tuition grants in legislatures across the South. (© Bettmann/CORBIS.)

Little Rock served as the backdrop to renewed resistance in the Pelican State. "The irresponsible and unwarranted invasion of Little Rock by federal storm troopers," resolved the Joint Legislative Committee, "is officially condemned and deplored." And the legislative response went beyond resolutions. When Louisiana passed its next round of school segregation laws in 1958, Rainach warned that "Little Rock is an example of what can happen when integration occurs. We are close to another Little Rock in New Orleans." To Louisiana segregationists, closed public schools were a reasonable response. In their view of developments in Arkansas, the federal government presented the larger problem, not closed schools. To avoid another Little Rock while preserving segregation, Rainach and others believed it was necessary for Louisiana to pass laws that prepared for every contingency in their fight with the federal government over school segregation, including plans for a private school system for white students. Rainach moved toward privatizing the schools with reluctance, however, hoping to "return to a full public school system just as fast as we can gather the political force necessary to reverse the illegal and disastrous trend in this country over the last few years."[20]

Other states with segregated public schools had already moved forward with privatization plans, including Virginia and Georgia. Now Louisiana joined them. Under the leadership of the Joint Legislative Committee, Louisiana passed its first private school plan in the summer of 1958. Governor Earl Long signed a series of three acts on July 2. The first authorized the governor to close "any racially mixed public school." The governor could also reopen public schools quickly, once the federal government backed down. The second provided for tax-exempt educational cooperatives "for the purpose of conducting private elementary or secondary schools." It set up guidelines for the establishment of educational cooperatives and also stipulated that "any corporation ... providing educational services and facilities, may be converted into a cooperative." Allowing for conversions to cooperatives was the most significant aspect of this act— public schools that the governor ordered closed could be quickly converted into private cooperatives, with parents at the helm.[21]

The third one, Act 258, established "education expense grants." The legislature limited the grants to places "where no racially separate public school is provided," but there were other stipulations. The grants were only available when it was "not reasonable and practical" to send a child to a nearby, segregated public school. The legislature excluded sectarian schools—it was not lost on the lawmakers that two years before, Archbishop Rummel floated a plan to desegregate the Catholic schools (Rummel backed down; the Catholic schools did not integrate in 1956). Moreover, providing vouchers to Catholic school students would have been expensive. In New Orleans alone, approximately one-third of its pupils attended Catholic schools. The size of the grants was "equal to the per-day, per-student amount of state and local funds expended on the public schools throughout the state during the preceding school year." The State Board of Education would regulate the education expense grants, but parents would apply to the parish school board, which would disburse the grants as vouchers signed by the president and treasurer of the local school board and made out to both the parent and the private school. The act stressed that the state had no authority or responsibility over the non-public schools. The legislature justified the education expense grants on the following grounds: since the "effective operation" of the state's schools relies on conformance with local customs, "our people need to be assured that no child will be forced to attend a school with children of another race in order to get an education."[22]

Advocates of the education expense grants believed that its primary purpose was not to abandon public education, but, rather, to demonstrate to Washington that the cost of federal efforts to desegregate the Louisiana public schools would be too high. "We won't have to close many schools, if any," insisted Representative John Garrett of the Joint Legislative Committee at a Citizens' Council rally in New Orleans that summer. "When those birds on the Supreme Court realize we mean business, we'll find we won't have to change our entire school system." In other words, Louisiana legislators looked with favor on the Private School Corporation that Arkansas created as a substitute for Little Rock's closed high schools because they saw public school closings as the strategy that would convince federal authorities to back down. To the solons, school closings marked a strategy in their fight with the federal government. To students and their families in the affected schools, however, school closings marked life-changing disruptions. In the wake of Little Rock, other states also created tuition grants schemes whereby segregation would be preserved by closing public schools and setting up private ones. By 1959, six states passed such legislation—Alabama, Arkansas, Georgia, Louisiana, North Carolina, and Virginia.[23]

THE 1960 SCHOOL CRISIS

To the chagrin of the Louisiana legislature, the federal government, personified by U.S. District Court Judge J. Skelly Wright, held firm. Even though the civil rights movement reeled from the onslaught of the Joint Legislative Committee and the Citizens' Councils, black leadership in New Orleans continued to press for integrated schools. By 1960, ground zero in the struggle over segregated education had shifted from Little Rock to New Orleans, a district with growing enrollments and changing racial demographics. Table 2.1 and Figure 2.1 refer to population changes in the Crescent City. In 1960, New Orleans population growth was leveling off; the city would lose approximately 30,000 white residents in the 1960s while gaining approximately 2,000 black residents. Table 2.2 and Figure 2.2 show changes in enrollment in the Orleans Parish Public Schools (the school district for New Orleans). In 1960, white enrollment in the district began to decline. Black enrollment increased sharply from 1950 to 1970, more than doubling in 20 years. The 1960 school crisis, therefore, came at a time of accelerating demographic change. Whites were leaving the public schools, but the ones who remained felt threatened by increasing black enrollment. Moreover they believed the public schools were under siege by the federal government.

Given whites' near-monolithic opposition to school desegregation in New Orleans, it seemed a distinct possibility that public education would collapse in the Crescent City and possibly across the state. Although the federal judiciary crushed most of the resistance to school desegregation

Table 2.1 New Orleans Population Changes, 1940–1970

Year	White	African American	Total Population
1940	345,374	149,163	494,537
1950	377,064	175,127	570,445
1960	387,810	204,573	627,525
1970	354,896	206,528	593,471

Source: U.S. Census.

Table 2.2 New Orleans Public School Enrollment Changes, 1940–1970

year	White	African American	Total Enrollment
1940	44,569	25,613	70,182
1950	34,590	30,740	65,330
1960	39,823	53,606	93,429
1970	35,627	78,116	113,743

Source: Ninety-Second Annual Report for the Session 1940–41. State Department of Public Education, 1941, 181–186; One Hundred Second Annual Report for the Session 1950–51. State Department of Public Education, 1951, 204–218; One Hundred Twelfth Annual Report for the Session 1960–61. State Department of Public Education, 1961, 304–333; One Hundred Twenty-Second Annual Report for the Session 1970–71; State Department of Public Education, 1971, 171–200.

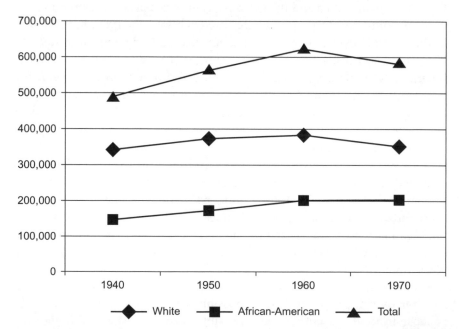

Figure 2.1 New Orleans Population Changes, 1940–1970. (*Source:* U.S. Census.)

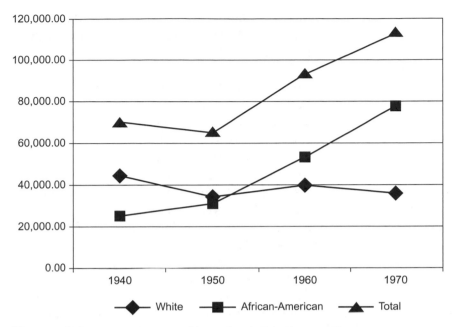

Figure 2.2 New Orleans Public School Enrollment Changes, 1940–1970. (*Source:* Ninety-Second Annual Report for the Session 1940–41. State Department of Public Education, 1941, 181–186; One Hundred Second Annual Report for the Session 1950–51. State Department of Public Education, 1951, 204–208; One Hundred Twelfth Annual Report for the Session 1960–61. State Department of Public Education, 1961, 304–333; One Hundred Twenty-Second Annual Report for the Session 1970–71. State Department of Public Education, 1971, 171–200.)

in the state legislature before the year was out, the direct action of protesting whites in New Orleans nevertheless brought desegregation to a standstill, courtesy of a near-total boycott of two elementary schools in the Ninth Ward.

African Americans had been working to furnish quality education to black children in the Crescent City prior to *Brown,* and they were well aware that the *Plessy* doctrine of "separate but equal" did little to generate equality between segregated schools. As blacks migrated to New Orleans in increasing numbers in the early 20th century, the Orleans Parish School Board responded by providing school facilities of the poorest quality. For example, in 1922 school authorities converted "a dance hall, barroom and motion picture house" into the John W. Hoffman School. In 1935, the board erected the Sylania Williams School. It had "electric lights in two rooms" and "two wash basins for 1000 pupils." By 1947, approximately 20,000 of the 44,000 pupils in the New Orleans public elementary schools were black, and school authorities advocated the construction of additional "Negro" schools. School Superintendent Lionel Bourgeois also planned to convert white schools with declining enrollments to Negro schools, but mostly he was thwarted in this endeavor by stiff opposition to conversion by white parents.[24]

In 1948 a black plaintiff from the Lower Ninth Ward, in an NAACP-sponsored lawsuit, challenged the equality of New Orleans public schools on grounds that they were separate but not equal. A year later, the New Orleans NAACP denounced the board's school expansion program in a 1949 petition, in part because of the board's policy of "erecting temporary Negro classrooms and allowing them to become permanent" instead of converting white schools to black student use. The board built portable classrooms at eight black schools that year. The lawsuits and the petitions that the NAACP filed in the late 1940s resulted in no new schools for black students, however.[25] Meanwhile, the increase in black enrollment in the public schools exceeded growth in white enrollment, putting additional pressures on school authorities to find classroom space for black students. "Between 1940 and 1958, the city's black population increased by almost 40 percent; the white population grew by 14 percent." The racial composition of the public schools was roughly one black student for each white student in the elementary schools by the 1952–1953 school year. At the time of the school crisis, black students were a clear majority in the public schools of New Orleans, "approximately 50,000 Negroes to 41,000 whites."[26]

In the 1950s, New Orleans' black community switched to new, riskier tactics that confronted racial segregation in the public schools head-on. Following on the heels of U.S. Supreme Court decisions ordering the desegregation of graduate and professional schools, NAACP attorney A. P. Tureaud lined up plaintiffs from the Ninth Ward and filed a lawsuit in federal court in 1952. In *Earl Bush v. Orleans Parish School Board* plaintiffs demanded the admission of black students to white schools, challenging the *Plessy* doctrine. Judge Wright decided *Bush* in 1956, ordering the public schools desegregate "with all deliberate speed." Direct action also became more commonplace. In 1954, black educators and parents lodged a formal protest of an annual, segregated parade of schoolchildren "in honor of John McDonogh, the slaveholder who had bequeathed his fortune to the public schools of Baltimore and New Orleans." When the school board rejected the educators' demands, black New Orleans organized successful boycotts of the parade.[27]

In spite of the petitions, the *Brown* decision, the parade boycotts, and Judge Wright's favorable ruling on *Bush,* in the 1950s the Orleans Parish Board of Education did nothing to integrate the public schools, choosing instead to appeal the *Bush* ruling repeatedly. The school board was aided in its segregation defense by Rainach's Joint Legislative Committee, which effectively shut down the NAACP throughout the state (the New Orleans branch began functioning again in early 1960, when a federal court lifted the ban). Moreover the board's legal counsel put up roadblocks that delayed implementation. In one of the choicer examples of delaying tactics, Leander Perez filed a motion for dismissal on grounds that the plaintiffs had not proved they were Negroes. He also encouraged white parents in New Orleans to establish cooperatives at their children's schools, paving the way to converting the schools from public to private.[28]

In spite of Perez's best efforts, however, desegregation of the public schools in New Orleans moved forward. And in statewide politics, the wheels seemed to be coming off Willie Rainach's segregationist bandwagon. The senator from Claiborne Parish ran for governor in 1959, facing a crowded field in the Democratic primary, the only election that mattered in a state where the Republican Party's chances of holding state and local office had dissipated with Reconstruction long ago. Rainach believed his very public stance as the most visible segregationist in the state would give him a good chance for victory—Louisianans would vote their fears. But in white Louisiana prior to the federal Voting Rights Act, all white Democrats stood for segregation. Rainach's problem was that he was a single-issue candidate without a machine base of support, unlike New Orleans Mayor Chep Morrison or the popular country-western singer Jimmie Davis, anointed Governor Earl Long's successor. In the Democratic primary, Rainach ran a distant third while Jimmie "you are my sunshine" Davis cruised to victory, with Morrison close behind. Rainach backed Davis in the run-off election, in exchange for what he thought was a guarantee that the new governor would let him run the new State Sovereignty Commission, successor to the Joint Legislative Committee.[29]

In May 1960, Judge Wright ended the foot dragging of the school board by crafting a school desegregation plan that, in distinction to Little Rock, would encompass the elementary schools first, beginning with grade one. Wright's plan had the potential of affecting some 11,000 first graders; hence the school board pressed the judge for a more limited desegregation order. The board's official position was for the governor to "interpose himself" between federal authorities and the school district, "to keep the public schools of New Orleans open on a segregated basis." But the school board majority also understood that interposition was dead, that keeping the schools open would entail a degree of integration, and directed its lawyers to negotiate a desegregation plan that would be as limited as possible. Judge Wright agreed to a compromise in which district authorities, under Louisiana's Pupil Placement Act, screened applicants whose families volunteered them to integrate the schools. He also agreed to postpone the start of integration to November, some two months after the start of the school year, and, more important for the Republican-appointed federal judge, after Election Day. By fall, school superintendent James Redmond had winnowed the list of black first graders seeking transfer to white schools from 137 to 5, and Judge Wright removed one other child. Among the reasons given for rejected applications: low scholastic aptitude, failure to comply with established procedure, incompatible readiness score compared to students in the new school, possible negative effect on family relationships, and negative psychological effect upon the pupil. The one white request to attend a black school was also denied. The identities of the four students whom the district selected to integrate the schools, all girls, were kept secret, and the school board, though divided, also refused to disclose the school locations.[30]

The two schools were located in the Ninth Ward, a "downtown," working-class area of the city. William Frantz School was a substantial school situated in the middle of the Upper Ninth Ward and McDonogh 19 School was located at the center of the Lower Ninth, east of the massive industrial canal that bisected the ward. Since the mid-19th century, the Ninth Ward's swampy location adjacent to the business district had attracted "mostly free people of color and immigrants seeking to profit from the city's commercial expansion but unable to afford property on higher ground." The swamp drainage and flood protection that industrialization fostered caused the population to skyrocket in the first half of the 20th century, but in the 1950s the Ninth Ward was already experiencing an out-migration of whites to the adjacent St. Bernard Parish. Meanwhile, the modest shotgun-style homes of the ward attracted a significant in-migration of blacks, especially to the Lower Ninth. By 1960, "fully one quarter of New Orleans blacks lived in the Ninth Ward." The region's relative isolation and the fact that working-class whites and blacks lived in close proximity to one another, but within a social order premised on racial segregation, gave rise to a regional identity that was almost schizophrenic. Ninth Ward residents distrusted the middle- and upper-class whites that seemed to run the city. They also exhibited a loyalty to their neighbors that sometimes crossed racial lines. But blacks and whites responded differently to the demographic and social changes that percolated through the Ninth Ward in the two decades that followed World War II. Blacks demanded better treatment, as witnessed by the two school desegregation cases—*Aubert* and *Bush*—that originated in the Ninth Ward.[31]

Whites demanded better treatment too, but the foundation of this desire for more respect rested upon white supremacy, a system of racial nationalism that was coming under increasing pressure. When the school board polled parents in the spring of 1960 about whether they favored closing the schools or integrating them, a small majority favored integration, "but,

s and license plate numbers of white sympathizers. Moreover, or-
resistance was not limited to school boycotts, demonstrations, and
king. Whites inside the Ninth Ward, in Greater New Orleans, and
tate legislature also laid groundwork for alternative, whites-only
, so that boycotters could exercise what they believed was their god-
eedom to segregate their children.[37]

NINTH WARD ELEMENTARY SCHOOL

other side of the Lower Ninth Ward's eastern border lay St. Bernard
, a center of power for Judge Perez. The Boss of the Delta insured
lack voting rights played no part in Parish politics: "between 1936
953 not a single Negro citizen had been enrolled" to vote, and with a
population of nearly 30 percent on the eve of the 1965 Voting Rights
Plaquemines contained just 95 registered black voters. Willy Rainach's
vas dimming in 1960, but that of his compatriot still burned brightly.
g with black disfranchisement, Perez viewed segregated education as a
of the social order. He lent his considerable public power and private
rces in his fight to protect white students from the horrors of integra-
A majority of residents in the Lower Ninth Ward were black; at the
et of the crisis, whites in the ward looked to Leader Perez as a powerful
efactor.[38]

he public schools in St. Bernard welcomed the boycotting students
mly. Just two weeks into the school boycott, the district absorbed
dents in the fifth and sixth grades into two St. Bernard schools, Arabi
mentary and Carolyn Park Elementary. Meanwhile, Ninth Ward par-
s scoped out possible buildings to convert to schools for the rest of
children. One possibility was the old Jai Alai Club in the St. Bernard
vn of Arabi, which bordered the Lower Ninth. The other building, also
Arabi, was a former motor rebuilding plant. One of the leaders of the
ycotting parents was Ninth Ward hardware store owner and Downtown
tizens' Council member Cullen Vetter. "Volunteer workers, mostly union
en," he boasted, "will work in the structures over the weekend." The next
y the organizers leased the motor rebuilding plant. Vetter supplied the
paint, lumber, and building materials" for the work. By all accounts, Judge
erez organized and bankrolled the boycotters' efforts in St. Bernard.
day after a crew of some 50 carpenters and others readied the build-
ng, students began registering at the new school. Administered by the
t. Bernard Parish School Board, on December 8 the Arabi Annex School
was ready to be occupied. Armand Duvio emerged as the boycotters' principal spokesperson.[39]

counting only the votes of white parents, the result was overwhelmingly
for closed schools." Indeed, at a raucous school board meeting in June,
"a representative of a Frantz School Father's Club stated that his group
wanted no integration in the schools." He represented "downtown people
with schools in areas where Negroes were all around." Parents from Frantz
School were not the only ones to address the board that evening. "There are
those who say closing the schools will interrupt the education of our children," claimed Lawrence Hennessey Jr., president of the Gentilly Parents
School Co-operative Club, an uptown group ready to convert their elementary school to co-op status according to state law. "But what about us that
fought for our country? My education was interrupted—and for what? For
the politicians and so a few rich persons could get richer!" At this, some
members of the audience shouted, "Treason!" But Hennessey continued:
"You may say this is treason, but we were supposed to fight for freedom,
and when I am deprived of that right of having my children associate with
whom they want, I am being deprived of my freedom." The president of the
Frantz School Cooperative, Armand Duvio, preferred closed schools to desegregated ones. "We urge you to close the schools," he wrote the governor.
"Be advised that we are willing to assist you."[32]

That summer and fall, state officials kept up a steady drumbeat of threats
to shut down the public schools rather than see them integrated. School
board members issued statements showing their undying support for segregated education. Board President Lloyd Rittiner urged parent groups to
ready their plans to convert public schools to co-op institutions, so that "if
Governor Davis is unable legally to maintain the segregated school system,
the plans for a private system would be ready." Citizens' Councils and other
community groups didn't need such encouragement; they lobbied for segregated private schools to replace the public ones.[33]

Corporate New Orleans was silent on the issue, even though some of
the businessmen's spouses were active on the two organizations seeking to
keep the public schools open, Save Our Schools (SOS) and the Committee
for Public Education. These two white, middle-class groups were largely
ineffectual, though, buried under the weight of near-monolithic support
for racially segregated schools. The white daily newspapers, the *Times
Picayune* and the *States-Item,* refused to endorse even token integration;
they editorialized that New Orleans should oppose both integration and
closed schools. The legislature, for its part, ordered all schools closed on
the first day of school desegregation, but the New Orleans schools, under
Judge Wright's order, remained open. That morning, crowds of whites gathered around elementary schools across New Orleans, speculating about
which schools might be "targeted for desegregation." Little wonder that on
November 14, 1960, when black first-grader Ruby Bridges arrived at the

Frantz school with her escort of federal marshals, and three more black girls arrived at McDonogh 19, white mothers "darted into the schools" to remove their children.[34]

The next evening, at a Citizens' Council rally in Municipal Auditorium that drew 5,000 people, speakers incited spectators to riot. "Let's use the 'scorched earth' policy. Let's empty the classrooms where they are integrated," suggested Willie Rainach. His compatriot Leander Perez wrapped up the rally" by reviling "Communists, 'Zionist Jews,' that 'smart-alec mulatto lawyer' Thurgood Marshall, and the 'weasel, snake-head mayor of yours.'" Perez "urged the audience to march on the school board's offices the next day." High school students and other whites rampaged through the central business district: they "assaulted blacks" and "pounded on the locked doors of the mayor's suite, with Morrison inside." Meanwhile, the boycott of the two schools was nearly complete. On the second day of integration, "Frantz counted 65 students...and McDonogh just 20." Enrollment at the two schools dropped steadily, and by the end of November no white children remained at McDonogh. When SOS organized a "carlift" for white children on December 1, it appeared that dozens would resume their attendance at Frantz. Demonstrators responded by stepping up the campaign of intimidation and violence, focusing their ire on the middle-class, Uptown liberals operating the carlift. White enrollment soon dropped back to eight.[35]

The national press could have focused on many aspects of the school crisis in 1960. There was the story of the four first grade girls at the center of the storm, who attended classrooms devoid of other students. There was the struggle between the federal government and the state legislature over which entity would prevail. There was the battle between the state legislature and the Orleans Parish School Board over whether the schools would stay open and the district would meet payroll. There was the movement of boycotting white students to public schools across the city line in St. Bernard's Parish. There was the renewed effort to bring tax support to the new public-private school sector. And then there were the Cheerleaders. Newspapers devoted most of their ink to them. "What made the newsmen love the story," according to the equally fascinated John Steinbeck, who visited New Orleans when the demonstrations were in full swing, "was a group of stout middle-aged women who, by some curious definition of the word 'mother,' gathered every day to scream invectives at children. Further, a small group of them had become so expert that they were known as the Cheerleaders, and a crowd gathered every day to enjoy and to applaud their performance." The Cheerleaders hurled invectives at the black girls and the federal marshals each school day, "but this was not the big show," observed Steinbeck. "The crowd was waiting for the white man who dared to bring his white child to school."[36]

The "Cheerleaders" in New Orleans's Ninth Ward attracted mu[ch] attention in late 1960. Boycotting parents sent their children to scho[ol in] St. Bernard Parish. (© Bettmann/CORBIS.)

Nationwide, the press and its audience were repulsed by t[hese moth]ers. Although they harassed white parents outside their hom[es and] schools and intimidated the white activists from SOS, the [Cheerleaders] also menaced the four young black girls: "We're going to pois[on you,] you choke to death," was one of the threats hurled Ruby Bridge[s. "The] gravest crime of these gorgons," intoned *Chicago Daily News* col[umnist] Robb, "is not against innocent children or against their com[munity but] against the nation." Enclosing a newspaper photograph of one o[f the Bible-] carrying Cheerleaders, one Johnny Hamlet, a black man from [Columbus,] Ohio, wrote to Mayor Morrison, "What breed of ANIMAL is thi[s?" Not] the most naive observers believed, however, that white mothers [in the] Ninth Ward acted alone. Demonstrations might have begun spont[aneously,] but the demonstrators soon turned to the Citizens' Councils for [help. The] Citizens' Councils pulled the necessary strings to rescind jobs, [cancel] livelihoods, acquire unlisted telephone numbers, and dissemina[te

A plumber with a daughter at the Frantz School prior to November 14, Duvio began participating in the Frantz School Fathers Club when it became evident that the federal government would force segregation on the public schools of New Orleans; in the spring of 1960 he organized a cooperative to take advantage of Louisiana's education expense grants, should the need arise. Once the school crisis was underway, Duvio became something of a media favorite who stressed the reasonableness of the boycotters, the hypocrisy of the white leaders, and the injustice of poor whites bearing the brunt of school desegregation. Wearing a plaid work shirt in a December television interview, for example, Duvio calmly stated that he didn't mind that two white families sent their children to Frantz School "if they're doing it in good faith and not being paid off." Judge Wright and Mayor Morrison were also free to integrate their children "instead of sending them to a big, swanky private school." He added that whites who acquiesced to school integration "thought they had a low, poor class of people down here that they could push this on, and they found out we were poor, most of us lacked money, but these people don't lack any spirit as you can see." To Duvio, the Arabi Annex School was testament to the ingenuity of Ninth Ward whites. He told the press on December 6 that the state would supply the teachers, mothers would prepare and serve the lunches, and nine newly acquired school buses would transport the children.[40] As to the volunteers that made the new school possible, some of them "don't even have children," Duvio gushed. While State Superintendent Shelby Jackson declined to back Duvio on supplying the teachers, he did promise textbooks, "as are pupils in all Louisiana schools." Duvio added that he would pay the teachers "somehow."[41]

Superintendent Jackson and co-op president Duvio didn't have to worry about the teachers for long. On December 7 the St. Bernard Parish School Board voted unanimously to operate the annex school. "In a day or two," stated Joseph Davies, the St. Bernard school superintendent, it will be hard to tell the difference between Arabi Elementary Annex and any other school." After allaying fears that the newly converted school might be a firetrap by praising the safety of the building and the quality of the workmanship, Davies surmised that his district could "take care" of all of the students from Frantz and McDonogh. "The only exception would be kindergarten," he added. "We don't have kindergartens in St. Bernard Parish." Many of the teachers came from New Orleans, according to the superintendent. Although teachers at Frantz and McDonogh "were offered alternative positions" in the St. Bernard schools, most remained at the empty schools"—"only one teacher at each school failed to complete the school year." The teacher from McDonogh 19 began teaching at Arabi Elementary School in January 1961. "It was the best thing that ever happened," he confided years later. "When I came to Arabi, I was kind of cheered."[42]

The St. Bernard superintendent claimed that the Arabi Annex School had 197 students and eight teachers in its first day of operation, and the regular Arabi Elementary School had 212. Across the border in New Orleans, Superintendent James Redmond reported in January that 608 students from Frantz and McDonogh were enrolled in public schools in St. Bernard Parish, not including 219 students who "have not asked for any records transfer." Redmond's estimate of enrollment at the Annex School was more modest—113 students, all from the Frantz School. But the flight to St. Bernard schools could not be a permanent solution. In early 1961, U.S. attorney M. Hepburn Many filed suit "aimed at stopping New Orleans white students from being educated in the St. Bernard Parish public schools." Concurrent with their efforts to open the Arabi Annex, Duvio and others pressed ahead with a plan for a private school in the Ninth Ward. Duvio told interested parents at a meeting at St. Mary's Italian Hall that the Ninth Ward school co-op looked to purchase land for a school to open for the 1961–1962 school year and accommodate "at least" 2,000 students. "We will need about $360 per child from the legislature for the grants-in-aid," he surmised.[43]

The Ninth Ward Private School Association also needed a capital campaign, which they launched in April, 1961. It began with a demonstration of mothers from the Ninth Ward who had withdrawn their children. They marched to the fundraising drive's headquarters on Commercial Place, where Duvio announced plans for a house-to-house canvass of the Ninth Ward—given the racial make-up of the ward, the canvassers presumably passed over quite a few Ninth Ward addresses. Donors received red, white, and blue stickers in the shape of a shield. "Buy a square foot of freedom for the Ninth Ward Private School," was the slogan. Boycott organizers also appealed to whites outside of the ward. The flyers that were mailed featured drawings of two white children, looking disappointed and confused that they could not attend their neighborhood school. "Dispossessed!" the flyer read. "When the Federal Court forced racial integration . . . these poor tots were driven away by the ensuing chaos." Now middle-class residents of New Orleans could also put their shoulders to the wheel: "As might be expected," the flyer continued, "the federal forced integration order is directed against one of the poorer sections of New Orleans. . . . The surest way to insure that *your* children will not be embroiled in this integration war is to help defend these children who are on the front line of this terrible mess."[44]

Boycotters raised the necessary funds, purchased a building site on Japonica Street near the dog pound, and built their school. For his part, Duvio was offended by the term "boycott." In a debate with Mary Sand, president of SOS, he argued that the federal government took the public school buildings from the citizens: "They were not our schools on Nov. 14, but they were on Nov. 13," he said. Duvio was also irked that Robert Kennedy's attorney general's office had pressured the St. Bernard Parish schools to reject the boycotting students. Describing desegregation as "Communistic," Duvio argued that "Mr. Kennedy says, in effect, that our children...now become the property of the federal government." Such sentiments were not Duvio's alone; he expressed the opinion of a majority of whites.[45]

The Ninth Ward's newest school was dedicated with much fanfare. At the ceremony Judge Perez pronounced the school a "monument to the brave spirit of Americans who refuse to yield to the tyranny and oppression of those mismanaging our government in Washington." He added that "this marks the people's answer to that fellow-traveler administration of misgovernment." New Orleans mayor Victor Schiro cut the ribbon to the new building, which contained 10 classrooms and had an enrollment of 443 students, most of whom came from Frantz and McDonogh 19. Fundraising efforts of the trustees and parents of the Ninth Ward Private School Association had worked. And for operating costs, the state legislature and the New Orleans Parish School Board obliged with tuition grants. The school board appointed one of its own, Citizens' Council member Emile Wagner, to chair the board of administrators to "supervise the city's projected private school cooperatives," of which Ninth Ward Elementary was the first. His New Orleans Educational Foundation's major responsibility was to administer state grants-in-aid for students residing within the boundaries of the Orleans Parish School Board.[46]

The state legislature supported the boycotters as best they could, but the federal government thwarted its efforts to close down the public schools in its quest to keep schooling segregated. The legislature resolved in early December "that the parents who withdrew their children...are commended for their courageous stand...which will long be remembered by the Legislature and the citizens of this state." Further, the legislature directed that its resolution be printed in every daily paper in New Orleans. But as the school crisis unfolded, it dawned on the Louisiana government that it could not prevail in a direct counterattack on the federal government's policy of racial desegregation. Much to former senator Rainach's disgust, political leaders and officials "caved in" rather than face jail for contempt of court. For example, State School Superintendent Shelby Jackson "meekly answered 'no' when Federal Judge Skelly Wright asked him if he intended to interfere further with the New Orleans schools." And unlike Governor George Wallace, who stood in the schoolhouse door at the University of Alabama three years later, the man Rainach had endorsed, Governor Davis, refused to make the New Orleans public schools his line in the sand.

Inside the Arabi Annex School, an industrial building converted for 256 students whose parents boycotted the Frantz and McDonogh 19 schools, 1960. Boycott leader Armand Duvio is on the left and St. Bernard School Superintendent Joseph Davies is on the right. (AP Photo/RWT.)

To add insult to injury, Davis also disbanded Rainach's Joint Legislative Committee and excluded him from the State Sovereignty Commission.[47]

Another segregationist who caved was Leander Perez—although he claimed "I'll stake my life" on preventing integration of the St. Bernard and Plaquemines public schools, this did not include the boycotters from the Ninth Ward, whose children sought refuge in the public schools of St. Bernard. After part of one school year, the public schools of Perez's kingdom turned those children away, under threat of a lawsuit from Robert Kennedy's Justice Department. And after months of haggling with the federal judiciary over the New Orleans Parish Schools, the legislature backed off its attempts to shut the public schools down. In Louisiana the power of the Citizens' Councils dissipated in the early 1960s in the wake of such setbacks. Desegregation continued in New Orleans, albeit at a snail's pace.[48]

SPREAD OF TUITION GRANTS

Instead of attacking desegregation head-on, most of Louisiana's white politicians took the lead of the boycotting students of the Ninth Ward—they turned to "Freedom of Choice." In the words of political scientist Earlean McCarrick, this was "the title given to a series of proposals designed to make vacating of desegregated schools economically and politically feasible—economically by giving pupils money, legally by making the grants available to any child, white or Negro, to attend any private, non-sectarian school...rather than restricting payment in such a way as to be clearly and obviously designed to avoid desegregation." Governor Davis signed into law an education expense grants act on December 2, 1960, as the New Orleans school crisis raged. The house supported it 84–0. Essentially, Act 3 of 1960 was the same as Act 258 of 1958, but stripped of any language the legislature believed associated it with support for racially segregated schools. For example, the legislature removed the damning sentence, "Our people need to be assured that no child will be forced to attend a school with children of another race in order to get an education." Eligibility was expanded beyond one who is "assigned to a public school attended by a child of another race against the wishes of his parent." Officially, the new legislation extended education expense grant eligibility to "any child residing in the state." As with the earlier legislation, the legislature limited the grants to those enrolled in "private, non-profit, non-sectarian" schools, and parents made application to local school district authorities. Like the 1958 legislation, Act 3 appropriated no state funds for the expense grants; rather, the law stipulated that it was "the policy of the State" to provide expense grants "from state and local funds."[49]

Louisiana provided steady funding for tuition grants beginning in 1961, when the legislature created an "expense grant fund" where it "transferred $2.5 million from the public welfare fund." The legislature also directed that $200,000 per month from the new state sales tax go toward tuition grants. During the first year of operation, the State Board of Education disbursed $104,465.20 for the grants-in-aid program; all of it went to the Ninth Ward Elementary School. Parent groups at other public schools began to demand tuition grants also, first in New Orleans, and then across the state.[50]

In 1962 the legislature created a new agency, the Louisiana Financial Assistance Commission, and transferred administrative authority from the State Board of Education to the new commission. With this change, lawmakers hoped the program would pass federal constitutional muster—they sought to insulate the program from the charge that the State Board of Education was running a new kind of dual school system, a segregated private system and an integrated public one. But the purpose of the legislation,

Table 2.3 Tuition Vouchers in Orleans Parish

Year	White	African American	Total
1962	6,812	281	7,093
1964	10,345	782	1,1270
1965	10,557	946	11,503
1966	14,131	959	15,090

Source: Loislaw Federal District Court Opinions, *Poindexter v. Louisiana Financial Assistance Comm.* (1967) 275 F. Supp. 833 (no data available for the year 1963).

the maintenance of racially segregated schools, remained the same. "We haven't changed our position one iota," said State Representative Triche. "This bill allows the voters to change to a private segregated system." Presumably, the legislature created the commission to avoid possible conflicts of interest with the State Board of Education (the state board did not preside over a voucher program that threatened public education). The 1962 legislation continued the $200,000 per month appropriation, which the legislature increased to $300,000 per month in 1963.[51]

The Louisiana Financial Assistance Commission distributed grants beginning with the 1962–1963 school year. Commissioners had expected to field requests from parents whose children attended public schools in the two parish school systems facing court ordered desegregation—St. Helena and Orleans. But the law stipulated that any child wishing to attend a private, non-sectarian school in Louisiana could apply for a grant. The commission "was faced with thousands of requests—more requests than students in the desegregated schools of New Orleans. Requests for applications for grants came not only from New Orleans but from parishes where segregated education had not even been challenged and from pupils who wished to attend expensive private schools in the New Orleans Metropolitan area." Table 2.3 and Figure 2.3 illustrate the growth in tuition grants in New Orleans from 1962 to 1966. Grants disbursed to white students more than doubled in this five-year period, increasing from 6,812 to 14,131. Grants disbursed to black students more than tripled in the same period, increasing from 281 students to 959. Tuition grants for black students began at a much smaller base that leveled off in 1965—from the 1965 to the 1966 school year there was an increase of 13 grants.[52]

All of the schools that accepted tuition grants in New Orleans (and across the state) were racially segregated; none of the schools accepted grants from both white and black children. In other words, all of the participating schools in New Orleans remained segregated for the duration of the program, which ended in the spring of 1967. Table 2.4 lists the New

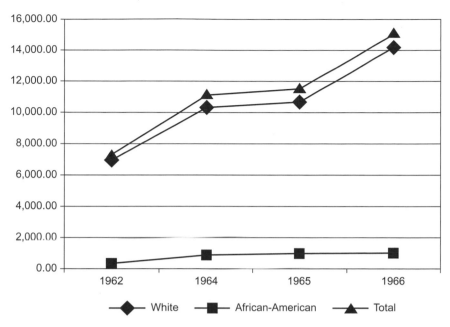

Figure 2.3 Tuition Grants in Orleans Parish, 1962–1966. (*Source:* Loislaw Federal District Court Opinions, *Poindexter v. Louisiana Financial Assistance Comm.* [1967], 275 F. Supp. 833. No data available for the year 1963.)

Orleans schools that participated in the tuition grants program in 1967 (by that time, Ninth Ward Elementary School changed its name to Riverview Preparatory School). In addition to Ninth Ward Elementary School, parents applied for grants to 17 other private schools established before 1962. Following the lead of the Ninth Ward Elementary School, white parents and educators created ten additional private schools in New Orleans, designed to take advantage of the Louisiana voucher program. Not surprisingly, in an era of intense black support for desegregating the schools, no new black schools were created. In the Crescent City there were, in addition, eleven "schools for retarded children" that also had students in attendance who were recipients of tuition grants. Nine of the 11 special needs schools enrolled blacks. Two of the schools established prior to 1962 that accepted vouchers, Jayne Primary and Bush Elementary, enrolled black students. During the 1966–1967 school year, 7,401 students in New Orleans received tuition grants from the state: 6521 at schools that accepted tuition grants only from whites, and 880 at schools that accepted tuition grants only from blacks. Statewide, the Louisiana Financial Assistance Commission disbursed grants to students at 85 schools. In its final year, white parents received $4,920,120 in tuition grants; black parents received $338,760.[53]

Table 2.4 Orleans Parish Grant-in-aid Schools

SCHOOLS STARTED PRIOR TO 1962	WHITE STUDENTS	BLACK STUDENTS
Connor-Parkview (1956)	125	0
Ecole Classique (1955)	403	0
Clifton Ganus (1950)	257	0
Louise McGehee (1912)	303	0
New Orleans Academy (1909)	272	0
Ferncrest (1953)	344	0
Rugby Academy (1894)	126	0
Bush Elementary (1939)	0	172
LaPetite Ecole (1944)	63	0
Newman (1903)	672	0
Jayne Primary (1949)	0	211
Westbank Academy (1955)	417	0
Garden District Academy (1959)	87	0
Vieux Carre (1957)	25	0
New Orleans Hebrew Academy (1960)	4	0
Lakewood (1960)	163	0
Prytania (1960)	625	0
SCHOOLS FOR RETARDED CHILDREN		
Louise Davis (1946)	67	0
Faith School (1956)	0	61
DIT School (1952)	0	102
Crescent City Retarded (1956)	0	28
Thel's School (1963)	0	87
Boyd School (1963)	0	70
New School Inc. (1963)	27	0
Mary Ellen Abbie (1963)	0	82
Star of Hope (1959)	0	17
Sacred Heart (1966)	0	18
Robertson School (1966)	0	32
SCHOOLS STARTED 1962 TO DATE		
United Elementary (1962)	135	0
First Educational Coop. (1962)	156	0
Riverview Preparatory School (1966)	574	0
Gentilly Private (1965)	277	0
Carrollton Ass'n (1962)	121	0
James Murphy School (1962)	79	0
Lake Castel School (1963)	280	0
Hart School (1962)	159	0
Uptown Elementary (1962)	127	0
Aurora Gardens Academy (1964)	439	0
New University School (1964)	194	0
TOTAL ENROLLMENT: 7401	6,521	880

Source: Louisiana Financial Assistance Commission, 1967.

Table 2.5 Non-sectarian Schools Enrolling; Grants-in-aid Students in Louisiana: A Partial List

John Curtis Christian High School
Grawood Christian School
Lake Charles Christian Institute
New Orleans Hebrew Academy
Promised Land Academy

Source: Alphabetical Index to School Statistics, Louisiana Financial Assistance Commission, 1967.

The Financial Assistance Commission did not approve Catholic schools for the grants-in-aid program. Since the Catholic schools in Louisiana took their first tentative steps to desegregate beginning in the 1961 school year, the state legislature wanted them excluded. Commenting on the precursor to the 1962 law, for example, floor leader Representative Risley Triche stated that "this bill allows the voters to change to a private segregated school system." Racial segregation was the litmus test for the approval of grants. Moreover, lawmakers knew that opening up the grants-in-aid program to Catholic schools would cost the state a considerable amount of money, since parochial schools made up the lion's share of the private schools. Nevertheless, the Financial Assistance Commission defined "non-sectarian" loosely. Of the 85 schools receiving tuition grants compiled by the Financial Assistance Commission, five of the non-special needs schools had names that could be readily construed as religious (see Table 2.5). For example, the curriculum of the John Curtis Christian School, located in the Carrollton Avenue Baptist Church Building, stressed "Christian character and faith" as it welcomed "students of all faiths." The principal made it clear, however, that there was another, higher purpose for its existence, not segregation per se, but rather parents' "God-given right to determine, with whom, by whom, and what their children shall be taught." The school repudiated "all socialistic thought which weakens self-government," and opposed "the ever-increasing powers, regulations, and control of the Federal government."[54]

While all of the schools were segregated for the duration of the tuition grants program, 1961–1967, one private school accepting tuition grants, Isidore Newman School, made plans to integrate for the next school year, but at this point the federal government had already shut the program down. Louisiana was to point to this example as evidence that its grant-in-aid program promoted racial integration. Founded in 1903 with roots in the Jewish community, Newman was an uptown, secular school with a progressive reputation. But in 1967, Newman and other private schools desegregated without the help of tuition grants. While tuition grants would make

reappearances in other programs in other states, their association with racial segregation doomed them in states that practiced legal segregation.[55]

LEGAL DEFENSE OF TUITION GRANTS

Under the leadership of A. P. Tureaud, the New Orleans NAACP moved
to stop Louisiana's grants-in-aid program. Interestingly, Tureaud might
have been kinder to the program had it allowed parochial schools to
participate—he suggested that tuition grants should be available "to all
or to none" (he had children in the Catholic schools). On January 24,
1964, Tureaud began laying the groundwork for the NAACP's challenge.
Together with their lawyer, parents of two black children visited the school
on Japonica Street and attempted to enroll their children. Reporters accompanied the group. The children did not register at the Ninth Ward
Elementary School that day: Duvio was "out" and, after "waiting a while,"
the group left. Responding to Tureaud two weeks later, Duvio rejected
his clients' request for admission for two reasons. First and foremost, he
didn't like their "attitude." Since the presence of "the press and television
people" created "turmoil" and interrupted the education of the other students for "at least one day," their purpose was not sincere. He also informed Tureaud that there was no room anyway, since Duvio had already
"made a commitment to another institution." Racism had nothing to do
with his decision: even "if they were white and displayed the attitude that
your clients have, they would also be refused admission to our school."
Black applicants, their parents, and their lawyers visited two other New
Orleans private schools that spring: Carrollton Private School and Garden
District Academy, where they were also turned away. Carrollton, like the
Ninth Ward Elementary School, was founded to avoid racial integration.
Garden District Academy, in existence since 1959, was founded in the
era of parent cooperatives that sprang up on the eve of the New Orleans
school crisis.[56]

Tureaud filed *Poindexter v. Louisiana Financial Assistance Commission*
on June 29, 1964. Rather than seeking to integrate the schools that admitted students on tuition grants, the suit sought an end to Louisiana's grants-
in-aid program. The plaintiffs' argument was simple: state tuition grants
create a separate, segregated school system that, in light of "the substantial
volume of funds being paid...is a public school system and not a private
one as labeled."[57]

Leander Perez headed up the defense along with three other lawyers,
two of whom represented directors of four of the black private schools in
New Orleans that accepted tuition grants, and one of whom represented

the Orleans Parish School Board. Presumably, educators and parents connected to the black schools were motivated by helping their schools rather
than helping the cause of Jim Crow. Lawyers for the state defended the
program by arguing that racial segregation was not the purpose of the creation in 1962 of the Louisiana Financial Assistance Commission. Its assistant director, James Fountain, even promised that Newman School in New
Orleans would continue to receive grants in the 1967–1968 school year
despite its decision to desegregate. The state made the argument that most
grants went to schools that were in existence prior to the formation of the
Louisiana Financial Assistance Commission in 1962. Since by state law all
the schools were segregated, the Commission couldn't be faulted for issuing grants for students to attend segregated schools. Defendants also pa-
pered over the existence of Ninth Ward Elementary School, claiming that
it was founded in 1966, the year the school changed its name. Louisiana
passed legislation in 1967 that gave the Commission itself a new name,
The Louisiana Education Commission for Needy Children. Supporters argued that the purpose of the new commission was to attack "juvenile delinquency" and give "special attention to retarded children." The U.S. District
Court was not persuaded. In 1967 it struck down the 1962 program, and
a year later it also ended the modified grants-in-aid program for needy
children. On both occasions, the Court ruled that Louisiana's tuition grants
were "the product of the State's traditional racial policy of providing segregated schools for white children," and, therefore, unconstitutional.[58]

When the federal courts struck down Louisiana's Grant-in-Aid program,
this sounded the death knell for the Ninth Ward Elementary School. Its
founders were unable to cope with the new reality of attracting enrollment and revenue to the school without benefit of grants-in-aid. Most
students simply couldn't afford tuition, and on top of this, the school's
leadership had its share of missteps. Duvio's father, Robert, took the school
over from his son in early 1966, because "it was losing money." Although
Robert Duvio ran the school frugally"—"like I run my plumbing business,"
he said—the school's finances continued to hemorrhage. Renamed the
Riverview Preparatory School, it adopted "Confederates" as its motto, and
Confederate battle flags graced the school's letterhead. Riverview limped
along a few more years, but lack of tuition support from the state was more
than its leaders could overcome. By 1970 Robert Duvio was approaching
prominent southern conservatives for money. Writing to W. J. Simmons,
president of the Southern Independent School Association in Montgomery,
Alabama, Duvio lamented that since the end of tuition grants, his students
"have been unable to pay and a large number are staying home and not
attending any school as their parents cannot afford to send them." For his
part, Simmons, who had ties to the Citizens' Councils of America, did

"not know of any organization...interested in acquiring a school in New Orleans." He let Rainach know that Duvio had contacted him, but Rainach chose not to help Riverview either.[59]

But there was another reason for the school's demise. One of the few white parents who continued to send children to Frantz during the 1960–1961 school year was Margaret O'Conner, a mother of nine children. But eventually she, too, left the Frantz School. "All the whites ran, including ourselves," O'Conner recollected in a 1982 interview with historian Alan Wieder. "I was sorry to leave [Frantz] school. I didn't want to desert it. On the other hand, I was headed out to the suburbs." Not all white parents living in the Ninth Ward joined the boycott. Of the hundreds of parents who boycotted the two schools, many of them did not enroll their children at Ninth Ward Elementary for long. Most white families with children simply moved out of the city. O'Conner's decision to move was one that parents made in significant numbers. And as white families left the Ninth Ward, they were replaced by black families. Such demographic changes, obviously, did not bode well for a school that not only excluded blacks, but also symbolized white racism. It would be a mistake to claim, however, that school desegregation triggered the exodus. O'Conner continued: "My sister lived out in the Parish and I had always wanted to live out there—it was called Little Farms." While the 1960 school crisis contributed to white migration out of the city, suburbanization was a process that had begun prior to desegregation, as evidenced by Margaret O'Conner's sister.[60]

In spite of a white electorate that preferred segregated education in the 1960s, public opinion on the tuition grants program was never monolithic. From the beginning lawmakers had concerns over costs. Moreover, white Catholics opposed the program because it bypassed parochial schools. Finally, public opinion began to sour on a system that encouraged lax educational standards—there was little oversight—and that provided grants to parents who would have sent their children to private schools anyway.[61]

FROM TUITION GRANTS TO SEGREGATED ACADEMIES

By the late 1960s desegregation of all of Louisiana's public school districts became inevitable. This development spurred William Rainach back to action, but this time as a private citizen rather than a lawmaker. Denied in his 1959 campaign for governor, in the early 1960s he retired to his northern Louisiana hometown of Summerfield and lived in relative obscurity. He had suffered from "near-total exhaustion" after his failed gubernatorial campaign, but with the help of medical treatment he returned to work as president of his company, Claiborne Butane. He committed suicide in 1978. But until the end, Rainach continued his fight to preserve racially segregated education.[62]

Following the *Poindexter* and *Green* rulings, which all but guaranteed widespread school desegregation across the South, Rainach organized a foundation to establish new, whites-only schools in his parish, disseminated advice to other groups seeking to start private academies, and helped to establish the Louisiana Independent Schools Association. The integration of the Claiborne Parish schools, where his home was located, was more than Rainach could stomach. The school board established a desegregation plan for the 1967–1968 school year that relied entirely on "Exercise of Choice"—this was bad enough. Then the U.S. Supreme Court ruled unconstitutional a desegregation plan similar to the one adopted in Claiborne Parish, and school desegregation, even in Northern Louisiana, accelerated. Reacting to the speed-up, Louisiana Governor John McKeithen declared October 13, 1969, "Freedom of Choice Day," which many still-segregated public school districts commemorated by closing the schools.[63]

For his part, Rainach responded to the speed-up by establishing the Claiborne Academy Foundation in July 1969. By September, its first school, the Homer Academy, opened on the grounds of the Calvary Baptist Church. The school admitted students "of the white race," grades one through eight. "Claiborne Parish's fine public schools once provided quality education," the Claiborne Academy directors told prospective parents. "That day is gone. Forced to integrate heavily by the federal courts, the Claiborne Parish public school system must now scale its educational level down to the average learning ability of the minority members of each class." In Rainach's view, and in the view of many white families in the parish, the only solution, for "the survival of our race," was a retreat to the private schools. The next semester the school admitted high school students, began "to recruit the better athletes," and negotiated with a divided school board over the use of the public school athletic facilities.[64]

Rainach became a major fundraiser for the Claiborne Academy: contributions to the school from individuals and institutions poured in—a donation from the staff at Homer Memorial Hospital, shares of stock, cash, etc. His spouse, Mabel Rainach, taught in the school for "no salary." Rainach coordinated his fundraising efforts with the Southern Independent School Association, an offshoot of the Citizens' Councils of America. Working with W. J. Simmons, head of the Southern Independent School Association, he connected wealthy segregationists to Louisiana's fledgling network of academies. At a November 1970 meeting of the Independent Schools Association in Acapulco, Mexico, Rainach could boast of the Claiborne

Academy—a school that outgrew its Baptist Church facility and enrolled 457 students in a "debt-free plant located on a 41 acre site." Even in the absence of tax-exempt status, the school operated in the black. Rainach's efforts were repeated in municipalities across the state.[65]

One would never learn of the white supremacist roots of the Claiborne Academy by perusing its website in 2011, however. According to its history page, "Claiborne Academy was founded in 1969 by a group of citizens [whose] goal was to provide a high quality educational facility that parents will choose as to where to educate their children." Photographs reveal white students participating in a variety of academic and extra-curricular activities. Interestingly, Claiborne Academy did not remain segregated: its website reveals one black student in attendance, a member of the football team. Presumably, other black parents enrolled their children at Claiborne Academy also, most likely for the same purpose to which its website alludes—that at Claiborne students received a high-quality education, presumably better than that provided by the local public schools. For them, educational opportunities trumped the origins of the school in the Citizens' Council and white reaction to the civil rights movement.[66]

The segregated, private academies founded by Rainach and others around 1970 were what remained of massive resistance—from refusal to compromise with the federal government in the 1950s, through the implementation of tuition grants programs in the 1960s, to the creation of segregated, whites-only academies in the 1970s. In the southern context of the 1950s and 1960s, supporters of school vouchers justified tuition grants first and foremost as a means to defend racial segregation and the southern way of life. Founders of Ninth Ward Elementary School viewed their institution as protecting their children from the dangers of integration. But behind this goal there lurked a more enduring justification for school vouchers: the freedom for parents to select the schools they viewed as in accordance with their values.

The link between southern tuition grants and northern school voucher proposals, often—but not always—emanating from conservative politicians and intellectuals, are murky. Economist Milton Friedman has been perceived as the most well-known advocate of school vouchers since the early 1960s. He helped to break the association of school vouchers with Jim Crow through his persistence in pairing them with the ideas of freedom for individuals and the superiority of markets over governments in meeting educational demands. In 1955 however, Friedman's advocacy of school vouchers was only a theoretical exercise. Yet, in the guise of tuition grants, school voucher proposals floated in several southern states the same year. As Friedman conceded in a footnote to his 1955 presentment of school vouchers on free enterprise grounds, "Essentially this proposal—public financing but private operation of education—has recently been suggested in several southern states as a means of evading the Supreme Court ruling against segregation." But in the reprinting of his 1955 work as a chapter in his best-selling book, *Capitalism and Freedom* (1962), he removed the footnote. In 2005 Friedman conjectured that he removed the footnote because southern states no longer offered tuition grants, though, in fact, tuition grants were still offered at that time.[67]

Southern officials in the Pelican State justified school vouchers for reasons other than the superiority of free-market competition in delivering educational value, however. At least, this was the case in the 1950s and early 1960s. Louisiana legislators did not intone Friedman or other free-market economists while arguing for tuition grants. In the years surrounding the New Orleans school crisis, the Crescent City was "flooded" with anti-Semitic literature—the linking together of Jews, Communists, and the NAACP in a northern conspiracy to harm the South was a staple of backlash, ultra-segregationist rhetoric. This may be part of the reason why the political climate was unreceptive to a free-market justification for tuition grants, since the principal advocate of this position was a northern-born, Jewish economist. But more than this, the civil rights struggle to end Jim Crow left little room for the market. To A. P. Tureaud and other civil rights activists, the movement meant abolishing Jim Crow in the existing public schools, not creating an educational marketplace where, in theory, racial oppression would have no place. And to Rainach, Perez, and other fervent white supremacists, the education marketplace was a second-best alternative to segregated public schools.[68]

Moreover, there was little support for vouchers as a means to support Catholic education. Indeed, segregationists viewed the Catholic schools with suspicion, since a handful of prominent church leaders, including Archbishop Joseph Francis Rummel, had stepped cautiously toward desegregation since the mid-1950s. Rather, Louisiana supporters were explicit in designing and supporting the tuition grants system as a means of defending racial segregation. Even when racial language was removed from the justifications for tuition grants, defense of white supremacy remained their driving force. White mothers and fathers in the Ninth Ward associated white supremacy with freedom—freedom to associate with whom they pleased and freedom from the edicts of federal, state, and local governments that they believed abandoned them. This rhetoric of freedom was mirrored in statements by high-ranking Louisiana politicians and officials, and it was prominent in the literature that the Citizen's Councils circulated. White supremacy began to shift, from official public policy to the private sphere—the result of individual choices. The establishment of tuition grants in Louisiana and elsewhere represented a way station, for whites, in this retreat to the private sphere. The similarity, then, between northern, Friedman-inspired programs for school vouchers and southern programs of grants-in-aid, was in freedom of association—both traditions argue for rights of parents to select the schools that they deem best for their children.

Advocates of school vouchers downplayed the significance of segregationist tuition grants in the gestation of 1960s voucher plans they began to popularize in the North. For example, in his leftist critique of American education, Christopher Jencks argued in *Dissent* that schools responsive to students and parents "could be realized either by making all [government] subsidies take the form of tuition grants or by paying public funds to schools and colleges according to the number, level, and...incapacity to pay of their students." To be sure, Jencks opposed vouchers to "all-white schools," but in his criticism of top-down, bureaucratic educational systems he glossed over tuition grants that operated in the 1960s to preserve racially segregated schools. The target of Jenck's attacks were the urban public schools, but his articles advocating school vouchers appeared in 1966, when tuition grants programs remained going concerns. From the right, Friedman removed his comments about southern grants-in-aid programs in the reprinting of his 1955 argument for education vouchers in his best-selling book. *Capitalism and Freedom* appeared in 1962, the same year that Louisiana created the Financial Assistance Commission. Later, Friedman portrayed school vouchers as a fresh idea in his efforts in the 1970s to establish federally sponsored vouchers projects in New Hampshire and elsewhere. Not only would school vouchers "moderate racial conflict," suggested Friedman in 1973 in the *New York Times Magazine,* they would also "completely eliminate the busing issue."[69]

Kevin Kruse examines white reactions to civil rights in *White Flight: Atlanta and the Making of Modern Conservatism.* His work is hugely useful in conceptualizing white resistance to school desegregation in the 1950s in terms of property rights, freedom of association, and retreat to the private sphere. Georgia pioneered the formulation of tuition grants in 1953, amending the state constitution to take Georgia's schools private should the federal government order them integrated. Kruse provides a succinct analysis of the role that tuition grants played in the establishment of Atlanta's segregation academies as well as the responses of long-established parochial and private schools to desegregation. In support for property rights, for freedom of association, and for the private sphere can be found the commonalities between southern tuition grants and northern voucher programs. The segregationist backlash to the civil rights movement helped to shape postwar conservative movement nationwide, and it is from conservative efforts that school vouchers derive much of their support.[70]

Undoubtedly, Louisiana's segregationists perceived the gains of the civil rights movement as the loss of a social order that seemed to them timeless and self-evident. Hence the trend that the NAACP and the Supreme Court initiated was, in Rainach's words, "disastrous"; the South faced racial "extinction." The title of both a 1960s country-music song and a recent book on the responses of ordinary whites to the end of Jim Crow, "There Goes My Everything"—certainly could be applied to Senator Rainach and others who sought to preserve Jim Crow. Historian Jason Sokol observes that most white southerners experienced civil rights movement gains as their losses. Responses ran the gamut, however. "For some, the law forced changes in practices....Others began to question deeply held views even though their lives looked much the same.... And for still others, change in any form—in law, mind-set, or lifestyle—was something to fear and resist, with denial and bitterness, all the way to the grave."[71]

Rainach's sense of loss translated into resistance rather than acceptance; in his public and private utterances, he spoke a language of restoration. As a candidate for governor, he perceived himself as taking "a strong stand toward working with the rest of the South...just as Louisiana, Florida and South Carolina did previously in 1876, when we overthrew carpetbagger rule." In the mid-1960s he saw himself as laying the groundwork for whites to "get together and restore control of this country." And in efforts to preserve segregated education in the early 1970s, he believed that a new network of private schools would lead "to the perpetuation of Western culture in America through a proper education of the white youth." Each of Rainach's projects, then, sought to shore up and restore power to those who wielded it prior to the Second Reconstruction. It remains an open question, the extent to which Rainach and his allies succeeded in this restoration.[72]

Presently, there are few places in the United States where racial segregation is absolute. Willie Rainach's vision proved fleeting—even his Claiborne Academy began admitting black students a generation after its founding. Yet in American public schools, racial segregation remains widespread. One of Rainach's cronies from 1955 proved prophetic. "The best way to keep segregation, not 100 percent but largely," he suggested, "is by districting or redistricting the school boards.... We have to avoid, of course, state action so far as possible.... [In this way] we could make certain districts which would be 90-odd percent white or 90-odd percent black." Another compatriot suggested that the rest could be privatized. "I fully agree with you," responded Rainach. "We will be forced to resort to the private system for schools, parks and recreation facilities before the matter progresses much further."[73]

This is an apt description of contemporary American education—public school districts and publicly supported private schools that are racially identifiable. Contemporary conservatives justify their support of public dollars for private schools on market-based grounds. And the market metaphor is also invoked as a method of reforming the public schools—competition, accountability, choice. But not to be discounted in this support for the educational marketplace are white supremacist roots. Beliefs in freedom of association inherent in the civil rights backlash, not an apolitical marketplace, is American education's invisible hand.

Free-market advocates of school vouchers wanted them implemented nonetheless, in settings outside the South and free from the racial segregation purpose of tuition grants. Their promoters believed that the competition for students that school vouchers could engender would help to improve the public schools, especially public schools in the large cities. The most fertile soil for free-market vouchers to germinate, however, turned out to be a state known for its rural traditions.

Chapter 3

DETOUR

The future looked bright for Nixon administration officials in early 1973. At the January 20 inauguration, the president put a new twist on Kennedy's famous plea for public service by urging Americans to ask "not just what will government do for me, but what can I do for myself?" With rumblings of the Watergate scandal still distant, a second term would widen the administration's efforts to apply conservative principles to a welfare state that was under increasing attack. For several Republican politicians and conservative officials with an interest in education, 1973 promised to be the year the federal government would open up the public school bureaucracy to market-based, "do for myself" routes to educational advancement such as vouchers. With Nixon's electoral landslide, conservative policy makers could up the ante in school reform: Not only could federal officials promote vouchers to deliver compensatory education to improve the academic achievement of working-class students and urban minorities, but they could also provide federal funding for voucher plans that had a non-compensatory, unregulated edge, thereby subsidizing the education expenses of families at all income levels.[1]

Outside of Washington, D.C., liberal policy analysts, leftist social commentators, and far-right politicians also saw vouchers' allure. Through the Center for the Study of Public Policy (1970), Christopher Jencks, an authority on anti-poverty initiatives, had already prepared a blueprint for the federal government on compensatory vouchers, while left-leaning author Jonathan Kozol and other backers of "free schools" saw vouchers as a means to subsidize small alternative schools for students hailing from the poorest areas of the big cities. Advocates of compensatory vouchers targeted them to families with low incomes—either excluding affluent parents from access to government-funded vouchers or indexing the vouchers according to income. Meanwhile, in New Hampshire, Governor Meldrim Thomson advocated the unregulated distribution of school vouchers as part of his conservative vision for a Granite State free from the social engineering, permissiveness, and liberalism that, in his eyes, characterized the federal government. The upstart Thomson's ultraconservative platform carried the state in 1972, when he was elected with the backing of the *Manchester Union Leader,* an influential, right-wing daily newspaper with circulation throughout the state. To conservative policy makers and their liberal allies, the early 1970s seemed a propitious time to introduce vouchers to the nation's public schools, whether in the guise of helping urban blacks obtain "a piece of the action" for their children or of helping rural whites free their children from heavily regulated public schools.[2]

At the urging of federal officials, the New Hampshire Department of Education applied for an Office of Economic Opportunity (OEO) grant in 1973, disseminated information to school district officials and voters throughout the state, and convinced voters in a handful of rural school districts to participate in a planning phase, with the proviso that voters would decide later whether to implement the voucher program. OEO and one of its successor agencies, the National Institute of Education, sought to showcase New Hampshire as an example of a "pure" voucher system. In this proposed, non-compensatory form, public schools competed with private schools to attract and retain students, with private schools maintaining their admissions standards, and with parents who could afford private schools paying the difference between tuition and the voucher amount. In spite of enthusiastic backing by free-market economists, federal officials, a libertarian governor, and prominent think tanks, however, the state's urban districts refused to take part in the voucher program. In the handful of rural districts that agreed to participate in the planning phase, voters rejected the program in the spring of 1976, essentially ending federal education voucher initiatives for the next twelve years.[3]

Conservative policy makers came to see this failed voucher initiative as a paradigm of how *not* to go about influencing education policy. Voucher supporters chalked up the New Hampshire reversal to voter apathy and opposition from the teachers' union, but deeper reasons for their failure were the exclusion of religious schools, Granite State opposition to federal interference, and the very real logistical difficulties of adapting voucher programs to the needs of rural areas. These obstacles overrode both ideological support for competitive markets in education and the motivation among leaders of financially strapped rural school districts to use vouchers as a way to obtain more federal funds. After the New Hampshire debacle, voucher promoters turned to state legislatures and bypassed local school districts as possible allies.

RIGHT TURN AT THE OFFICE
OF ECONOMIC OPPORTUNITY

The federal agency that led the voucher charge was an unlikely one. President Johnson created the OEO as the "national headquarters" of the War on Poverty, and the agency had evolved into a liberal bastion. Beginning in the mid-1960s, the OEO coordinated a variety of anti-poverty initiatives large and small, most directed at cities. In Roxbury, Massachusetts, for example, a group of African American parents secured an OEO grant for the free school that hired Jonathan Kozol. The largest OEO programs were Head Start, Job Corps, Model Cities, VISTA, Legal Services, and Community Action—all premised on linking federal resources to local activists in order to stimulate grassroots public services. In line with the spirit of experimentation that pervaded OEO, school vouchers attracted the attention of staffers interested in compensatory education. "Possible techniques for inducing successful education," according to economist Robert A. Levine, an OEO assistant director in the Johnson administration, "include the provision of special grants to families to buy for their children the best education they think they can buy." Levine also advocated "contracts with profit-making organizations to take slum children as inputs and produce better-educated citizens as outputs." Levine was not the only official at OEO interested in public-private innovations in education. His boss, OEO Director Sargent Shriver, was a longtime supporter of tax credits for parents with children in private schools. Late in the Johnson administration, the OEO offered federal funding to school districts willing to experiment with compensatory vouchers but received no takers, perhaps because OEO offered nothing in the way of guidance for prospective school districts that might have been interested in crafting voucher plans. Vouchers were to prove the only OEO perspective on education reform that the new Republican administration retained and cultivated.[4]

When Nixon assumed the reigns of government in 1969, his administration tapped Donald Rumsfeld, an ambitious Republican Congressman from the Chicago suburbs, to run the OEO. As a conservative lawmaker skeptical of the welfare state who had "voted to revise the poverty and the Model Cities programs," Rumsfeld's appointment invited speculation that the days of the OEO were numbered. During his year at the helm, Rumsfeld and his assistant Richard Cheney opposed on ideological grounds the grassroots focus of OEO and sought to restrict the power of

Richard Nixon introduces Donald Rumsfeld as director of the Office of Economic Opportunities (OEO), 1969. Rumsfeld's OEO favored performance contracting, teaching machines, and school vouchers. (© White House/Handout/CNP/Corbis.)

OEO's existing services. They began by limiting the Civil Rights Division and Legal Services, two programs that enabled poor people to challenge local power structures. Meanwhile, Nixon transferred Head Start and Job Corps to the Department of Housing and Urban Development and the Department of Labor, respectively.[5]

In common cause with many of the liberal staffers at OEO, however, Rumsfeld defied predictions and did not move aggressively to dismantle his agency. Instead, Rumsfeld's OEO awarded grants that championed experimental social programs based on free-market principles and individualism. In education, for example, OEO funded "performance contracting," in which incentive payments for academic achievement went to "students, teachers, and private educational contractors." The OEO also supported experiments that featured "teaching machines," the very latest in educational technology that allowed "students to learn at their own speed." But the most important free-market experiment by far was the education voucher. The OEO commissioned a feasibility study of vouchers in 1969, awarding the grant to a Cambridge, Massachusetts, think tank, the Center for the Study of Public Policy, where Harvard education professor Christopher Jencks served as co-director. The resulting report came out a year later.[6]

Entitled "Education Vouchers" and authored by Jencks, it served as the blueprint for federal voucher initiatives. Jencks began his advocacy of education vouchers in 1966, before there was real accomplishment in the racial desegregation of the public schools, and when school vouchers, in the form of tuition grants programs, were still active in the South, as a means for parents to continue sending their children to segregated schools. In his articles in *The Public Interest* and *Dissent*, Jencks criticized the public school bureaucracy, particularly as it stood in the way of equalizing educational opportunities. In Jencks's view, a voucher system would promote desegregation: In order for the public bureaucracy to fulfill its proper role of protecting parents from fraud and discrimination in a market-driven system of "tuition grants" or enrollment-driven public funding, all schools receiving public funds would "be open to public inspection." Thus, no public funds could go to schools that discriminated on the basis of race, religion, or academic ability.[7]

His support for school vouchers reached a wider audience in 1968, as the Black Power movement gained credibility in liberal quarters in the wake of the assassination of Martin Luther King, Jr. "The best alternative I can see," suggested Jencks in the *New York Times Sunday Magazine*, "is to follow the Catholic precedent and allow [black] nationalists to create their own private schools, outside the regular public system, and to encourage this by making such schools eligible for substantial public support." In the 1970 "Education Vouchers" report for OEO, Jencks discussed several models for school vouchers, but favored compensatory programs in which participating private schools had limited selectivity and voucher amounts compensated for limited family income to pay private tuition. In contrast to the "pure" or unregulated voucher model advocated by the right, in which anyone could request a voucher, compensatory vouchers would either be indexed to family income or only be available to economically disadvantaged families who could not otherwise afford private school tuition. Jencks's report came down squarely against an unregulated voucher model, arguing that giving vouchers to everyone would not correct existing inequities in families' access to good schools. To Jencks, the utility of vouchers for disadvantaged students was "all in the details."[8]

OEO staffers in the early 1970s were intrigued by the revolutionary potential of the education voucher to radically reorganize public education.

To be sure, OEO officials were well aware of the association of vouchers with southern school segregation in the late 1950s and early 1960s. But the Supreme Court clearly prohibited their use for segregative purposes, and the lure of the market and the desire to innovate overrode the segregationist taint. The "anti-poverty experts" at OEO hoped to offer vouchers in selected school districts by the fall of 1971. Staff at Jencks's think tank contacted superintendents of big city school districts around the nation seeking sponsors for demonstration projects. Five of them—Gary, Indiana; Seattle, Washington; Alum Rock, California; New Rochelle, New York; and Rochester, New York—accepted planning funds from the OEO. In 1972, one of the districts, Alum Rock, moved out of the planning stage and began to offer vouchers, but participation was limited to public schools. Alum Rock's model was essentially an open-enrollment system for conventional and alternative elementary school programs. The RAND Corporation, a prominent West Coast think tank with roots in the defense industry, won the OEO contract to evaluate the Alum Rock program. In spite of RAND's conservative credentials, to voucher advocates and private school supporters Alum Rock's scope was too limited to serve as a proper test-case for vouchers.[9]

Despite urban school districts' hesitancy to use federal funds to bring public and private schools into direct competition for students, education vouchers became a showcase policy for OEO in the early 1970s, symbolizing its shift from an underwriter of left-leaning organizations that used the grassroots to challenge well entrenched political and economic interests, to an agency that applied free-market solutions to the poverty problem. Under the leadership of Rumsfeld (1969–1971) and his successors Frank Carlucci (1971–1972) and Phillip Sanchez (1972–1973), OEO's free-market strategy supplemented its more pedestrian tactic of favoring grant applications from local community groups that tilted right and could deliver votes to Nixon.[10]

Conservative forces still wanted OEO dismantled, however. The highest echelons of the Nixon administration viewed the agency with suspicion, and its origins in President Johnson's "Great Society" initiative ultimately doomed it. Adding insult to injury, liberal activists often found employment in the Great Society agencies, of which OEO symbolized to conservatives the worst excesses of liberalism. The director in the OEO's final months in 1973, Howard Phillips, sought the termination of the entire agency and most of its programs: Not only was "the place infested with left-wingers," he said, but there was also "unconstitutional" lack of accountability in how community action programs spent federal dollars. In early 1973, with the election over, Nixon asked his domestic policy advisor John Ehrlichman to come up with "10 or 15 horrible examples of how money has been wasted in model cities, community action, etc." After Ehrlichman reported that OEO funds had reached left-wing stalwarts such as the American Indian Movement and the National Welfare Rights Organization, the president announced "his intention to dismantle OEO by mid-year."[11]

As OEO neared its end, Republican staffers and conservative supporters moved forcefully to establish a voucher experiment that would introduce an open market of private schools into the public education system. Although a handful of big city school districts had accepted OEO funds to study the feasibility of vouchers, urban school superintendents did not exactly beat a path to OEO's door. Moreover, the voucher proposals that did interest the city districts were compensatory in nature and almost always excluded private schools. (An exception to avoiding private schools occurred in cases where school districts looked to contract with them to enroll their most difficult to educate students.) In addition, each of the school districts that expressed interest in vouchers was located in a city that voted Democratic. It appeared to conservatives within OEO that funds earmarked for voucher plans that included private schools would go unused. With northern cities reluctant to adopt vouchers, southern states and school districts under desegregation orders that prohibited vouchers, and most suburbanites satisfied with their public schools, there were few options available for conservative free marketeers. In such a climate, a small northern state with a conservative political tradition—New Hampshire— began to look appealing to Phillips's OEO.[12]

Phillips and other OEO officials lobbied New Hampshire's governor hard in the spring of 1973 to encourage him to apply for federal funds. Phillips also shielded the New Hampshire proposal from the agency's more liberal Voucher Office. The OEO director was already on cordial terms with Governor Thomson due to their mutual interest in right-wing causes. Indeed, after Phillips' resignation from the federal government that summer, he tapped Thomson to lead his new political organization, the Conservative Caucus. Phillips' aide, Daniel Joy, handled the negotiations between the federal government and the state. Joy cited OEO's track record of funding for Alum Rock when he guaranteed three-and-a-half years of funding in a meeting with the New Hampshire State Board of Education in April 1973. The hastily put-together application for the New Hampshire Voucher Project had powerful backers outside of OEO: Department of Health, Education and Welfare (HEW) secretary Casper Weinberger; the American Enterprise Institute's William Baroody; and several conservative Congressmen, including Jack Kemp. They protected this "pure" voucher initiative from liberal career bureaucrats who wanted to kill it.[13]

In the summer of 1973, when the OEO was finally dismantled, the New Hampshire Voucher Project, along with Alum Rock and the other urban

voucher initiatives, moved to the National Institute of Education (NIE), a
new education research agency within HEW that Congress had established
in 1972. Several young voucher enthusiasts, most of them political appoin-
tees who had worked on Nixon's 1972 campaign, accompanied the voucher
demonstration projects to the NIE and shuttled between Washington and
Concord to oversee the program.[14]

THE FRIEDMANITE VOUCHER

The voucher advocates' most important ideological ally was Milton Friedman, a Nixon advisor whose advocacy of school vouchers dated to the
1950s. Vouchers had grown in popularity in the South in the 1950s, in the
form of "tuition grants" designed to maintain racially separate and unequal
schools in the face of the civil rights movement and the *Brown v. Board of
Education* decision. That same decade, Friedman, part of a small group of
free-market economists and philosophers disillusioned with postwar liberalism and the welfare state, advocated school vouchers as one of the routes
to free individuals from unnecessary government control. Friedman's stature as a free-market economist and a public intellectual survived the failed
presidential campaign of Barry Goldwater (Friedman served as one of
Goldwater's advisors). The Arizona senator and presidential candidate opposed the growth in federal authority on school matters. Education policies
were best resolved by state and local governments, according to Goldwater,
and in the early 1960s the racial implications of his position were not lost
on southern voters. But Goldwater did not take a further step and campaign on a platform with an education voucher plank. Friedman's reputation continued to grow after the Goldwater debacle. As a part-time Nixon
advisor, for example, he worked to replace the draft with an all-volunteer
military—a market-based development that drew support from across the
political spectrum.[15]

Intellectually, Friedman did not consider rural states such as New Hampshire a promising location for a voucher experiment, at least at first blush.
"In small communities and rural areas," argued Friedman in 1955, "the
number of children may be too small to justify more than one school
of reasonable size, so that competition cannot be relied on to protect
the interests of parents and children." In 1973 Friedman continued to
argue that vouchers with minimal regulation would be most benefi-
cial to "those living in slums." Friedman also asserted with consistency
that vouchers would be of special benefit to African American families:
"My sympathies are wholly with the black parents in NY and Watts and
Chicago who say they want to run their own school," noted Friedman

Economist Milton Friedman in 1969. Over a 50-year period, Friedman advocated for vouchers on free-market grounds, rather than basing his support on religious freedom or racial nationalism. (© Bettmann/CORBIS.)

in 1968, at the height of the movement for community control of public schools. "Many of them will do a lousy job—but the governmental authorities are doing a lousy job. There will be some among them who will do a good job and they will help pull up the rest." Provided that governments prohibit segregationist schools from using vouchers, Friedman suggested in 1973 that "freedom to choose" schools would "completely eliminate the busing issue." Moreover vouchers would "moderate racial conflict" and violence in the schools because parents would "desert in droves any school that could not maintain order."[16]

With a rural reputation and an African American population of 0.3 percent, the Granite State was not an ideal test case for Friedman's belief that urban, multicultural settings would make the best proving ground for education vouchers. Moreover, the Jencks report on education vouchers—which many OEO staffers used as both a "Blue Book" for planning and a "gospel" for ideology—took a dim view of Friedman's "Unregulated Market

Model," which would "redistribute resources away from the poor…increase economic segregation in the schools…and exacerbate the problems of existing public schools."[17]

But voucher proposals that prohibited racial segregation had been attracting the support of liberal and conservative policy makers since the mid-1960s, symbolized in the advocacy of Christopher Jencks and Milton Friedman. Other scholars of varied political stripe were also intrigued by education vouchers in this era, including Theodore Sizer (Harvard Graduate School of Education dean), Thomas Sowell (economist and conservative public intellectual), Henry Levin (economist and left-leaning academic), James Coleman (sociologist and author of the Equality of Opportunity federal study of education), and John Coons and Stephen Sugarman (law professors and policy specialists). In the OEO of the early 1970s, liberal voucher advocates sought Friedman's support for compensatory vouchers, something to which the free-market economist acquiesced.[18]

Nevertheless, Friedman's first choice remained a voucher model that was open to a wide range of private schools, and he argued that federally funded voucher experiments should include both free-market models (such as New Hampshire) and public-school-only models (such as Alum Rock). Helped along by his *Newsweek* columns and 1973 *Playboy* interview, as well as a *New York Times Sunday Magazine* article, Friedman was instrumental in keeping interest in unregulated vouchers alive in conservative circles and in bringing new converts into the fold. He advocated vouchers of equal value regardless of household income, leeway for parents to top off the voucher with additional tuition, and the inclusion of religious schools. Indeed, the "Friedmanite voucher" was the term policy makers used in the 1970s to refer to plans near the unregulated end of the continuum. In an era of growing government expenditures and regulations, Friedman's position stressed the individual rights of parents, and for conservative leaders in New Hampshire, the unregulated voucher promised to hold big government at bay.[19]

THE NEW HAMPSHIRE CONTEXT

Friedman's personal relationships with New Hampshire policy makers also helped connect school vouchers to the Granite State. Not inconsequentially, the University of Chicago economist had summer homes in New England from 1950 to 1980, first in New Hampshire and then just across the Connecticut River in Vermont, where he cultivated relationships with New Hampshire politicians and Dartmouth College professors. Friedman's home from 1950 to 1967 was located in Orford near Mt. Cube Farm, the residence of Governor Meldrim Thomson, whom Friedman knew person-ally. In spite of their similar libertarian beliefs and the "personal and of-ficial interest" that Governor Thomson took in the OEO vouchers grant, Friedman's relationship with Thomson was strained. But Thomson's per-sonal disagreement with Freidman—the two quarreled over alleged tres-passing—did not extend to ideological differences.[20]

Besides, the well-connected Friedman had additional New Hampshire allies. Friedman found his biggest admirer to be William Bittenbender, a former businessman whom Thomson appointed Chair of the State Board of Education in 1973. Thomson also appointed Bittenbender to the Governor's Commission on Public Education the same year. Bittenbender contacted Friedman shortly after OEO staffers began wooing New Hampshire offi-cials, and soon Bittenbender was relying on Friedman and another eco-nomics professor, John Menge of Dartmouth College, for advice. That summer, Bittenbender broke a 3–3 tie vote at the Board of Education to authorize the state to apply for federal funds for vouchers and to prepare a voucher feasibility study.[21]

New Hampshire was a promising site for school vouchers in the early 1970s. First, belying its rural reputation, New Hampshire had long been an urbanized state, a consequence of 19th-century industrialization. New Hampshire's shoe and textile mills concentrated the population into several cities, Manchester being the largest. All was not lost economically when the mills began to close their doors in the 1950s; the industrial population was augmented by the movement of people and businesses from Massachusetts and other New England states attracted to New Hampshire's low taxes and charming geography.[22]

Second, an extensive system of urban parochial schools, along with non-sectarian private academies, provided the state with a ready supply of alter-natives to the public schools. Like other parochial school systems across the nation, enrollments in New Hampshire's Catholic schools began to decline in the late 1960s: The Catholic system enrolled 35,614 students in 1966, but by 1973 enrollment had dropped to 21,687. To staunch the decline, the state passed dual enrollment provisions in 1969, whereby students could simultaneously attend public and private schools part-time, with the sum meeting full-time attendance requirements. Dual enrollment allowed city school districts to assign some of their teachers to parochial schools to teach secular subjects, while the state and the local school districts also paid parochial schools to rent classroom space for the public school teach-ers. Dual enrollment provisions defrayed instructional expenses at the Catholic schools and generally encouraged public–private cooperation. Parochial school supporters viewed vouchers as a similar avenue of pub-lic support, particularly since dual enrollment was challenged in federal court. Indeed, the U.S. District Court struck down New Hampshire's dual enrollment program in May 1973 as "an excessive governmental entanglement with religion."[23]

Third, the state already had voucher-like policies in place for the smallest school districts, for which maintaining high schools or even elementary schools was too expensive. Local school boards could elect to pay tuition for their students to enroll in other districts. At the elementary level, district tuition payments equaled the state-average cost per student, with parents having the option of topping off their payments if they selected schools that spent more per student than the statewide average. At the secondary level, the state required the sending district to pay the receiving district the full tuition at any public school. In the town of Lyme, for example, the district based its secondary education budget on a poll of eighth-grade parents' high school preferences. Although most parents chose nearby Hannover High School for their children, some selected high schools across the river in Vermont.[24]

Most important, New Hampshire's political climate was far enough to the right to produce demand for a Friedmanite voucher plan among the leadership and, potentially, in the grassroots. Governor Meldrim Thomson's radical conservative credentials were well-known. After running unsuccessfully for governor in 1970 on "George Wallace's American Party ticket," he was elected in 1972 on an "Ax the Tax" platform. As governor he headed the national Conservative Caucus, where he campaigned to remove United Nations Ambassador Andrew Young. A strident Cold Warrior abroad—he believed the New Hampshire National Guard should train to use nuclear weapons, and he considered apartheid South Africa a strategic ally—at home Thomson argued for law and order, capital punishment, a return to self-reliance, and low taxes for New Hampshire residents. His educational policies favored school prayer and neighborhood schools, and he based such positions on local control. Much like Goldwater, Thomson believed the school districts, not the federal government, should determine educational policy. Indeed, he first came to the attention of *Union Leader* publisher William Loeb in 1968 when, as a school board member in Orford, he sought to return federal funds for his district's remedial reading program.[25]

The *Union Leader* was among the most conservative newspapers in the nation. For example, in 1957, it was one of the few daily newspapers in the North to oppose federal intervention in the Little Rock crisis. That year, Elizabeth Scripps "Nackey" Loeb, William Loeb's spouse, drew and published a cartoon showing U.S. paratroopers forcing together a black girl and a white girl, with the title "Brotherhood by Bayonet." Underneath, the caption read "Start loving each other. That's a Court Order!" The cartoon

was reprinted widely in the South: the image could be found on segregationist pamphlets, bumper stickers, and flyers. By the early 1970s the
backlash to school desegregation, especially busing, had spread nationwide—according to historian Rick Perlstein, it was "the one growth area
of mass political participation." In spite of a minuscule African American
population in New Hampshire, anti-busing swayed voters in the Granite
State also. Governor Thomson opposed busing for purposes of racial desegregation and sought state and federal legislation to keep the practice out
of his state. Although Thomson, his appointee William Bittenbender, and
his political mentor, William Loeb, provided most of the statewide muscle
in spreading the voucher message, several school superintendents, school
board members, clergy, and other local leaders also worked to introduce
vouchers.[26]

Beginning in June 1973, Thomson and Bittenbender put federal funds to
work to bring the Friedmanite voucher to the Granite State. Bittenbender
established a Voucher Project Office that was closely connected to the
Governor's Commission on Public Education—the two offices shared a telephone number. With the governor's input, Bittenbender enlisted the help
of the state commissioner of education, Newell Paire, and hired a project
director, staff members, and consultants, including those at the Center for
the Study of Public Policy. The Center's new director, Frank Overlan, had
warmed to the idea of a Friedmanite voucher experiment, even though
the viewpoint that had carried the Center under Jencks's tenure was that
"a voucher system which does not include... effective safeguards would be
worse than no voucher system at all." Staffers at the Center and in the New
Hampshire Vouchers Project Office, along with Professor Menge, produced feasibility studies in the summer and fall. In 1973, Thomson also
pressed for an enabling law in the General Court, New Hampshire's legislative body. The enabling legislation was passed two years later.[27]

At its inception, the New Hampshire voucher project suffered a serious
setback when the U.S. Supreme Court handed down two decisions that essentially ended programs of state tax support for tuition at religious elementary and secondary schools. On June 25, 1973, the Supreme Court ruled
that tuition reimbursements for parents and tuition grants for students
enrolled in sectarian schools were unconstitutional (*Sloan v. Lemon* and
Committee for Public Education and Religious Liberty v. Nyquist). Based on
its 1971 *Lemon v. Kurtzman* decision, the Supreme Court curtailed a variety
of strategies states had devised to assist their parochial schools, ruling that
such policies "had the (primary) effect of promoting religion" or caused "excessive entanglement" between church and state. "History may thus record
Nyquist and *Lemon* as the last shot in the long battle over specific state aid for
religious education," boasted a lawyer retained by the National Educational

New Hampshire governor Meldrim Thomson and Attorney General David Souter in 1977. Thomson introduced vouchers to the Granite State in 1973. Three decades later, Supreme Court Justice Souter opposed them for religious schools. (AP Photo.)

Association who filed friend-of-the-court briefs. Due to the *Nyquist* ruling, the federal government forced New Hampshire officials to submit a new voucher feasibility study, one that excluded religious institutions. The Supreme Court decision caused more than a delay for the Voucher Project, however. It also knocked out the most readily available supply of non-public schools in the state. In response, the Catholic League for Religious and Civil Rights threatened to sue the state because its revised voucher proposal "discriminated against parochial schools."[28]

By early 1974 Bittenbender and other state officials seemed to be back on track. They crisscrossed the state to disseminate information to voters and to generate interest in local voucher votes at various district meetings scheduled for later that spring. Bittenbender playfully used Cold War concerns as a foundation for free-market vouchers. "There's a clear and present danger out there," he told an audience in Jefferson, New Hampshire. "There are some groups of dissidents who would like to take us backward in time to an earlier America—there are, in fact, parents who would like to make free choices with their children's futures uppermost in their minds!"[29]

Meanwhile, the Catholic lawsuit never materialized. Nonetheless, even with the exclusion of parochial schools, a nominally Catholic organization, the New Hampshire Citizens for a Pure Voucher System, worked for vouchers at the grassroots level, and the school superintendent for the Manchester Diocese, Reverend Joseph P. Duffy, S. J., continued to serve on the Voucher Project Advisory Board, along with two presidents of Catholic colleges.[30]

William Loeb's *Union Leader* pushed for vouchers with a series of favorable editorials. Loeb's advocacy culminated in the spring of 1974, when he added an eight-page insert to the *Union Leader* that staffers at the New Hampshire Voucher Project prepared. Five other supportive New Hampshire newspapers followed Loeb's lead. Called *The Voucher,* the purpose of the tabloid was "to inform the citizens…particularly those in the 17 communities considering adoption of the voucher test." It included an announcement from the governor, a lead story by Professor Menge ("How Free Can a Free Education Be?"), an explanation of vouchers by State Board of Education Chair Bittenbender, commentary from pundits from around the country (e.g., William F. Buckley termed the New Hampshire project "the most exciting educational experiment of the century"), a supportive resolution by the National Council on Educational Research (the NIE governing body), a favorable commentary from the Diocese of Manchester, and a series of questions and answers. The insert also announced the times and places for the school district meetings at which residents could vote on the proposal. Officials at the Voucher Office allotted one page of the insert for a rebuttal by the state affiliate of the National Education Association. Its author, Thomas Adams, was photographed with long hair and a beard, while the others—Weinberger, Thomson, Bittenbender, Menge—appeared clean-shaven with short hair. Along with the 130,000 newspaper inserts, school districts and private schools distributed copies "to parents through their school children." Radio stations also spread the word in the spring of 1974, as school districts and voters considered participating in earnest.[31]

Academics did their part too. In addition to Menge, who also served as a project consultant, two other Dartmouth professors served on the voucher project advisory board. Menge and Bittenbender "pressed" Washington for funding commitments, and Menge also coordinated the activities of Frank Overlan with Milton Friedman and Denis Doyle of NIE. In addition, Menge secured funding from the Smith Richardson Foundation to encourage private school participation and to underwrite a summer 1974 voucher symposium in Hannover to spread the free-market voucher idea to the public. The speakers were Frank Overlan, Denis Doyle, Stephen Sugarman (law professor at UCLA and a prominent advocate of compensatory vouchers), and, of course, Milton Friedman.[32]

Academics from Cambridge, Massachusetts assisted with the project, but perhaps with less of a free-market edge than the professors at Dartmouth. The state hired the Center for Contemporary Public Policy to serve as the primary consultant on the project. The viewpoint of its director, Frank Overlan, swayed many of the liberal staffers at NIE to support the New Hampshire voucher experiment even though it did not include compensatory safeguards. The Center prepared detailed strategies along with a series of progress reports. It was the analysts at the Cambridge think tank who enabled New Hampshire policy makers to meet the federal guidelines for the project, which required adequate public information, informed consent of the voters, and at least one alternative for each pre-existing public school.[33]

As one of its first uses of federal money, the state commissioned Cambridge Survey Research to conduct a poll in the summer of 1973. Poll takers visited eight hundred homes in eight of the state's cities, with results that were promising for voucher advocates. Majorities favored vouchers because they would force teachers to work harder to keep students and because they would enable children of modest means to "choose their schools just like the rich do." The survey also uncovered viewpoints that pointed to obstacles for vouchers supporters. For example, a majority of respondents believed, in distinction to the June 1973 Supreme Court rulings that excluded parochial schools, that religious schools should nonetheless participate in the event of a voucher program. Majorities also predicted that they would not consider establishing schools with other parents should vouchers become a reality.[34]

YANKEE DEMOCRACY

In the end, however, conservative politicians and liberal policy wonks were not the ultimate arbiters of school vouchers. Federal guidelines insisted on "informed consent," and in New Hampshire that responsibility fell upon the voters. Yankee democracy, at least as it was practiced in New Hampshire, included voting on a variety of issues that in other states would have been considered by elected representatives or public administrators only. New Hampshire's tradition of town meetings, which dated back to the Colonial era, encompassed district schools as well. Each spring, school districts held open meetings in which residents cast votes on how to best spend public dollars. Residents might decide whether to add a wing to the elementary school, for example, or to contract with a different transportation company. Some of the districts were (and are) so small that they joined together in supervisory school unions to provide elementary and/or secondary education. The smallest districts maintained no schools at all, electing instead to send their students to schools outside the district. Still other districts were quite urban. But all offered spring meetings where residents could weigh in on pressing educational concerns.[35]

Bittenbender began soliciting school district participation in the summer of 1973 and put out a state Board of Education press release in January 1974 for local school districts to express an interest in vouchers. Thirty districts responded—ten declined participation, and twenty requested informational meetings. School boards declined for "many and varied reasons," which included more important priorities, lack of assurances of specific state and federal funding, lack of private school alternatives, and unwillingness to become part of an experiment. Ideological differences did not figure in the justifications for the rejections that district officials sent to the Vouchers Office. "Members of the Concord School Board were not against the voucher project," explained its superintendent. "They did, however, feel that local needs were more pressing at this time."[36]

Many of the boards that expressed interest did so because of the promise of federal funding for innovative programming or to meet expanding enrollments. The Dover superintendent, for example, gave his "main reason" as "the incentive funds amounting to $1,400,000+." Most significantly, the boards of nearly all of the city districts—including Manchester—declined to participate. Presumably, the Manchester Board of Education, heading the largest school district in the state, saw no clear benefits for its students, since the largest contingency of private school students, by far, enrolled in the Catholic schools. In the late spring of 1974, seventeen school districts held votes on whether to participate in the planning phase of the voucher experiment. Three of those school districts were urban.[37]

The most important opponents of vouchers were the National Education Association (NEA) and its New Hampshire affiliate. The national organization had opposed school vouchers since 1970, when, in response to the OEO voucher initiative, it resolved that "the so-called 'voucher plan'... could lead to racial, economic, and social isolation of children and weaken or destroy the public school system." In conjunction with sixteen other organizations, including the American Federation of Teachers, NEA officials had even met with Rumsfeld and other OEO officials in the fall of 1970 and "attempt[ed] to change their plans." Since representatives of the NEA-led coalition believed the executive branch was bypassing Congress, it also urged the House Education and Labor Committee "to order the Office of Economic Opportunity to discontinue all grants for feasibility studies and funding of voucher programs" until Congress had conducted thorough hearings. Rumsfeld claimed that the coalition "border[ed] on the irrational" and doubted "that these people speak for most teachers." The NEA's executive secretary, Sam M. Lambert, rallied the membership by predicting a ruined public school system should vouchers prevail: "It would...reduce public education to a position of being the 'school of last resort,'" he stated. "In all likelihood," he added with a hint of racism, those attending the public schools would consist mainly of minority groups, 'problem children,' and children of disadvantaged parents."[38]

The NEA's New Hampshire affiliate opposed the state voucher plan on a variety of fronts. It distributed position papers to teachers, helping to persuade NEA members to denounce the vouchers measure at district meetings. It encouraged teachers to disobey orders to distribute voucher flyers and newspaper inserts for students to take home to their parents. It sponsored a conference on alternative education that highlighted reforms other than vouchers and complained that the Voucher Office prevented important opponents of vouchers, such as the National Congress of Parents and Teachers (later, the Parent Teacher Association) and the New Hampshire Council of Churches, from publishing articles in the statewide newspaper insert. Occasionally, the state affiliate used racist imagery to bolster opposition. For example, Director of Professional Development Thomas Adams reminded voters in his newspaper insert article that "40 percent of the families" in the Alum Rock district "are supported by welfare funds." He added that, according to the *Wall Street Journal,* the most popular course offerings in Alum Rock involve "multicultural field trips" where students "prepare soul-food dinners and luau celebrations for their parents."[39]

Ground zero of the voucher battle turned out to be the city of Berlin, "The City that Trees Built." There was a strong Catholic and French-Canadian presence in Berlin; immigrants settled to work in the lumber and paper mills, but Berlin's population peaked in the 1920s—its major industry had suffered setbacks since the Depression. Berlin was the only North Country district to consider school vouchers; nearly all of the other interested school districts were located near the state's southern border with Massachusetts, where population growth was strong. Map 3.1 shows Berlin, the capital city of Concord, and the school districts that authorized participating in the phase of the New Hampshire Education Voucher Project.[40]

Hearing of the voucher plan from the newspapers in the spring of 1973, the Chair of Berlin Regional Catholic Schools, Reverend Michael J. Griffen, asked William Bittenbender to include Berlin in the OEO voucher experiment. He was joined by the Superintendent of the Berlin Public Schools, Lawrence Dwyer. The Catholic schools already had several cooperative arrangements with Berlin's public school district. The dual enrollment

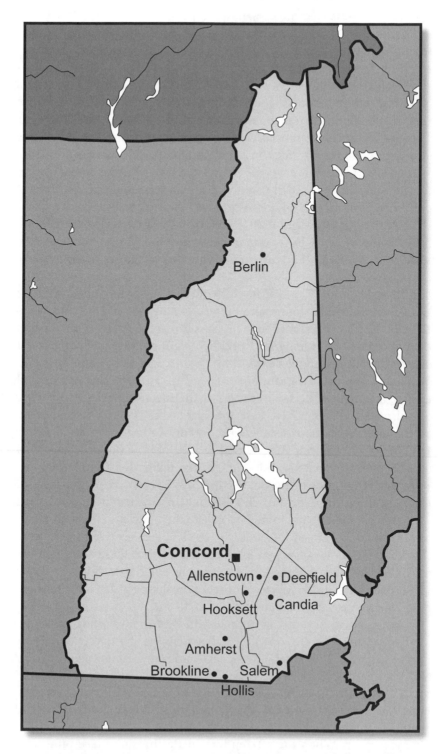

Map 3.1 New Hampshire: Concord, Berlin, and School Districts Participating in Voucher Program.

program had been going strong there for the past three years, with public school teachers teaching secular subjects in the Catholic schools. Conversely, the Catholic Church provided afterschool religious instruction in the public schools. Teachers of both systems attended workshops together, and the two school boards, public and Catholic, held joint annual meetings. These collaborations were in addition to the usual arrangement of tax-supported bus service and school lunches for children in all schools. In June 1973, the Berlin mayor also contacted Bittenbender, informing him that the Berlin City Council voted to accept a recommendation from the public and Catholic school boards to have "Berlin considered as a site for the 'Experimental Voucher Plan.'" The school leaders based their request on the high prevalence of poverty in Berlin and the North Country, and on the deleterious effects that the abolition of dual enrollment would have on both school systems.[41]

In the spring of 1974, advocates for vouchers in Berlin pulled out all the stops. The local radio station aired interviews by Bittenbender and James Leonard, the state director of the Vouchers Project in its first year. The local newspaper, the *Berlin Reporter,* published eight editorials of support. The chair of the public school board, John Vezina, was one of the prominent advocates. Skeptical of the authority of education professionals to serve the needs of all children, he saw vouchers as the means for parents to "regain control of their schools." He also anticipated that federal voucher funds could enable Berlin to furnish better programs for "handicapped children." Members of a new group, Concerned Parents for the Berlin Voucher, distributed bumper stickers and other pro-vouchers literature, canvassed Berlin neighborhoods by telephone, and drove voters to the polls. In spite of the exclusion of parochial schools, educators distributed copies of the state's voucher tabloid for children to give to their parents. The pro-voucher literature held out hope for Catholic parents. It is likely that some Catholic school supporters were swayed by its assertions that there were still ways around the Supreme Court—Catholic schools could participate by becoming non-sectarian, with religious instruction taking place after school or being relegated to elective status.[42]

Opponents also mounted a campaign in Berlin. Radio talk shows provided one forum, and two open meetings organized by the school districts provided another. Public school teachers came out strongly against vouchers at the meetings and in the press. In alignment with the organization's national position, the president of the local NEA affiliate, Robert Verge, opposed vouchers on the grounds that private schools could exclude difficult-to-educate students and that the voucher itself would serve as a subsidy to affluent parents. When the referendum in Berlin took place on May 23, 1974, voters narrowly rejected vouchers, 557 to 520.[43]

In other parts of the state, when the dust settled from the school district meetings and referenda in the spring of 1974, supporters had convinced only a handful of rural school districts to sign on to develop detailed voucher plans, with the proviso that voters would decide later whether to implement them. The reluctance of most district school boards to put vouchers to the voters, coupled with negative votes in twelve of the districts that considered participating, essentially ended school vouchers in the Granite State. Even so, the project limped along for two more years. The seven districts that did authorize participation—Candia, Allenstsown, Hooksett, Deerfield, Brookline, Amherst, and Hollis—served a 1970 population of just under 20,000 people and made up parts of three supervisory unions in southern New Hampshire. Only four of the districts were contiguous to each other. Hooksett was the largest district, with 1,570 students. This included 92 students enrolled in parochial schools and 72 students in other private schools. The Voucher Project office went ahead and applied for federal funds anyway, treating the seven districts as a single entity. Over the next two years, two of the districts dropped out of the program, but one urban district on the Massachusetts border, Salem, joined in. Because of its status as a city with nearly 6,000 students, Salem's participation gave voucher advocates hope that a viable voucher system would be implemented. But in the spring of 1976, voters in all the remaining districts, including Salem, rejected the program. Voucher advocates at the federal and state levels had overreached—demand from the grassroots, for a variety of reasons, did not match their enthusiasm.[44]

AFTERMATH OF NEW HAMPSHIRE VOUCHERS

Contemporary observers and participants posited several reasons for the rejection of education vouchers in the Granite State. Many of the reasons given for the defeat were managerial in nature. It was a question of leadership (there was turnover in the voucher director's position at the state level), or clarity (the information disseminated to voters was confusing), or timing (there were too many delays at federal and state levels), or ambivalence (the voucher leadership quarreled over the details). For partisans it was the powerful teachers unions that scuttled the plan. The NEA state affiliate bragged that "The New Hampshire Education Association scored a smashing victory against Republican governor Meldrim Thomson and the arch-conservative state board majority who saw vouchers as a way to funnel public money into private schools." Looking back on the plan some forty years later, Milton Friedman believed that "the ambitious attempt to introduce vouchers to the large cities of New Hampshire ... was aborted by the opposition of the teachers unions and the local administrators."[45]

Although voucher supporters tended to chalk up the reversal to voter confusion or opposition from the teachers organizations, there were other, more immediate reasons that school vouchers failed to take root in the Granite State. The exclusion of parochial schools due to the federal Supreme Court rulings of *Lemon* and especially *Nyquist* removed a considerable base of electoral support in cities that were predominantly Catholic. Manchester, the seat of the state's Catholic diocese, did not participate, and, with the exception of Salem, neither did any other New Hampshire city. The city with the closest vote in 1974 was Berlin, which had the support of the public school board and, in spite of the Supreme Court rulings excluding parochial schools, the Berlin Regional Catholic School Board. Had the proposal included sectarian schools, it is an open question whether the vote would have gone the other way. On one hand, the parochial school enrollment was nearly as large as the public school enrollment in Berlin, and hence parents of Catholic school students would have good reason to go to the polls. On the other hand, so would supporters of the status quo in the public schools, since vouchers almost certainly would have cost the district revenue and enrollments in the long run. At the very least, the inclusion of religious schools would have raised the visibility of vouchers in urban New Hampshire.

In the rural parts of the state, concerns about viability of public–private vouchers almost certainly detracted from the program. Although some voters in the rural districts might have supported vouchers initially because of a belief in free-market competition, as the details firmed up voters became aware of the practical difficulties of creating even a single institutional alternative to the closest public school. The educational realities of low population density—namely, long distances from home to school and the disincentive to build new schools—made it difficult to convince voters that alternatives could materialize. Even schools-within-schools were a hard sell in districts with elementary schools and high schools that had small enrollments to begin with. Some rural voters in growing districts saw the potential of using federal funding to improve educational programs. But the more complicated and expensive the administrative and transportation systems became, the less funding would be available for innovative programming.

Finally, the political baggage that school vouchers had taken on by 1976—as an imported federal program spearheaded by the disgraced Nixon and Ford administrations rather than an initiative home grown in the Granite State—also caused voters to lose interest. The most indirect explanation for the rejection of school vouchers was Watergate: Had the Nixon administration not imploded in scandal, vouchers might have received higher priority in the executive branch and retained their political legitimacy for voters in at least a handful of New Hampshire school districts. Some of the school superintendents had viewed vouchers as an opportunity to create new public school programs with federal money, much as Alum Rock had done. Presidential scandal probably tipped the balance against this strategy in a state whose voters were already famously leery of federal control. And certainly, Watergate postponed the resurgence of federal interest in vouchers until the election of Ronald Reagan to the presidency (he proposed compensatory vouchers in his second term). But presidential scandal was a red herring compared to the structural obstacles facing vouchers in the Granite State—most important, interpretations of the First Amendment that excluded parochial schools in urban New Hampshire, as well as the low population density of rural regions, which made alternative schools impractical. Such obstacles outweighed the attractiveness of "free" federal funds or free-market ideology.[46]

It would be easy to overemphasize the importance of the New Hampshire Voucher Project to federal and state education policy in the 1970s. For the Nixon and Ford administrations, putting breaks on court-ordered desegregation plans received much more attention than did the still-quirky notion of school vouchers. Indeed, in Richard Nixon's memoirs, published in 1978, school vouchers did not merit a mention. Rather, the education topics he deemed "most explosive" were the civil rights questions of "school desegregation and busing." According to Ehrlichman, "Busing was a virulent issue much of the time. The federal courts were ordering the busing of white kids and black kids, and Richard Nixon wanted every one of their parents to know that he opposed it." Even among President Nixon's proposals for aid to non-public schools, the cause célèbre was tuition tax credits, not vouchers. And in spite of the importance of school desegregation during the Nixon and Ford years, Americans more broadly did not view education as a pressing federal concern. According to Roper Polls conducted during the 1972 federal election, respondents ranked education 26th out of 26 problems facing the nation; during the 1976 election, education was not even listed as a concern.[47]

At the local level, the voucher project failed to generate interest beyond small circles of supporters and detractors. The close Berlin vote in 1974 represented less than 11 percent of the registered voters, and this was the highest rate of voter participation in the state. Just 27 voters in the little district of Allenstown, in a 15–12 vote, determined preliminary participation in the Voucher Project, and this in a school district with a population of nearly 3,000 people. School vouchers mattered a great deal to free-market ideologues, conservative politicians, innovative policy makers, school board members, and teacher union leaders, but in New Hampshire their importance failed to resonate much beyond these partisan circles.[48]

A core group of advocates loyal to the market model in education worked hard to convince Granite State voters and school boards to put school vouchers into practice at the local level. But in the end the New Hampshire episode was a diversion in the efforts of voucher advocates, from a legislative and populist movement at the state level to an effort by a handful of powerbrokers to sway voters at the school-district level. In the 1950s and early 1960s, vouchers in the form of tuition grants fell under the purview of southern state governments spurred to action by the popular reaction in the white South to school desegregation. In the 1980s and 1990s, legislatures in northern states like Wisconsin (1990) and Ohio (1995) developed voucher legislation for particular cities, this time in the form of "parental choice," but without the input of local school boards or voters. In the 1970s, by contrast, voucher strategists went directly to the local districts to win support.[49]

In the Wisconsin program targeted to Milwaukee, an alliance between a conservative Republican governor and a liberal state representative moved voucher legislation—dubbed the Milwaukee Parental Choice Program—through the statehouse. Undergirding this alliance was considerable dissatisfaction with the Milwaukee Public Schools, support for a pre-existing cluster of non-sectarian schools serving African American and Hispanic Milwaukeeans, and significant backing by conservative foundations and think tanks. Black lawmakers supported the program. In Ohio the Cleveland Scholarship and Tutoring Program had a similar pedigree, although the vouchers push in Ohio included support from the Catholic Church. Significantly, it lacked the same degree of support by black lawmakers in the legislature, though it had the support of the Cleveland mayor and a city councilwoman. Both programs were compensatory and for both, the arena for the voucher fight was the state legislature, not the city school district. The New Hampshire effort, with its Friedmanite voucher and its canvassing of local districts for votes and school board support, represented a detour in the larger movement.[50]

Of the advocates who have been attracted to vouchers over the past 50 years, the ones with the most loyalty to the market model seem to be those who look at education from conservative perspectives. For Christopher Jencks, Jonathan Kozol, and many others on the political left, the voucher mystique might have been fleeting; not so for Milton Friedman and other like-minded free-marketeers and social conservatives. Political conservatives, although they experienced a setback in New Hampshire, succeeded in implementing vouchers once they hitched their proposals not just to an ideological belief in the superiority of competitive markets, but also to the concerns parents had regarding the difficulties of the urban public schools. In a sense, then, Christopher Jencks and Milton Friedman both had it right, in that they predicted that the most fertile ground for education vouchers was the cities. But it was coalitions headed by conservatives—often with the support of urban parents and their state elected officials—that persuaded state legislatures to institute vouchers as a tangible alternative to the urban public schools.

Besides the challenge of holding these unlikely coalitions of voucher supporters (and themselves) together, conservatives faced two additional obstacles in their struggle to bring education vouchers to the mainstream. First, electorates trailed behind the ambitions of voucher supporters—in New Hampshire, and, for the last 30 years, in other states. In state referenda on the voucher question, vouchers have gone down to defeat at the polls (Utah in 2007, for example). Second, the New Hampshire voucher episode demonstrates that Americans were ambivalent about allowing the federal government to set the agenda in education: New Hampshire voters and educational leaders seemed wary of this federal initiative in the 1970s, just as many Americans today share this same ambivalence to federal initiatives in education. Interestingly, both New Hampshire and Utah voters had considered Friedmanite voucher plans, with little or no restrictions on the income levels of participants. Since the 1970s, however, legislators tended to give more support for vouchers programs that were, to some degree, compensatory.

The New Hampshire voucher project provided guidance for conservative advocates: Local districts, whether in the guise of school boards or voters, were not reliable voucher allies. Rather, the more favorable terrain lay at the statehouse. More important, advocates learned from the New Hampshire experience that for vouchers to be viable, urban settings were essential. In this, two trends in urban education tended to favor the growth of compensatory voucher plans. Dissatisfaction with the urban public schools had, if anything, widened since the 1970s, providing a ready supply of potential participants. And with the Supreme Court's upholding of the Cleveland, Ohio, plan in *Zelman v. Simmons-Harris* (2002), parochial schools, the most readily available alternative to public education in cities, were legal recipients of students' education vouchers. The New Hampshire voucher experience was a detour, an effort that tempted rural districts but, ultimately, failed to generate support outside of a small coterie of free-market voucher advocates.[51]

When school vouchers burst back on the scene in the late 1980s, their promoters from conservative circles no longer attempted to persuade local school districts to sign on. Their efforts, rather, flowed in two directions: lawmakers and governors began promoting vouchers as a viable school reform at the state level, something to be legislated in statehouses rather than voted on by the people. Promoters also began to cultivate parent supporters at the grassroots, by tapping into the concerns parents had about the public educations their children received. While many suburban and rural parents were satisfied enough with the public schools their children attended, the same could not be said about public schools in the big cities.

Chapter 4

THE URBAN SCHOOL CRISIS

"If you're drowning and a hand is extended to you, you don't ask if the hand is attached to a Democrat or a Republican," Wisconsin State Representative Annette "Polly" Williams stated at a 1990 American Opportunities Workshop. "From the African American position—at the bottom, looking up—there's not much difference between the Democrats and the Republicans anyway. Whoever is sincere about working with us, our door is open." Williams, a Democrat, authored the 1990 legislation that brought school vouchers to Milwaukee. Her bill followed on the heels of proposals by Republican Governor Tommy Thompson that sought vouchers for low-income Milwaukee public school students to attend secular and religious private schools in Milwaukee County. Williams's support for non-sectarian private schools in the city of Milwaukee and her leadership of black elected officials on this issue put school vouchers over the top in the Badger State. In the 1980s blacks and Catholics in Milwaukee looked to vouchers as an alternative to the public schools and as means to maintain private and parochial schools. Racial minorities supported Milwaukee's fledgling network of private community schools from the 1970s, whereas Catholics began promoting school vouchers in the 1950s in support of parochial schools. By the 1980s, concerns over urban schools moved vouchers to the big city, but unlike the New Hampshire efforts, in Wisconsin the battleground was the state legislature.[1]

The so-called urban school crisis, of course, did not begin in the 1980s. In *Slums and Suburbs* (1961), the author, Harvard University President James Conant, was convinced that the contrasting quality between "prosperous suburban schools" and "big city slum schools" allowed for "social dynamite to accumulate in our large cities." And historian David Tyack, after exhaustive inquiries into urban schools of the early 20th century—supposedly the glory days of urban education—concluded that "schools have rarely taught the children of the poor effectively—and this failure has been systematic, not idiosyncratic." Whereas compensatory educational programs and racial desegregation formed the pillars of education strategies designed to ameliorate the crisis, by the 1970s and 1980s such strategies lost the political consensus necessary for complete implementation. Milwaukeeans disillusioned with urban public schools looked to other strategies. Some continued to vote with their feet, either relocating to the suburbs or enrolling their children in private schools. But others looked to school vouchers to fill what they believed were voids in the public system.[2]

The Milwaukee Parental Choice Program of 1990 (MPCP) was the first publicly funded voucher program to be implemented outside the South. Intended to provide Milwaukee residents of modest means—mostly blacks and Latinos—with alternatives to the public schools, MPCP enabled up to 1 percent of city students to attend non-sectarian private schools free of charge. The ferment of the urban school crisis in the post–World War II era—and the efforts of Milwaukeeans and statewide leaders to blunt this crisis within a context of economic stagnation and the growing popularity of political conservatism—were preconditions for MPCP.

But the tradition of school choice in Milwaukee stretches back further, to the 1950s and the efforts of a Jesuit priest, Reverend Virgil C. Blum, who galvanized Catholics and other religious supporters to seek public funding for parochial school students on grounds of religious freedom. Blum did not see his dream realized. He died just before the MPCP became law, and, as compromise legislation funding for tuition at parochial schools ended up on the cutting room floor. Blum's writings and activism helped break the association of school vouchers with massive resistance to school desegregation in the South. His efforts in the 1950s and 1960s kept school vouchers in the public eye as an alternative method of funding schools in spite of the durability of New Deal–style welfare state liberalism that held sway over Midwestern educational policy makers in those decades. He sought to build a multi-religious, conservative coalition through the politics of parental choice and defense of religion. However, his organizational style and political outlook precluded him from finding common cause with school voucher supporters among racial and linguistic minorities as the civil rights movement accelerated and then fragmented in the late 1960s.[3]

REVEREND VIRGIL BLUM'S VOUCHERS CRUSADE

Blum was a professor at Marquette University in Milwaukee from 1956 until his death in 1990. He authored one of the earliest treatises on school vouchers, *Freedom of Choice in Education* which, together with economist Milton Freedman's *Capitalism and Freedom*, helped popularize school vouchers outside of the South. Blum also helped to found an advocacy group for school vouchers in 1959, called Citizens for Educational Freedom. Initially an organization of Catholic school parents in St. Louis, with Blum's assistance the group evolved into a national, non-denominational organization that lobbied the federal Office of Education as well as state governments for school vouchers on free-market and freedom-of-religion grounds.

Blum earned his Ph.D. in political science from St. Louis University in 1954. Along the way, he studied constitutional law with two conservative professors at the University of Chicago, Robert Horn and C. Herman Pritchett. In his dissertation, "Legal Aspects of Equality and Religious Liberty," Blum mounted constitutional arguments in favor of public aid to parochial schools that, in their broadest contours, remained fixed until his death in 1990. Blum shied away from "attacking the doctrine of absolute separation of church and state" that inhered in the Establishment Clause of the First Amendment, since he believed this doctrine was accepted "by the majority of the American people." Rather, he based his rationale on the Free Exercise Clause of the First Amendment and the Equal Protection Clause of the Fourteenth Amendment. He believed that parents who exercised their right to enroll their children in religious schools should have access to the same educational benefits that public school students received. One such benefit that Blum believed was not equally distributed to public and parochial school students was bus transportation. The other, more important benefit was schooling that was tuition-free.[4]

Blum saw his dissertation as more than a constitutional argument for public aid to parochial schools or, as he put it, "the right of the child to attend a parochial school without suffering the imposition of economic reprisals." He also viewed it as an opening gambit in his effort to educate the Catholic laity on the importance of political struggle and coalition building in support for parochial schools. "We must have well-trained Catholic lay leaders," he wrote, "who can speak and write authoritatively—that is, in the language of...the judicial opinions of the Supreme Court of the United States." Blum admired the Jehovah's Witnesses and the National Association for the Advancement of Colored People (NAACP), who utilized constitutional arguments in winning their court cases, implying that Catholics could do the same. He asked in 1956, "Had the Witnesses and the NAACP appealed merely to tradition, would their rights have been sustained?" In the realm of public opinion, both Catholic and non-Catholics mattered in defense of religious education. "For their own good," Blum informed his Jesuit Provincial, "they must unite in defending their mutual constitutional rights." And the parochial schools were just one facet in Blum's political struggle. He also saw his mission as rallying the religious faithful to battle the forces of secularism and permissiveness in a wider culture war.[5]

Blum's *Freedom of Choice in Education,* published by MacMillan in 1958, was part of a growing Cold War consensus on the importance of religious belief in protecting American cultural identity from the forces of Communism. President Dwight D. Eisenhower perhaps summed up this growing consensus best: "a deeply felt religious faith" is essential for Americans—"and I don't care what it is." True to this new consensus on religion, Blum's book included a forward by the neoconservative Jewish theologian Will Herberg, author of *Protestant-Catholic-Jew.* Blum began his book with the following sentence: "The USSR challenge to world freedom is a challenge to America to solve its educational problems." To Blum, lack of religious liberty was the number one educational problem in America, but there were others: teacher education programs that taught "there is no eternal truth," the mediocrity of "life adjustment" education, the lack of educational choices for gifted children, and the "danger" of the welfare state "submersion of the individual."[6]

The solution to the lack of religious liberty in America was "the certificate plan," in which the government would provide vouchers or grants to parents valid for partial tuition at approved private and parochial schools. Blum credited University of Chicago professors for giving "a new impetus" to education certificates in separate 1955 publications: Milton Friedman of the Department of Economics and Procter Thomson of the Department of Education. If state governments were reluctant to provide education certificates, then Blum advised state and federal governments to furnish tax credits to parents paying tuition at private schools. As a book that advocated a new method to fund the schools, Blum blended together the alleged efficacy of the free market with a defense of religious freedom for parents. "Freedom to choose a God-centered education"—this was paramount for an American culture that was under foreign attack by the Soviet Union and domestic attack through secularism. Indeed, Blum quoted approvingly from FBI Director J. Edgar Hoover on the cause of juvenile delinquency: "There is a necessary connection between crime and the decline of faith and religious practice."[7]

In the 1950s, however, the school voucher as championed by Blum, Friedman, and Thomson had little traction in the mainstream media and in popular culture. The "grand expectations" of many Americans benefitting from the postwar economic boom and the guarantees of the growing liberal-democratic state made school vouchers seem radical and out of step. In addition, conservatives were divided on the utility of the school voucher. Some sided with Blum. For example, in 1957 *U.S. News and World Report* reprinted one of Blum's articles that advocated his certificate plan. Other conservatives believed that the growing welfare state necessitated a *defense* of the right of families to pay for private schools themselves rather than an *offense* of compelling the state to reimburse parents for parochial and private school tuition. *Wall Street Journal* editors worried in 1959, for example, that "the next socio-political issue" in education "will be a battle by the public educators to abolish private schools" even though middle-income parents "are willing to take on the additional burden of paying private school tuition."[8]

But this was not the biggest division among conservatives over education policy in the 1950s—the biggest divide was sectional. Ground zero in the battle for education vouchers was not found in the writings of Catholic conservatives or free-market ideologues disillusioned with the New Deal. Ground zero was the unfolding struggle in the South over civil rights, with southern conservatives defending the social order against civil rights activists seeking to dismantle segregation. One of the more prominent tools segregationists used to keep the schools racially separate, of course, was the school voucher. Blum was well aware that southern states turned to voucher programs in the late 1950s, under the guise of freedom of choice, but he, like Friedman, maintained a careful aloofness from southern voucher programs, even as he corresponded with some of the advocates of tuition grants.

In 1958, Governor Lindsay Almond of Virginia closed public schools in three districts under court-orders to desegregate. One of the outcomes of the school closings was tuition grants. In Prince Edward County, for example, segregationists created a private school system for white children beginning 1959, and its private school foundation sought state aid for the 1960–1961 school year. One of Virginia's most vocal supporters was journalist Leon Dure. In 1958 he insisted that "segregation by free individual choice...can be maintained in schools in spite of the Supreme Court decision." The state needed only to provide "tuition grants for the per capita average expenditure in public schools to any parents—white or Negro—who prefer to arrange their own private schooling." Segregation would be maintained on the basis of freedom of association: since "most white people do not want Negro association," private schools could be maintained on a segregated basis.[9]

In his efforts to seek allies outside the South, Dure wrote to Blum in June 1959. After receiving *Freedom of Choice in Education* as a present from a Virginia Catholic priest, he "was startled to find" arguments similar to those he had "been waging in Virginia for a long time." Dure was particularly "interested in the origin of the phrase 'freedom of choice.'" The Jesuit took a year and a half to respond. While his response was lengthy and cordial, Blum nevertheless told Dure that he believed the "non-sectarian restriction" in the Virginia Direct-Grant program was unconstitutional, because it imposed "a religious test upon the receiving of educational grants." Dure conceded that the religious restriction in the Virginia tuition grants legislation was a mistake, one that he was working to correct. But he also suggested that Blum and other Catholic leaders should act with logical consistency when seeking federal education dollars: "The Southern delegation in Congress" would be in accord with Catholic lobbyists "provided, of course, that the weird loan idea is replaced by direct-to-individual grants." The loans were a proposal for the federal government to help build more parochial schools. Dure suggested that Catholic leaders shift their lobbying strategy to aiding families exercising religious liberty rather than aiding capital projects. He believed that if Blum and other Catholics jumped on the southern states' "freedom of assembly" bandwagon, both would benefit, since "all our first amendment freedoms are just facets of the same jewel."[10]

Blum neither supported nor condemned southern tuition grants publicly. But his private correspondence was more nuanced. The heart of the matter for Blum was that the southern plans excluded religious schools. Yet, he lamented the actions of Attorney General (and co-religionist) Robert Kennedy, who worked to dismantle tuition grants programs as simple evasions of *Brown v. Board* before they had a chance to demonstrate their utility as a mechanism for freedom of choice. Moreover, he also opposed plans that excluded black families. In his correspondence with John Donovan, a Virginia state senator and self-identified racial moderate, Blum hoped "that the white people of Prince Edward County would take positive action to supply private schools for the colored people." (In Prince Edward County, unlike Charlotte and Norfolk, tuition grants were for whites only). And Blum was aware that tuition grants, theoretically, could also be awarded in racially integrated settings. Dure informed him, for example, that "57 grants are being given in segregated Albemarle County to go to the integrated schools in Charlottesville." In the end, Blum took the same tack that Milton Friedman adopted after 1955 regarding southern tuition grants—in his published writings, they did not exist.[11]

The U.S. Congress in the 1950s considered a succession of bills seeking increased federal aid to elementary and secondary education. And while one of the reasons Congress failed to pass most legislation prior to 1965 was disagreement over the question of federal aid to religious schools (the question of aid to racially segregated schools was the other), the debates nevertheless spawned spirited discussions among Catholics as how best to win support for parochial schools. The National Catholic Welfare Conference (NCWC), the lobbying arm of the American Catholic Church, favored federal aid to public schools provided Catholic schools received support for targeted programs, but Catholic bishops "had diverse opinions about federal aid." The NCWC and its director, Monsignor Howard Carroll, tended to keep Blum at arm's length—he threaten their negotiated efforts in Washington because of his pat answers to complex education problems and because his certificate plan would, in essence, upset the way the U.S. federal system funded and controlled public education. The NCWC legal counsel, George E. Reed, went further, labeling Blum "an overzealous Jesuit with no legal background."[12]

The Catholic bishops and clergy did not necessarily side with Blum either. In many dioceses, for example, parish elementary schools charged no tuition prior to the 1970s. Therefore, the voucher model made less sense to some bishops than lobbying states to increase the allotments states set aside for non-public schools. Others opposed government aid for private schools because they believed that adding those schools to the public ones that already received support would raise taxes for everyone, resulting in little savings for parochial school parents in the end. And there was the suspicion, shared by Milton Friedman and others outside the Catholic Church, that some Catholic leaders opposed vouchers because "in the resulting competition the parochial schools" might lose ground to other private schools.[13]

Lay Catholics who sent their children to parochial schools were another matter; this was where Blum focused his political strategy. Since Catholics taught in and sent their children to both public and Catholic schools, lay sentiment was, if anything, even more diverse. Blum tended to focus on the parents of parochial school students. In 1954, Blum proposed that his bishop organize a "Committee for Obtaining Religious Liberty" so that the Church could "assume the offensive" on parochial school aid. By the late 1950s, however, Blum believed that a bishop-led parochial school advocacy organization would have little traction in national politics because Americans would identify it with the Church hierarchy. The better strategy, in Blum's eyes, was to encourage lay Catholics to create an advocacy organization with membership open to non-Catholics.[14]

The organization that Blum chose to shepherd from its conception was Citizens for Educational Freedom (CEF). The group began at Blum's urging in May 1959 in St. Louis, as Congress debated the Murray-Metcalf bill to provide federal grants to public schools in support of building projects and teacher salaries. Originally calling themselves "The Fair Share Plan," the group, headed by husband-and-wife team Mae and Martin Duggan, opposed the bill because it excluded aid to parochial schools. Mae and Martin Duggan were also concerned that the St. Louis Archdiocese might begin closing some city schools due to faltering enrollments. Blum served as their mentor. He met the Duggans while in St. Louis visiting his brother, also a priest. In May, Blum advised the Duggans that the emphasis of their organization should not be "fairness." Rather, their group should argue for "freedom of mind and freedom of religion." Blum prevailed upon Mae and Martin Duggan to rename their group; by August, they were calling themselves the Citizens for Educational Freedom. (CEF's periodical, "Fair Share News," continued under the old name until 1963, when it was renamed "Educational Freedom.")[15]

In late 1959 and early 1960, CEF grew rapidly, publishing articles in the Catholic press, staging rallies, and establishing chapters in several states. However, Blum continued to push Mae and Martin Duggan and the rest of the leadership in St. Louis to open their membership to non-Catholics and to make sure that the group disengaged with the Catholic bishops. By December, the organization had "wonderful news." Martin Duggan had a "personal conversation" with Archbishop Ritter, who "explained that the bishops now think it is wise to let the laity go it on their own as citizens. Ritter also stopped sponsoring CEF workshops "so that the Church would not be publicly identified with the movement." One of the goals of CEF was to have chapters in every state, and by 1962, CEF was active in 45 of them.[16]

Unlike private school groups active in the tuition grants movements in the South, CEF was not an organization that sought public funding in support of racially segregated schools. Nor was CEF a civil rights organization. Perhaps a photograph highlights these distinctions best. In 1961, one appeared in *Fair Share News* with the title "Get the Picture, Congressman?" It shows 30 or so parochial school students, of which four are black, the balance white. The accompanying article describes a kick-off rally to have parochial school parents send photographs of their children to federal lawmakers, asking them "why don't we count?" in the debate to increase federal aid to elementary and secondary schools. It was inconceivable that southern advocates of tuition grants in Virginia or any other state in 1961 would lobby the federal government for increased aid to education. More to the point, neither would they endorse a photograph depicting school-children in an integrated scene—in contrast, CEF accepted integrated schools. The St. Louis Archdiocese desegregated its schools in the 1940s. The black students in the photograph are holding a sign identifying the Kinloch School District, a segregated, black school district in one of the St. Louis suburbs. Because of the school uniforms, most likely, the black students in the photograph attended a parochial school that remained all black. The CEF leadership welcomed participants at the rally from the segregated and black school district, but did not seek to extend desegregation in public or private schools in St. Louis.[17]

Eventually, CEF established a state affiliate in Louisiana. But the reason was to attract parents whose children attended Catholic schools in

"Why Don't We Count?" Students at a Citizens for Educational Freedom (CEF) rally, St. Louis, 1961. In the debates over federal aid for education, parents wanted a "fair share" of aid to parochial schools. Meanwhile, CEF created state affiliates to lobby for vouchers. (Courtesy of Mae Duggan/CEF.)

the Pelican State, rather than organizing parents benefiting from the nondenominational grants-in-aid program that operated there. The CEF leadership also kept the civil rights movement at arm's length. For example, Martin Duggan wrote an opinion piece in 1965 that lambasted priests and nuns in four Milwaukee parishes in the ghetto for setting up freedom schools in support of a public school boycott. On the surface, Duggan opposed Father Groppi and the other freedom school clergy who defied their bishop because religious instruction was not part of the curriculum. But Duggan also argued that it was "ridiculous" to blame the public schools for de facto segregation. And of course, the solution to racial segregation for Duggan was a simple one—school vouchers.[18]

The 1960s were heady times for Blum and the CEF. In 1961, Mac Duggan provided Congressional testimony, urging federal lawmakers "to provide equal grants-in-aid in education for students who attend non-state but fully accredited voluntary schools." Fundraising proceeded at a brisk clip, spurred on, in part, by Supreme Court rulings that banned organized prayer and bible reading in the public schools. According to CEF records membership grew to 125,000 and non-Catholics joined the CEF and served in leadership positions. In 1965, the headquarters of the national organization relocated from St. Louis to Washington at Blum's urging, and the group's governing board, which included Blum, hired a salaried national director. Throughout the 1960s CEF's profile grew as an organization bringing increased government funding to parents with children in private schools.[19]

Despite Blum's best efforts, however, the organization had trouble shedding its denominational image. CEF added Protestants to its governing board in 1962. Indeed, the first chairperson of the national board was Glenn Andreas, of the National Union of Christian Schools. Since Lutherans had a reasonably well-organized system of parochial schools, they were represented in the CEF membership on the national board. There was also Jewish representation in the CEF leadership. During the run-up to, and after the passage of the 1965 Elementary and Secondary Education Act, Orthodox Jewish leaders who operated schools in New York and elsewhere broke with most other Jewish organizations to lobby for government assistance for their schools. Blum courted Jewish organizations such as the National Society for Hebrew Day Schools and Agudath Israel of America, and beginning in 1964 Orthodox Jews served on CEF's executive committee. Since the executive committee met on Saturdays, however, the two Jewish members did not attend, so it is debatable the extent to which Orthodox Jewish membership in CEF went beyond the political expediency of projecting a non-denominational image. In spite of the efforts of Blum and others to present CEF as a non-denominational organization, there was widespread skepticism. For example, a widely reprinted cartoon in *Church and State* in 1962 shows a Catholic priest pushing a CEF official in front of him to ask Uncle Sam for tax dollars: "Our priests must have tax funds for their—I mean our—schools."[20]

Divisions also cropped up between Blum and Mae and Martin Duggan over control of the organization. In the early 1960s, there were already disagreements over strategy. Mae and Martin Duggan wanted CEF to instigate a civil rights lawsuit in a heavily Catholic state that would compel the government to share education funds with private schools because of equal protection. Blum disagreed. Partly it was the expense of litigating. But more important, Blum was convinced that sponsoring such a lawsuit would be counterproductive because of the risk that a state court, and ultimately the Supreme Court, could rule that government was under no obligation to subsidize religious schools. Such a lawsuit, according to Blum, would be akin to the CEF "placing a neck in a noose and daring [Supreme Court] justices such as Black and Douglas to kick the barrel out from under our feet." To Blum, the best route was the legislative process, not the judicial one. This disagreement brewed into the 1970s.[21]

Mae and Martin Duggan also had problems with some of the results of CEF's outreach to non-Catholics. For them the biggest problem was CEF member William Stringfellow, whom Mae Duggan deemed "impossible." Stringfellow was a radical Episcopal theologian, an editor of *Ramparts* magazine, and a civil rights lawyer and leader who wanted CEF to go on record in favor of busing for the racial desegregation of public schools. While Blum lamented that Stringfellow identified himself as a CEF "spokesperson," to Blum the benefits of positioning CEF as a national, non-denominational organization outweighed Stringfellow's outspokenness.[22]

Most of all, Blum wanted Mae and Martin Duggan's influence reduced, creating dissent between the Duggans and CEF leadership. "Martin and I have never been so deeply hurt in all our lives," Mae Duggan complained to Father Blum in 1965. "After working our heads off for six years, our [CEF] big shots in Washington...want to get rid of us." The national director wanted Mae and Martin Duggan to relinquish one of their seats on the executive board. Blum shot back that as a national organization, each region must have equitable representation, and "Missouri is in no way entitled to have two people on the executive committee." In Blum's reckoning, Missouri only contributed 5 percent to the CEF membership, but held 17 percent of the leadership positions. After 1965, Mae and Martin Duggan's influence waned; CEF was essentially Blum's organization until 1973, when unfavorable Supreme Court decisions on aid to parochial schools undermined CEF's most important objective. After these decisions, Blum greatly reduced his role, opting instead to found a new organization in 1973 with a wider scope than school politics, the Catholic League for Religious and Civil Rights. This explicitly Catholic organization defended Catholic teachings and values on a variety of fronts. Mae and Martin Duggan reasserted their authority, but after 1973 CEF lost much of its influence. CEF succeeded in its goal of including parochial schools in federal aid to education, a far cry from the 1959 Murray-Metcalf bill that excluded parochial schools. But the Second Vatican Council of the early 1960s brought centripetal changes to the American Catholic Church, something that CEF leader Mae Duggan had difficulty accepting.[23]

In his home state of Wisconsin, the ongoing objective of Blum's activism was school vouchers and tuition tax credits. Blum also led efforts in the early 1960s to establish state-sponsored busing of parochial and private school students. Government-funded school transportation was also an early objective of CEF, both nationally and in the various state chapters. In 1959, a mother and six children died when their car was hit by a train en route to a Minnesota parochial school. This Zimmerman family tragedy became something of a cause célèbre for parochial school parents, many of whom felt the accident could have been avoided had public school buses been available. Working through the Wisconsin chapter of CEF, which he founded, Blum succeeded in 1962 in lobbying the state legislature to pass "a fair bus ride bill," only to have the Wisconsin Supreme Court strike it down "as an unconstitutional aid to 'religious seminaries.'" The next year, Blum helped secure the passage of a joint resolution in the state legislature calling for a constitutional amendment allowing state aid to parochial schools for the purpose of student transportation. Blum took credit for leading the amendment campaign and the passage of a more inclusive school transportation law. Wisconsin joined several states that permitted school bus

Reverend Virgil Blum, S.J. at Milwaukee's Marquette University in the 1960s. Blum organized CEF and his 1958 book, *Freedom of Choice in Education*, helped reduce the association of school vouchers with the maintenance of racial segregation. (© Department of Special Collections and University Archives, Marquette University Libraries. Reprinted with permission.)

transportation for parochial school students in the 1950s and 1960s, something that the U.S. Supreme Court had ruled constitutional in 1947.[24]

In contrast to the ultimate success of the bus ride legislation, Blum experienced nothing but setbacks for school vouchers in Wisconsin in the 1960s and 1970s, in spite of a promising political climate after Richard Nixon's election to the presidency in 1968. Blum set 1969 as his goal for a federal enactment of a voucher program for elementary and secondary private and parochial schools. In March of 1969, state representatives in Wisconsin introduced a bill that provided $100 and $50 tuition grants to students enrolled in private high schools and elementary schools, respectively. Blum participated on television panel discussions and met with editorial writers at the major Milwaukee newspapers in support of the bill. CEF sponsored rallies in several Wisconsin cities, and the Wisconsin Catholic Welfare Conference supported the bill. There was steep opposition, however. Organized labor (the teachers unions, the AFL-CIO) opposed the measure, as did the Greater Milwaukee Council of Churches. In January 1970, it failed in the Assembly. Similar legislation throughout the rest of the decade also went down to defeat. And at the national level, although Nixon's Office of Economic Opportunity solicited support from public school districts in several cities, including Milwaukee, the public schools refused to participate in a voucher project, even though the federal initiative had support among some black and white activists who backed independent community schools.[25]

As a coalition builder, Blum had trouble conceiving of a coalition that went beyond the identity politics of Judeo-Christian educators and parents. For Blum, freedom of choice in education meant freedom of religion—a government obligation to fund education equally and in spite of parental decisions to enroll children in sectarian schools. Blum's center of gravity was the Catholic Church and its schools, and just as he was unwilling to unite with southern segregationists who favored tuition grants as a form of freedom of association, he was unwilling to unite with northern civil rights leaders who favored policies such as racial desegregation or community control as promising reforms that would lead to better outcomes for black students. To be sure, Blum had an acerbic personal style, and so, perhaps, this confined his warmest interactions to religious and political conservatives. But Blum was also impatient with people who were his natural allies. For example, he repeatedly referred to Catholics who disagreed with his aims as "political eunuchs" and even "political pygmies." From the late 1960s to the end of his life, struggles over school vouchers centered on the urban schools. For the most part, Blum was unable to make the jump from vouchers in support of parochial schools to vouchers in support of urban students. For this reason, he was an intellectual and political pioneer who was ahead of the voucher curve in the 1950s but behind it by the 1970s, when a hand-ful of black leaders and others in Milwaukee's central city began to consider vouchers.[26]

PUBLIC AND PRIVATE EDUCATION IN MILWAUKEE

Several factors contributed to the enactment of the Milwaukee Parental Choice Program (MPCP) in 1990. The continued urban school crisis laid bare the limitations of Milwaukee desegregation policies. Discriminatory implementation, continued segregation of the metropolitan area, tenuous links between desegregation and increased academic achievement for mi-nority youth, and federal government retrenchment removed desegrega-tion from the set of educational policies around which many reformers mobilized. Indeed, disillusionment with Milwaukee Public Schools (MPS) transfer policies that required higher percentages of black children to change schools, coupled with low achievement levels of black students in MPS, led to support from many black leaders for alternatives to MPS.

Other developments unique to Wisconsin also contributed to the politi-cal climate necessary for the voucher program's passage. First, from 1970 onward, Milwaukee's central city already contained a handful of indepen-dent community schools that sought local, state, and national funding. Hence, a group of non-sectarian private schools, with strong cultural ties to Milwaukee's black and Latino communities, were already willing to enroll underprivileged MPS students in exchange for state funding. Second, black political power in 1980s Milwaukee increased to a point where some white politicians at the municipal and state levels increased their efforts to gar-ner black support. State Representative Annette "Polly" Williams authored MPCP and generated support for it among black and white lawmakers. Significant minority support for state funding of non-sectarian private schools operating in the central city was one means whereby Republican legislators could ally with black Democrats and split the Democratic Party along liberal versus conservative lines.

Third, the election of Tommy Thompson as governor in 1986 extended the Republican ascendancy to Wisconsin and guaranteed that proposals for state support of private education would emanate from the governor's office. Previously, voucher plans were only backed by private and parochial school lobbyists and their legislative supporters. Finally, the wealth amassed by the Bradley Foundation in 1985 meant that this Milwaukee grant-maker became the nation's largest financial backer of conservative intellectuals and causes. The Bradley Foundation could bring sizeable resources to bear in direct and indirect support for voucher programs in Wisconsin and nationally. This support helped create a climate conducive to the legislative and legal success of MPCP.

Responses to desegregation and low academic achievement levels in MPS, the existence of independent community schools, increased black political power in Milwaukee, the influence of the Thompson administration, and the growth of the Bradley Foundation all played a role in the formulation and passage of MPCP. Moreover, the efforts of Virgil Blum and other Catholic conservatives laid the groundwork for Catholic advocacy of school vouchers in Milwaukee. And while the 1990 legislation excluded parochial schools, the Wisconsin legislature, with the support of Williams and Milwaukee's Democratic Mayor, John Norquist, expanded the program to include parochial schools five years later.

Like many northern cities, in the post–World War II era Milwaukee experienced a significant out-migration of white residents to the suburbs and elsewhere, and a significant in-migration of blacks and other minority groups. Unlike Cleveland and a handful of other Midwestern cities, however, these migration streams did not produce a city population in which minority groups outnumbered whites. Table 4.1 and Figure 4.1 illustrate the changing demographics of the city, 1960–1990.

Enrollments in the Milwaukee Public Schools did not mirror changes to the city population. In the public schools, a much higher percentage of white students left the system in the postwar years, and a much higher percentage of black and other minority students enrolled. The availability of parochial schools partly explained the sharp decline in white enrollments. Higher rates of poverty coupled with higher percentages of children of school age among black families compared to white families also accounted for some of the differences in demographic patterns between city population and public school enrollments. Table 4.2 and Figure 4.2 show changing enrollments in the MPS.

Table 4.1 Milwaukee Population Changes, 1960–1990

Year	White	African American	Hispanic	Other	Total
1960	1,127,383	63,132	N/A	3,775	1,194,290
1970	605,372	105,088	N/A	6,639	717,099
1980	468,064	147,055	26,487	5,396	636,210
1990	397,827	191,597	37,420	1,244	628,088

Source: U.S. Census.

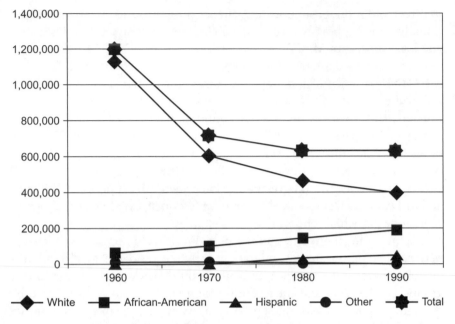

Figure 4.1 Milwaukee Population Changes, 1960–1990. (*Source:* U.S. Census.)

Table 4.2 Milwaukee Public Schools Enrollment, 1960–1990

Year	White	African American	Hispanic	Other	Total
1960	N/A	N/A	N/A	N/A	103,341
1970	93,315	34,512	N/A	N/A	132,739
1980	39,540	41,861	N/A	7,856	89,257
1990	30,293	55,186	9,148	3,744	98,371

Source: Proceedings of the Milwaukee Board of School Directors (Milwaukee: Milwaukee Public Schools): October 4, 1960, pp. 172–174; October 6, 1970, pp. 166–169; October 29, 1980, pp. 1111–1114. In William J. Kritek and Delbert K. Clear, "Teachers and Principals in the Milwaukee Public Schools," ed. John L. Rury and Frank A. Cassell, *Seeds of Crisis: Public Schooling in Milwaukee since 1920* (Madison: University of Wisconsin Press, 1993), p. 157.

RESPONSES TO SCHOOL DESEGREGATION

In the 1960s and 1970s, desegregation was the hub around which many Milwaukee reformers seeking improved opportunities for black students organized. The civil rights campaign to desegregate MPS dated at least to 1963, with the years of greatest popular protest—demonstrations, sit-ins, student boycotts, freedom schools, the blocking of school buses, and other

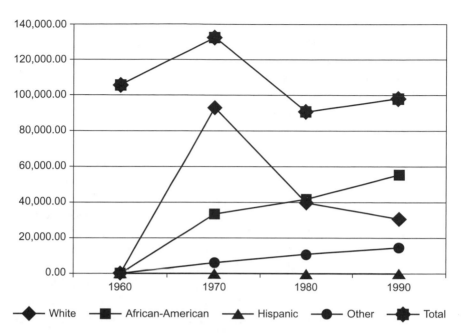

Figure 4.2 Milwaukee Public School Enrollment, 1960–1990. (Proceedings of the Milwaukee Board of School Directors [Milwaukee: Milwaukee Public Schools]: October 4, 1960, pp. 172–174; October 6, 1970, pp. 166–169; October 29, 1980, pp. 1111–1114. In William J. Kritek and Delbert K. Clear, "Teachers and Principals in the Milwaukee Public Schools," ed. John L. Rury and Frank A. Cassell, Seeds of Crisis: Public Schooling in Milwaukee since 1920 [Madison: University of Wisconsin Press, 1993], p. 157.)

forms of civil disobedience, being 1963–1966. After these years, direct action shifted in part to open housing and employment opportunities, and in part to Black Power and community control of public institutions.[27]

In the litigation phases of school desegregation, civil rights activists filed suit in federal district court in 1965; the case was argued in 1973 and 1974. Federal Judge John Reynolds ruled in 1976 that MPS, but not the state of Wisconsin, created and maintained an unconstitutionally segregated school system, and ordered school authorities to formulate a plan to desegregate. School board appeals to the Supreme Court extended the final ruling to 1979, when plaintiffs and defendants signed a consent decree. This phase of litigation ended in 1980, when the federal court rejected an appeal by the NAACP arguing that the consent decree did not go far enough because it allowed 25 percent of MPS students to remain at predominantly black schools. The 15 motions, countermotions, amendments, and appeals (mostly by the school board) made the *Amos v. Board* case one of the most costly desegregation suits ever.[28]

The second round of litigation took place in the 1980s. The Wisconsin legislature, in 1976 and in anticipation of the *Amos* ruling, had enacted a student transfer and transportation program, known as Chapter 220, which stimulated a small degree of school desegregation between the city and its predominantly white suburbs. The Milwaukee school board, now with an integrationist majority, sued its suburban counterparts in 1984 to compel them to accept more African American students into their schools, on grounds that suburban districts declined to participate fully for racially exclusionary reasons. The federal district court arranged a consent decree for Greater Milwaukee school districts in 1987 that encouraged suburbs to accept higher numbers of African American students.[29]

As implemented in Milwaukee in the late 1970s and early 1980s, desegregation policy was crafted by professional educators who sought to maintain white enrollment in MPS and did so by attempting to bypass most community input, especially from black Milwaukee. Under the new system of "forced-voluntary" transfers and magnet schools, the burden of desegregation fell disproportionately on black students—school authorities closed or converted to magnet schools those schools with predominantly black enrollments and required a disproportionate percentage of black students to transfer to schools in white attendance areas. As to Chapter 220, financial incentives were put in place for MPS to rely heavily on transportation to desegregate Milwaukee schools, and this limited compensatory aid to schools in black attendance areas. By the 1990s, Chapter 220 grew to the third-largest category of state school aid in Wisconsin.[30]

From the perspective of many school reformers seeking to bring high-quality education to minority students, desegregation lost its luster. MPS authorities had closed schools in the predominantly black North Side during a time of increasing black enrollments and decreasing white enrollments. Black students were transported to schools throughout Milwaukee while higher percentages of white students could remain at their previous schools. Money spent on transportation could have been utilized for compensatory programs in central city schools. Chapter 220 also took academically talented students from city schools, and the receiving districts could augment their budgets by accepting small numbers of non-white students.

One consequence of 1960s demands for desegregation was that the civil rights movement underscored the limited power that blacks and other minorities wielded in Milwaukee and in MPS. This lack of political power, together with the problematic nature of desegregation policies and the continued flagging achievement levels of minority students, helped to generate a reform movement within Milwaukee's black community that embraced local control of public schools as a means to raise minority achievement.

Two black education reforms in particular demonstrated the shift in goals among many of Milwaukee's black educational activists and reformers, from desegregation to community control. The two causes were the campaign to save North Division High School in the late 1970s and the effort to create a new school district with a predominantly black enrollment out of MPS in the late 1980s. Geographically, the proposed district would be comprised of the core of the near-North Side ghetto.

As part of the original desegregation plan developed in 1976, Superintendent Lee McMurrin recommended that North Division High School close. In response to demands from black leaders, the school board reversed this recommendation and replaced the turn-of-the-century high school with a new structure built on the same site. This predominantly black high school opened in 1978 "as an attendance area school with a medical specialty as a part of the program." The next year, the school board voted to turn North Division into a citywide specialty school that, in effect, would deny access to a substantial portion of black students within its attendance area, forcing them to attend high schools in other areas of the city. The extension of Lee McMurrin and Deputy Superintendent David Bennett's policy of "forced-voluntary" desegregation to North Division generated backlash among black residents. North Division students staged a walk-out in protest; concerned parents and community members presented the school board with a proposal to maintain North Division as a comprehensive, "*integrated* school, but a *predominantly black* one (60 percent black/40 percent white)."[31]

When the school board rejected this proposal, parents and activists organized the Coalition to Save North Division (CSND). Prominent among the African American leadership of the CSND was activist Howard Fuller. Future State Representative Polly Williams also played a role (both were classmates at North Division in the 1950s). CSND was successful in elevating the issue to citywide importance. Among other strategies, the coalition staged large rallies at North Division High School and the School Administration Building, convinced the editorial boards of the largest white dailies, the *Milwaukee Journal* and the *Milwaukee Sentinel,* to urge the school board to reconsider its action, and brought legal action against the board. In 1980, the school board reversed its position and approved an agreement with CSND that was similar to the original community proposal.[32]

Beginning in the summer of 1987, black activists and educators who were critical of MPS policies regarding black students, together with a handful of white supporters, attempted to carve a nearly all-black (97 percent) school district out of MPS. Called The Steering Committee for New North Division School District, black proponents of the plan included

Milwaukee. Urban Day School and Harambee Community School served a predominantly black student body on the near-North Side and Bruce Guadelupe Community School served a predominantly Latino student body on the near-South Side. In the inaugural year, 228 out of 347 students participating in the voucher program attended these schools. In the second year of operation, 486 MPCP students, or 88 percent of all students participating in the choice program, attended Harambee, Urban Day, or Bruce Guadelupe.[39]

Milwaukee's independent community schools were forged out of the intersection of two developments: the movement of Catholic schools away from the Central City, and efforts of residents, activists, educators, and parents to maintain the former parochial schools as independent community schools. The legacies of these two movements remained for decades at some of the surviving schools: a few women who worked in the schools were members in Catholic religious orders, the governing boards of the schools consisted of local residents, and the curricula of the schools, which were non-religious, contained multicultural elements.

After World War II, the Catholic Archdiocese of Milwaukee and its parish-based school system adapted to the migrations of Catholics and others into and out of Milwaukee's central city. Parishes built many Catholic schools in the Milwaukee suburbs following the migration of white, Catholic Milwaukeeans away from the city in the 1950s and 1960s. At the same time, central city parochial schools adjusted to the in-migration of blacks to the North Side. In five Catholic schools located on the near-North Side, enrollments declined from nearly 1,000 students in 1945 to less than 200 by 1970. The majority of black migrants to Milwaukee were non-Catholic, but, more significantly, many could not afford tuition. Even after Catholic schools changed their admissions policies to admit non-Catholics, enrollments continued to decline. Central city Catholic schools were closing; it was up to the congregations to accept the decisions of the Archdiocese or to attempt to reopen the schools under different governance.[40]

The first formerly Catholic school to become autonomous from the Archdiocese was Urban Day. Milwaukee's first black parish, St. Benedict-the-Moor, had operated a boarding school and a day school since the 1920s. The exclusive boarding school had a national reputation. "Entertainer Redd Foxx and Chicago Mayor Harold Washington had attended." But church and school buildings were razed in 1965 to make room for an expressway. In 1967, the Racine Dominican Sisters, along with interested parents, reorganized St. Benedict's day school at another location as an independent community school, Urban Day. As other formerly Catholic Schools broke ties with the Archdiocese in the late 1960s, Urban Day served as a model. By 1970, eight other schools made the transition from Catholic to non-sectarian status. Urban Day was relatively successful in attracting foundation support and some public support. Compared to most of the other independent community schools, Urban Day maintained relatively secure finances.[41]

To keep its central city parish schools solvent, the Archdiocese began subsidizing the heretofore self-supporting parish schools in the 1960s. Historian William Dahlk reports that white opposition within the Archdiocese to continuing subsidization "was strong enough to cause Archdiocesan officials to warn inner-city parish leaders in 1967–1968 that subsidization could not continue indefinitely and alternatives must be considered, including possibly closing the schools." During the ensuing negotiations among the parties connected with the threatened parish schools—parents, community activists, clergy, and archdiocesan representatives—the dominant faction that emerged concluded that the best route would be to reorganize the schools along independent lines governed by a parent board. White supporters included Patrick Flood and Dismas Becker of the Archdiocese Council on Urban Life, and black supporters included activist Larry Harwell, who later became Williams's policy director, and Jesse Wray, leader of a parents group who became coordinator of the Federation of Independent Community Schools (FICS).[42]

Others argued to maintain religious curricula and affiliation. Staff and parents at one of the independent community schools eventually re-affiliated with the Archdiocese. However, most parents, activists, supporters, and outside advisors were convinced that public and foundation funding for the schools would be forthcoming if ties to the Archdiocese were severed. This was not an idle hope, since the Wisconsin legislature entertained school voucher bills beginning in 1969, and Nixon's Office of Economic Opportunity sought to establish a voucher program in Milwaukee in 1970.[43]

Parents, community activists, and religious leaders connected with 14 parish elementary schools facing severe financial pressure—seven of them predominantly non-white—formed Parents for Educational Progress (PEP). Supporters of the schools with the majority non-white student enrollments formed the nucleus of the FICS, but in its first year the Wisconsin branch of CEF put pressure on PEP. Representatives from the seven predominantly white parish schools located in transition neighborhoods on the periphery of the expanding ghetto were connected with PEP, but did not, in the end, become independent community schools. Through PEP efforts, three parish schools re-opened in the fall of 1969 as independent community schools. Predominantly black St. Boniface (Fr. James Groppi's former parish) was one of them. It became DePorres Community School. St. Francis (also predominantly black) became St. Francis Community School. And predominantly Latino Holy Trinity-Our Lady of Guadelupe became Bruce

Guadelupe Community School. The next year, four other predominantly black parish schools reorganized: St. Leo, St. Michael, St. Gall (Martin Luther King Community School), and St. Elizabeth (Harambee Community School).[44]

For the independent community schools, fundraising was an ongoing challenge. The Archdiocese rented the buildings to the schools for one dollar per year. The Archdiocese also provided the formerly Catholic schools with approximately $400,000 in transition funds the first year and cut support in half the second year. By the third year, the Archdiocese ended financial support; financial advisors and lenders to the Archdiocese deemed its funding of the independent community schools as financially unwise.[45]

FICS pursued public funding as well as foundation grants and other private support. Several federation members envisioned that MPS would eventually fund the community schools—FICS would become a part of MPS but would retain an autonomous governance structure. In short, FICS would complement MPS by offering a network of schools similar to the magnet schools that MPS eventually adopted as part of desegregation. The schools sought federal assistance through the Model Cities program, but the mayor's office prevented most Model Cities funds from being channeled to the community schools. Some of this money did reach the schools indirectly, however, through contracts with MPS for students that the public schools found difficult to educate. There were also federal funds available for crime prevention and other social programs, and the independent community schools tapped these sources.[46]

Many black residents were supportive of public funding for the independent community schools in the early 1970s, but some opposed public support. This division, in general, was between black leaders who were supportive of Mayor Maier, and those who were not. Many Protestant ministers opposed public funding of the independent schools; the issue also divided the executive board of the NAACP. In the meantime, blacks increased their presence in teaching and administrative ranks of the public schools. Since MPS officials and most members of the school board viewed vouchers as a threat, many black educators working in the district also believed that vouchers put public education in jeopardy.[47]

FICS and other community school supporters lobbied unsuccessfully in the state legislature for state support for the schools. In the 1969, 1971, and 1973 legislative sessions in Madison, a series of bills designed to assist the independent community schools and other private and parochial schools were proposed. Some were specific to Milwaukee, and one was directed to the independent community schools. In the 1969 session, an assembly bill "relating to providing direct state aid to private, non-sectarian schools which are controlled by parents or neighborhoods" made the rounds. Ultimately

Wisconsin governor Tommy Thompson (right) with Milwaukee parent Janette Williams and George H. W. Bush in 1992. The president wanted the federal government to enact school vouchers. Governor Thompson was more successful, working with black elected officials to establish the 1990 Milwaukee Parental Choice Program and expanding it in 1995 to include religious schools. (AP Photo/ Dennis Cook.)

defeated, this bill would have provided $200 grants for low-income pupils. The FICS supported this bill, which was opposed by the Wisconsin branch of the American Civil Liberties Union on the grounds that the bill was a stalking horse for public aid to parochial schools. It was defeated.[48]

Father Blum's relationship with the independent community schools was distant. He supported vouchers for students enrolled in these schools, but only as a byproduct of legislation that would also bring vouchers to parochial school students. To some extent, Blum's stance mirrored his relationship to black civil rights generally—he supported non-discrimination in principle, but avoided black civil rights advocacy organizations in practice. Since Catholics represented large proportions of public school enrollments in the nation's largest cities, desegregation served as a wedge issue that divided them between those who remained loyal to the labor-liberal-New Deal wing of the Democratic Party and those unable to accept increasing numbers of African Americans in the same neighborhoods and schools. Put another way, Catholic leaders, such as Blum, faced difficulties propagating an official policy of racial non-discrimination on a reluctant and

divided rank-and-file. Blum also had a tin ear when it came to black identity politics and political activism. In the weeks following the assassination
of Martin Luther King, Jr., for example, he penned an article entitled "We
Need a Martin Luther King." Blum argued that "the disadvantaged poor"
sorely needed "a Martin Luther King." Whereas "Citizens for Educational
Freedom has repeatedly proposed legislation," Blum added, "these poor
people today have no eloquent voice to plead their cause." Several magazines rejected Blum's manuscript, and perhaps the most likely reason for
the rejections was the critique noted by one of Blum's colleagues, who
wrote in the margin of one of the drafts, "You open yourself to the charge
of 'using' [King] at a time of intense emotionalism after his death."[49]

During the debates on the 1969 Wisconsin school voucher bill, there was
no correspondence between Blum and representatives of the Independent
Community Schools. And when Blum commented on urban schools that
enrolled blacks, he clearly favored Catholic schools. For example, the one
Milwaukee Independent Community School that he wrote about was St. Leo,
which "became Leo Community School, declined to seventy students,
and went bankrupt." For Blum the greatest moment came in 1977, when
the Catholic parish reopened the school "with 280 students, 98 percent
black...and with a waiting list of some 500 hopeful families."[50]

Among other failed bills that the Wisconsin legislature considered in
the 1969 session: an assembly bill sought federal aid by which "education-
ally deprived children attending non-public schools may receive federal
educational welfare benefits to children in economically deprived areas."
A senate bill would have provided "state grants to parents for students attending state-supervised private schools." The amounts would increase for
low-income students. In the 1971 session, two assembly bills would have
provided state aid to non-sectarian schools for low-income pupils. Another
assembly bill would have authorized MPS "to provide audio-visual materials and services to private schools." In the 1973 session, the assembly failed
to pass a resolution requesting that the attorney general state its position
on "the constitutionality of a public school system providing services to
private schools." The assembly also failed to authorize a study of the feasibility and constitutionality of loaning public school textbooks to private
school students."[51]

Another promising source of funding was the federal government's
school voucher initiative. In 1970 the OEO approached the FICS to take
part in a school vouchers pilot project to be funded through a federal grant,
an idea with support in the Central City. In October an OEO representative, Robert Bothwell of the Center for the Study of Public Policy traveled to
Milwaukee to build local support for the program. Blum supported vouchers, of course, but so did the FICS and also the Urban League. Supporters

justified vouchers for several reasons: growth of a diverse array of schools, improvements to MPS due to competition with the independent schools, and meaningful choices for parents to select the best education for their children. Because the guidelines of the federal government required a local government authority to coordinate the program, supporters worked to bring MPS on board. Indeed, two school board members supported a voucher demonstration project for Milwaukee.[52]

A majority of the Milwaukee School Board committee that considered vouchers voted against the program, however. After the first vote, Bothwell, Wray, and the two members of the school board agreed to remove parochial schools from the grant proposal, but this alienated Blum and other religious leaders in the heavily Catholic city. It also eroded support among African Americans who educated their children in Catholic schools. At the same time, the shift to secular schools failed to persuade the Milwaukee NAACP and major education organizations to back the program. In spite of an endorsement from the *Milwaukee Journal,* another school board committee voted against the proposal, so Bothwell and the OEO looked elsewhere.[53]

In 1978, Dismas Becker, by now a state representative from Milwaukee, introduced a private school options bill, whereby parents who could prove that MPS was not educating their children could arrange to enroll them in independent community schools and other private schools, with MPS and the state paying tuition. This proposal, in modified form, was passed in 1983. Although MPS allowed no students to transfer directly to a community school, it contracted with community schools and other private schools to educate students that MPS found difficult to manage. Williams became a supporter of Becker's initiative, as did State Representative John Norquist. Hence, from the 1960s to the 1980s, lawmakers devised various methods of generating state support for independent community schools.[54]

The independent community schools and their efforts to gain state funding garnered national attention. Jonathan Kozol came to Milwaukee at FICS invitation to speak about free schools. Academics were also interested in the movement. Within Milwaukee, Larry Harwell campaigned "for the Milwaukee School Board on a platform calling for MPS to contract with the Independent Community Schools." In the early 1970s, the force behind vouchers in urban areas were activists within central cities who sought state support for community schools, allied with left-leaning academics such as Christopher Jencks and writers such as Jonathan Kozol. Religious leaders and political conservatives were sotto voce regarding vouchers for urban schools. In the late 1980s, by contrast, the outside actors changed, from liberal academics and writers to conservative ones. And by the 1990s, religious leaders re-entered the field.[55]

Without public funding, four of the original PEP schools closed in the 1970s—Francis Community School, Michael Community School, DePorres Community School, and Martin Luther King Community School. Another community school unaffiliated with PEP, Clifford McKissick, closed in 1974. But Harambee, Urban Day, and Bruce Guadelupe survived. These three remaining schools retained their image as successful minority-run educational institutions and functioned as educational alternatives for minority youth to MPS and to the parochial school system. Over the years, as the personnel at the schools changed, school authorities no longer sought to become an autonomous division of MPS, valuing their independence instead. In the 1970s, efforts on behalf of independent community schools to access federal and state funding had less to do with advocacy of educational privatization and school vouchers, and more to do with efforts to deliver quality education to low-income minority children as an alternative to the options available within the public schools. Harambee and Urban Day became successful, black-led educational institutions in the central city.[56]

For Bruce Guadelupe Community School, however, financial difficulties brought the school to the brink of closure. In 1990, just before passage of the MPCP, "the school's board of directors voted to close the school down because of a financial crisis." After passage of the choice program, Bruce Guadelupe instead merged with a South Side Latino community organization and school called the United Community Center. The merger entailed relocating the school to the United Community Center, and in 1993 Bruce Guadelupe moved to a new facility at the center. School vouchers kept Bruce Guadelupe afloat.[57]

The other schools that enrolled significant numbers of MPCP students, Woodlands School and Highland Community School, had different origins. Alverno College, a small Catholic women's school located on the South Side, severed most ties with its lab school, called Alverno Campus Elementary School, in 1986. Parents, school directors, and staff wishing to continue this urban school reorganized it as the Woodlands School; it moved to an off-campus location in 1988, in a building that once housed Notre Dame High School. Woodlands enrolled a racially and socio-economically diverse student body from all over the city. As a non-sectarian school seeking to provide elementary education for an integrated student body, Woodlands enrolled MPS students who participated in the choice program. Principal Susan Wing stated that MCPC "allow[ed] us to keep our [economic] diversity." Highland began as a Montessori school in the late 1960s. Soon after, it joined the FICS.[58]

In the late 1980s, school leaders at Harambee, Urban Day, Bruce Guadelupe, and Woodlands met under the auspices of Family Services of

Wisconsin, a social service agency, to discuss methods to gain public support for their educational programs serving low-income students, while maintaining their independent status. School vouchers were discussed. Dr. Janet Ereth, of Family Services, had been director of the Independent Learning Center, an alternative secondary school that contracted with MPS to educate students who were not succeeding in MPS programs. These schools coordinated some of their fundraising efforts through the Coalition of Alternative Schools. According to Harambee Principal Callista Robinson, this coalition replaced FICS in the 1970s. In 1990, after passage of MPCP, the coalition was replaced by a Pupil Assignment Committee made up of the principals of the participating schools.[59]

BLACK POLITICAL POWER IN MILWAUKEE

The modest growth of black political power in Milwaukee in the 1980s helped to renew interest in public funding for Milwaukee's independent central city schools. African Americans were grossly under-represented in Milwaukee electoral politics prior to the 1980s, in spite of the sharp growth of Milwaukee's black population in the 1950s, "the highest rate of increase for any major U.S. city during that decade." In 1960, only one black served on Milwaukee's 19-member city council; by the early 1970s this representation increased to two. And on the school board, at-large elections limited black representation: from 1966 to 1970, no blacks were elected, but in 1975 three African Americans won the election, still a minority on the nine-member board. Limited black representation reflected voting strength, in part due to the youthfulness of Milwaukee's black population compared to the aging white population. Black representation was also a reflection of black voter registration and voting, which were both lower compared to whites. In spite of the population increase, Milwaukee's black population remained relatively small, contributing "less than one-fifth of the city's potential electorate in 1980." For several years, Lloyd Barbee was Milwaukee's sole black assemblyperson in the legislature. Black representation increased in the 1970s and 1980s, however. By 1988, black Milwaukee state legislators included four representatives and one senator. By the early 1990s, black representation in the common council increased to four out of 17. The number of seats on the school board remained at three.[60]

Although blacks remained under-represented, with the election of Democrat John Norquist as Mayor of Milwaukee in 1988, the new administration courted the black vote to a greater extent than the administration of Henry Maier, 1960–1988, a machine politician who largely ignored the Central City. In the state legislature, of course, the overwhelming white majority could pass laws with or without the support of black legislators. With parental choice legislation, however, black Democratic and white Republican interests dovetailed. This bipartisan support for the voucher plan helped create a rift among the legislature's Democrats, with conservative Democrats supporting MPCP and liberal Democrats opposing it.

The state representative who authored MPCP, Polly Williams, wrote the legislation with help from her policy director Larry Harwell and representatives of Harambee and Urban Day. Williams's election to the state assembly in 1980 reflected a modest increase in black political power. Williams moved from Mississippi to Milwaukee just after World War II; her father and uncle worked in the tanneries. An early supporter of the independent community schools, Williams sent her children to Urban Day and chaired Urban Day's Board of Directors.[61]

Beginning in 1969, Williams worked for federally funded urban programs, "first for an inner-city employment project, then for a community-based mental health program." During this period, many federally funded social welfare programs followed the "maximum feasible participation" model and with significant community input. Williams then switched to politics, defeating State Representative Walter Ward in 1980. One of the reasons that Williams switched from community social services to electoral politics was because she believed the professionalization taking place in federally funded poverty programs might block her occupational advancement. Williams argued that "social welfare has become a kind of alternate industry for college-educated, largely white, young professionals." Unlike some of her conservative allies who argued that social welfare programs ought to be trimmed back or eliminated, Williams believed that blacks needed to take control of publicly funded programs targeting their communities.[62]

Williams was perhaps the most high-profile African American opponent of MPS desegregation policies in the state. She believed that mandatory reassignment of black students at non-neighborhood MPS schools did nothing to improve academic achievement. During a 1990 community forum convened by the Wisconsin Advisory Committee to the U.S. Commission on Civil Rights, Williams stated that white students were "the only kids" who benefitted from desegregation in Milwaukee. "We don't want this desegregation," she continued. "Desegregation in the city of Milwaukee is terrible, and I'd like to see it abolished and go back to educating our children in our neighborhood schools regardless of color. And it doesn't matter if they're all black schools. I think black kids can learn in an all-black situation." In another 1990 context, the first day of the school year for participating "choice" students, Williams told a reporter that MPS has put "the emphasis on desegregation when you need to be talking about education."[63]

Although black politicians within the Democratic Party allied with white liberals from the time of the New Deal, to Williams there were limitations to the New Deal consensus, since access to decent employment, housing, and education remained problematic to so many of her constituents. Continued reliance on white-liberal Democratic support, then, held little promise for Williams. Rather, she believed that social policies that could benefit her constituents could come from either major political party. In Wisconsin in the late 1980s, Williams and other black politicians began to work more closely with Republican power brokers. After all, at the state and national levels, Republicans, rather than Democrats, were in control of executive branches. Moreover a conservative Democrat, John Norquist, was in control of the mayor's office. For black politicians such as Williams to move legislation that represented the interests of a majority of central city residents, compromise and coalition with Republicans and conservative Democrats was necessary.[64]

Due to her advocacy for school vouchers, coupled with her race and liberal credentials, Williams became something of a favorite of political conservatives on this issue. In Wisconsin her supporters included Governor Thompson, prominent Republican Party contributor Terry Kohler, and Bradley Foundation director Michael Joyce. At the national level, President George H. W. Bush, education secretaries William Bennett, Lauro Cavazos, and Lamar Alexander, and Minority Leader Newt Gingrich raised her stature. The Heritage Foundation, the *Washington Times,* and the editorial staff of the *Wall Street Journal* wrote sympathetic portrayals of Williams, also burnishing her image. Williams was a featured speaker at conferences around the country sponsored by the U.S. Department of Education, the Bradley Foundation, the Heritage Foundation and the *Washington Times.* Representative Newt Gingrich's political action committee, GOPAC, featured Williams on its "American Opportunities Workshop," which aired on the Christian Broadcasting Network's family channel. However, while Williams accepted financial backing by conservatives, she nevertheless opposed most of their other causes.[65]

GOVERNOR TOMMY THOMPSON

Tommy Thompson unseated Democratic incumbent Tony Earl in 1986. Almost immediately, Thompson sponsored legislation that protected wealth, with legislation in accord with the Reagan administration's "trickle-down" tax policies. Through Thompson's initiatives, state government phased out inheritance taxes, preserved a 60 percent capital gains exclusion that was eliminated at the federal level, and pared back the income tax.

Thompson also succeeded in scaling back business taxes and regulations to encourage corporations to remain and/or expand in Wisconsin and to encourage other employers to relocate to the state.[66]

Thompson developed a national reputation as a Republican reform governor through his efforts on social policy by applying populist appeal to neoliberal and neoconservative ends. On the neoliberal side, the Thompson administration underscored and exploited the belief that private markets rather than entitlements from the state ameliorated poverty most efficiently. On the neoconservative side, the administration sought to modify poor people's behavior, seemingly operating under the belief that poverty was largely the product of individual shortcomings. Hence, the Thompson administration began to require certain behaviors in exchange for welfare benefits under the federal Aid to Families with Dependent Children (AFDC) program. Undesirable behaviors resulted in reduced welfare benefits. According to Chief of Staff Scott Jensen, "We're trying to reinforce behavior that leads to success—school, work, families."[67]

Two of Thompson's best-known social policy initiatives, passed by the Democrat-controlled legislature, were popularly referred to as "Workfare" and "Learnfare." The federal government waived regulations for these programs; in fact, President Reagan telephoned Thompson in 1987 to tell him that federal waivers would be forthcoming should Learnfare pass. (A third Thompson-backed program, "Bridefare," was also proposed. Bridefare referred to changes in the AFDC program that would not penalize mothers who marry while collecting AFDC. It would also have held welfare benefits steady for mothers who have an additional child). "Workfare" required welfare recipients to participate in job training programs. "Learnfare" linked school attendance to welfare payments. Under this program, the state began monitoring students aged 13–19 with 10 or more unexcused absences the previous semester. If those students accumulated two days of absences in any following month, the state reduced AFDC monthly benefits by approximately $100 for each truant child.[68]

The Wisconsin legislature selected Milwaukee as the target for "Learnfare" and "Workfare," since it had the largest concentration of poor families (and the highest percentages of minority residents). The "Workfare" law exempted rural areas and small cities. The "Learnfare" law affected MPS, Wisconsin's largest school district, more than any other. In the late 1980s, the Wisconsin government, under Thompson's leadership, used Milwaukee as the laboratory for its social reform legislation. Williams was one of several legislators who opposed Learnfare. She argued that it unfairly punished mothers for their children's truancy, multiplied problems of poverty, and pitted family members against one another. "They are making education a punishment," she declared.[69]

School vouchers became another social reform that the Thompson administration favored, one that also fulfilled neoliberal and neoconservative goals. Potentially, school vouchers could fulfill neoconservative goals by rewarding the behavior of those parents able to secure places for their children in private schools. And making vouchers available to religious schools would expand the reach of traditional authorities, such as religious leaders, to more people. Moreover, wealth could be protected through state subsidization of private school tuition if all private school students were allowed to participate. On the neoliberal side, businesses in the form of private schools could expand through state subsidies, private educational markets would be extended, educational regulations would be reduced, and, allegedly, increased competition for students would be an effective incentive for all schools, public and private, to improve.

Political opposition to state reimbursement for the tuition payments of affluent parents, along with concerns about the separation of church and state, meant that Thompson's parental choice initiatives would not occupy the extreme Friedmanite end of the parental choice continuum—such bills that did died in the legislature. For example, Thompson's initial 1988 proposal included vouchers for religious and non-religious schools in Milwaukee. Markets would extend gradually due to the exclusion of parochial schools, which made up the overwhelming majority of private school enrollment. Nonetheless, on a symbolic level, neoconservative aims translated into social policy through MPCP. "Good behavior"—parents taking the necessary steps to secure quality education in non-public schools—was codified; "the deserving poor" were rewarded.

At the same time, the Thompson administration opposed most education initiatives that emanated from the Democratic Party. Although one of Thompson's 1986 campaign promises in the education arena was to boost state aid to elementary and secondary education to 50 percent of the total cost, a position favored by many Democratic legislators, state aid remained at 46 percent in Thompson's first two years in office. In the 1980s, before Williams and other Democratic politicians in favor of state aid for independent community schools got involved, the school voucher, even those of the compensatory variety, was a partisan political issue in Wisconsin. Complicating matters, MPS authorities and their supporters developed their own parental choice plan in 1989, causing more Democrats to become more favorably inclined to vote for school vouchers.[70]

In 1988, Thompson vetoed a requirement that MPS donate $75,000 to the Marshall Plan Committee (a group studying urban school problems), vetoed provisions for four-year-old kindergarten, and opposed various other early childhood and elementary grant programs for MPS students. According to State Representative Marcia Coggs, a black Democrat who represented a central city Milwaukee district, Thompson vetoed the provisions because the Marshall Plan Committee was the result of Democratic leadership and the MPS grants went against Thompson's strategies for working with MPS. The following year, Thompson vetoed Democratic-sponsored legislation that would have reduced class sizes in lower elementary school grades by providing state funding for additional classroom teachers. Thompson stated in his veto message that a need for lower class sizes was not demonstrated. Parental choice became an education reform the Thompson administration embraced to the exclusion of increased state funding, reforms in curriculum and instruction, and the New North Division District proposal.[71]

THE BRADLEY FOUNDATION

Philanthropic foundations and think tanks have often played crucial roles in the development of education systems and the shaping of school reform in the United States. In the case of MPCP, Milwaukee's Bradley Foundation helped to legitimate vouchers as a school reform strategy, helped establish a climate necessary for the bill's passage, and contributed to the program's legal defense. More broadly, Bradley funded programs and projects that promoted educational privatization at the national, state, and local levels. Among U.S. philanthropic foundations with conservative aims, the Bradley Foundation was the largest, with total fair market value assets of over $410 million in 1992 (the next-largest conservative foundation was Olin, with $100 million). For comparison, the largest U.S. foundation was Ford, with assets of over $6 billion. Bradley Foundation President Michael Joyce moved to Bradley from the helm of the Olin Foundation in 1986. He was a member of the Reagan Administration transition team in 1980/1981. Because of his position at the Bradley Foundation, he was one of the nation's most powerful conservatives.[72]

The Bradley Foundation attained its position of national prominence in 1984, after aerospace and defense conglomerate Rockwell International purchased the privately held Allen-Bradley Company of Milwaukee, the leading U.S. manufacturer of automation control equipment. Prior to the sale, Bradley was a small regional foundation with assets of $11 million. The foundation's assets jumped to $326 million after Rockwell International bought out the company. The Bradley Foundation's history of support for conservative causes dated to the political orientation of Allen-Bradley founders Harry Bradley and Fred Loock. According to John Gurda's *The Bradley Legacy: Lynde and Harry Bradley, Their Company, and Their Foundation,* both men "gravitated to the far-reaches of the right wing"—for example, they were active supporters of the John Birch Society. CEO Tiny Rader, who engineered the sale of Allen-Bradley, shared the Bradleys' views on free enterprise and private ownership; Rader was responsible for bringing Michael Joyce to Milwaukee.[73]

To maintain its tax-exempt status, Bradley was forbidden to "attempt to influence any national, state, or local legislation" or "otherwise attempt to influence legislation by attempting to affect the opinion of the general public or any segment thereof." The Bradley Foundation helped nurture an intellectual climate that increased the credibility of educational privatization, vouchers, parental choice, and the like. It bankrolled research in the late 1980s that for the most part, advocated vouchers and other forms of educational privatization. At the same time, Bradley-funded educational research tended to both disparage public education (especially MPS) and discredit other strategies of education reform. According to Michael Joyce, parental choice was the only school reform worth pursuing: "All the rest are palliatives. They are incremental at best. They palliate and disguise." Much of the research bolstering vouchers was carried out by the Wisconsin Policy Research Institute (WPRI), a think tank established and funded by Bradley since 1987 to disseminate research germane to state and local government policies "so that...elected representatives are able to make informed decisions."[74]

As one example of WPRI research, in a survey testing support for vouchers in Wisconsin, pollster Gordon Black found that 48 percent of those surveyed favored a state-supported voucher program (59 percent of Milwaukee residents responded this way). The question read, "Many people believe that poor children in urban areas are having problems in the public schools. One idea to improve their educational opportunities is for the state to give tax money to poor parents and allow them to choose which public, private, or parochial school to send their child to. This idea would not cost more than current public education. Would you like to see this idea adopted in Wisconsin?" The publication of this survey coincided with the timing of Governor Thompson's 1989 voucher proposals, and Wisconsin newspapers ran the results of the poll. Bradley also helped to sponsor research by John Chubb and Terry Moe that compared the governance structures of public and private schools. The resulting *Politics, Markets, and America's Schools* was influential in the United States and internationally, receiving attention from the U.S. news media, business groups, educators, and government officials.[75]

More specific to the genesis of MPCP, Bradley helped sponsor conferences on parental choice in Milwaukee and Madison in the late 1980s, contributed to the State of Wisconsin in support of Thompson's reform initiatives, and contributed to the legal foundation that successfully defended MPCP in the Wisconsin courts. The Bradley Foundation paid $65,000 for a conference on "Educational Decentralization" convened by the Robert M. La Follette Institute of Public Affairs at the University of Wisconsin-Madison in the spring of 1989. In 1990, Professors John Witte and William Clune edited a two-volume compilation of these conference papers, entitled *Choice and Control in American Education.* Researchers who received Bradley grants attended the March 1988 forum on parental choice at Milwaukee Area Technical College, at which parental choice initiatives were discussed. In attendance were John Chubb, Terry Moe, Howard Fuller, and Assistant Secretary of Education Chester Finn. At the conference Finn stated that the strongest outcry for "freedom of choice" came from the nation's poor and that "schools of choice are always better schools." He also called Thompson's voucher proposal "imaginative and bold." Following the conference, Milwaukee's largest black newspaper, the *Milwaukee Community Journal,* opined that the "parental choice idea is worthy of passage." In the editorial, the paper argued that black support for parental choice stems from the dissatisfaction of black and poor families with MPS.[76]

In 1990 and 1992, Bradley donated a total of $200,000 to the state of Wisconsin, "to support work on the state's education initiatives." This work was under the Wisconsin Department of Administration rather than under the auspices of the Department of Public Instruction (State Superintendent of Public Instruction Herbert Grover opposed vouchers). In December 1990, the state Commission of Schools for the 21st Century, which the Bradley Foundation helped to support, recommended that private school choice programs similar to MPCP should extend to three other sites around the state. Bradley also donated to the Landmark Legal Foundation in the early 1990s. Plaintiffs, who supported MPCP in the Wisconsin courts, hired this Kansas City-based legal foundation to represent them, through Polly Williams's office. The lead attorney was Clint Bolick, a former Reagan Justice Department official and a prominent conservative. From 1990 to 1992, the years of litigation, Bradley donated $350,700 to Landmark.[77]

In Milwaukee, Bradley donated hundreds of thousands of dollars to Marquette University over the years; some of this funding established, in 1992, the pro-voucher Center for Parental Freedom in Education, under the direction of Professor Quentin Quade and dedicated to the memory of Reverend Virgil Blum. Bradley has also contributed to the National Center for Neighborhood Enterprises, an organization that stressed self-reliance for impoverished communities. Through the Center's auspices, Bradley donated $83,361 in 1991 and 1992 to establish the Milwaukee Parental Assistance Center, headed for eight months by Larry Harwell. The Parental Assistance Center opposed an unsuccessful school building referendum in

Table 4.3 Foundation Support of Community Schools, 1988–1992
(In Thousands of Dollars)

	Urban Day	Harambee	Bruce Guadelupe	Highland	Woodlands
Bradley	31.8	48.2	53*	36.8	22.8
Pettit	60	1683.8	110	12	5
McBeath	12	—	95	89.1	—
*Cudahy***	185	—	—	—	—
Milwaukee	93.9	36.3	46	94.3	20
Smith	10	—	—	—	—
Totals:	392.7	1768.3	304	232.2	47.8

Sources: IRS Returns, 1988–1992, Bradley Foundation, Pettit Foundation, McBeath
Foundation, Cudahy Fund, Milwaukee Foundation, A. O. Smith Foundation.

*Does not include $275,000 to the United Community Center.
**The 1992 return was "unlocatable" by the IRS.

Milwaukee in 1993. According to Harwell, in the late 1980s and early 1990s
the Bradley Foundation was "moving everybody."[78]

In contrast, Bradley Foundation support of independent community
schools that participated in MPCP was modest. During the five years
spanning 1988–1992, Bradley contributed, in descending order, $53,000
to Bruce Guadelupe, $48,250 to Harambee, $36,820 to Highlands, $31,850
to Urban Day, and $22,850 to Woodlands. On June 6, 1990, the Bradley
Foundation made small contributions to four community schools to support "publications projects" that advertised the schools to MPS parents
and guardians: Urban Day received $3,250, Harambee received $1,500,
and Highland and Woodlands each received $1,820. Table 4.3 details foun-
dation commitments to the participating voucher schools. Compared with
the support of Milwaukee's other large foundations, total Bradley grants
to the five community schools were small. For example, during the same
five-year period, the Pettit Foundation (also a recipient of proceeds from
the Allen-Bradley sale) granted Harambee $1,683,787. Pettit also donated
$1,386,500 during the same five-year period to University School, an exclu-
sive Milwaukee-area secondary school that charged tuition of over $7,000
per student in 1990.[79]

VOUCHERS COME TO MILWAUKEE

Beginning in 1988, a flurry of parental choice proposals made their way
around the legislature. In January, Governor Tommy Thompson presented
parental choice legislation as a part of his state budget proposal. Although

Polly Williams discussed parental choice in the legislature for several years as a means of generating public support for Milwaukee's independent community schools, she remained on the sidelines of Thompson's proposed legislation, believing her education proposals made more sense. Thompson's recommendation called for educational vouchers for a limited number of underprivileged MPS students to attend any private or public school in Milwaukee County. The parental choice provision for Milwaukee would have created vouchers for up to 1,000 low-income students to attend any school in Milwaukee county—private, parochial, or public. Under this proposal, the state would pay tuition and reduce its funding of MPS by an equal amount.[80]

Political support for Thompson's parental choice initiatives was not forthcoming in the legislature, however. In April 1988, the legislature's Joint Finance Committee, under Democratic control, deleted the Thompson administration parental choice initiatives from the budget bill. Senator Gary George, finance committee co-chair, did not favor the plan. His educational policy advisor, Professor Walter Farrell of the University of Wisconsin-Milwaukee, objected to the program because of its reliance on vouchers. "We are for choice, but not for vouchers," he stated a year later. In essence, the Democratic-controlled state assembly rejected the Republican-crafted education proposals embedded in the budget bill. Chair of the Senate Education Committee Joseph Czarnezki described the proposal as "dead on arrival." The initiative was also opposed by Herbert Grover's Department of Public Instruction, the Wisconsin Education Association Council, MPS, the Milwaukee Afro American Council, the Milwaukee NAACP, and the Milwaukee Teachers Education Association. The National Education Association's state affiliate, the Wisconsin Education Association Council (WEAC) opposed the Thompson parental choice proposal on a variety of grounds. One objection was that public funds to parochial schools raised the specter of First Amendment debates on the limits to separation of church and state. The potential high cost to the state in paying tuition to private schools that charged tuition at a higher rate than per capita state funding to MPS was another objection. But the most vociferous objection was that the redirection of state funds from MPS to private schools would undermine public education in Milwaukee.[81]

The other 1988 development affecting the school voucher debate in Wisconsin was the appointment of Robert Peterkin as Superintendent of MPS, to succeed Lee McMurrin. Peterkin was Milwaukee's first black superintendent of schools. He had been superintendent of schools in Cambridge, Massachusetts, a district that received national attention for its system of "Controlled Choice." The new superintendent, cognizant of the MPS transportation programs that caused longer bus rides for black students on average, brought desegregation expert and Harvard professor Charles Willie to Milwaukee to help design a redistricting plan to reduce busing. Willie helped to introduce "Controlled Choice" plans in Boston and Cambridge, Massachusetts, and Little Rock, Arkansas. Due to Peterkin's background in the Cambridge Public Schools, he was familiar with the concept of choice.[82]

For the remainder of 1988, Polly Williams, although open to Thompson's choice initiative, put her energy into other reforms of MPS. In November, she and Larry Harwell organized a meeting in Milwaukee to elect a third black school board member. Williams also designed legislation to redirect some state funds under the Chapter 220 program away from transportation and toward compensatory programs in predominantly black schools. Another Williams proposal required parental consent before MPS could transport students to schools outside of the inner-city. Finally, she worked on an alternative redistricting plan to proposals drawn up by MPS.[83]

As a backdrop to unveil his updated voucher proposal, Thompson selected a federal Workshop on Choice in Education, held in Washington, D.C., on January 9, 1989. President Reagan and President-elect Bush also addressed the White House workshop. Polly Williams along with other parental choice advocates from around the nation attended. "The first part of my plan is designed to help the Milwaukee public school system," stated Thompson. "The proposal allows low-income children enrolled in kindergarten through sixth grade in Milwaukee public schools to attend any public or non-sectarian private school in Milwaukee County. The second part of the plan expands the concept of parental choice to the rest of the state." The Thompson administration looked to neighboring Minnesota and its statewide parental choice system of inter-district transfers in creating a statewide open enrollment provision for Wisconsin.[84]

Thompson's January 1989 plan, later introduced in the legislature through Thompson's budget proposal, streamlined the MPS voucher component to include only non-sectarian private schools and public schools in Milwaukee County. This was the only significant modification of Thompson's 1988 proposal. The removal of parochial schools disappointed parochial school boosters and voucher proponents who attended the White House workshop. When asked by a member of the audience why Thompson "backed down," he responded, "Why not include religious? I want to win." Thompson reminded the audience that when he included religious schools in his 1988 plan, "the legislation unfortunately went nowhere." He added that he would attempt to extend vouchers to religious schools once his latest proposal passed.[85]

Williams remained uncommitted even though Thompson helped enable Williams to attend the White House conference. Although agreeing with

Thompson that parental choices of schools should be expanded, she stated at the conference that her own plan, which would require MPS to obtain parental consent before transporting children to schools outside of their neighborhoods, would reach more people than Thompson's proposal. This redistricting plan, unveiled in mid-January, was an alternative to Peterkin's plan. It would reduce busing and transportation costs, and funds freed up by the reform would go central city public schools. Since Thompson did not support Williams over the creation of a North Division school district, and since he backed Learnfare legislation Williams opposed, it appears that Williams was unwilling to support an educational initiative that was so closely identified with the governor. Nevertheless, several black parents testified that they supported the bill at a legislative hearing.[86]

Prior to unveiling his choice proposals at the White House, Thompson contacted Robert Peterkin to enlist his support on parental choice. Peterkin and Thompson agreed that some form of parental choice legislation to send MPS students to independent schools in Milwaukee would be an educational policy that both men could support. Peterkin agreed to help draft an MPS proposal for the legislature. Thompson recognized that voucher-like legislation would fail to pass the Wisconsin legislature unless he could expand his support for parental choice beyond the Republican Party and a handful of conservative Democrats. Thus, Thompson attempted to enlist the support of two prominent black Milwaukee policy makers—MPS Superintendent Robert Peterkin, and one of MPS's best-known critics, Polly Williams.[87]

Once again, Tommy Thompson's parental choice plans died in the legislature. The Joint Finance Committee deleted both initiatives from the state budget in April 1989. WEAC Director Morris Andrews told a Joint Finance Committee hearing on February 28 that "WEAC says no to choice," and that he would not work with those interested in shaping an alternative plan. According to Assemblyman David Travis (D-Madison), Thompson's proposals stood a better chance in the legislature as separate bills. "There's a fair amount of sentiment that perhaps something special might be appropriate for Milwaukee, but the rest of the state wasn't particularly interested in doing it." On June 8, two Republican representatives reintroduced Thompson's proposals as separate legislation, but the education committee tabled the bills. In 1988 and again in early 1989, Thompson's choice proposals had Republican Party sponsorship, but the bills did not move out of committee.[88]

In late June MPS introduced its own parental choice plan in the legislature. This bill, with the support of Thompson, Peterkin, and Norquist, was similar to a proposal drafted by the Milwaukee School Board in April. A white Democratic Milwaukee Assemblyman, Thomas Seery, sponsored the bill.

The MPS plan, drafted by Peterkin and other administrative personnel, also earned the qualified support of Walter Farrell, policy director to state Senator Gary George, who termed it "a step in the right direction" while raising concerns about MPS retention of administrative costs and the threatened autonomy of receiving schools. Farrell was a critic of Thompson's earlier proposals. In this choice plan, independent and non-sectarian Milwaukee schools, pre-kindergarten through eighth grade, could contract with MPS to enroll up to 1,000 MPS students in their schools. Eighty percent of Wisconsin per pupil state aid would follow the student to the private school and MPS would retain 20 percent of this aid. The MPS proposal sought to maintain administrative control of the voucher system, just as it maintained contracting authority with partnership schools. In its parental choice proposal, MPS attempted to fold vouchers into an "at-risk" definition— behavioral and academic requirements took their places alongside the original Thompson proposals of vouchers for low-income MPS students.[89]

POLLY WILLIAMS AND THE PARENTAL CHOICE DEBATE

It was the submission of the MPS proposal to the state legislature that caused Polly Williams to counter with a bill of her own. She opposed the MPS bill on three grounds. She did not want MPS to have financial and administrative authority over a Milwaukee voucher program. She viewed the 20 percent retention of state funds as excessive. And most important, she viewed the MPS plan as an attempt to place disruptive, problem students elsewhere. "MPS and the Democrats proposed a plan to dump kids, and then we went into action," stated Larry Harwell. "We did all of the organizing. We got the schools together, the people together, and we got the other assembly people into line.... We blocked the MPS plan and made one similar to Thompson's." Williams made connections between MPS desegregation policies, bureaucratic growth, and parental choice. "As long as they can continue busing our children all around the city, MPS gets paid by the state," she said. "Black people have to understand that this has little to do with desegregation anymore."[90]

The Williams-sponsored parental choice bill, submitted shortly after the MPS proposal, removed the "at risk" criteria of the MPS bill and raised the income ceiling to 1.75 times the poverty line. In her bill, participating students would not be counted as MPS students to determine state categorical aid, unlike the MPS proposal, whereby the students in the "partnership" schools would still be considered MPS students. Unlike the Peterkin Bill, her proposal was supported by parents and personnel at the independent community schools: currently enrolled students could qualify for vouchers and MPS would not regulate the schools.[91]

The assembly defeated both bills, however. The MPS proposal went down 58–41. All four black representatives from Milwaukee voted against it. Assembly speaker Tom Loftus also voted against the proposal, perhaps as payback for Thompson's veto of a bill reducing class sizes that the legislature recently passed. Williams's bill was defeated by a narrower margin, 54–44. Three of the assembly's four black representatives voted for the bill. The only black opponent was Marcia Coggs, who succeeded Lloyd Barbee in the assembly in 1976. The bill did not have support from the assembly's Democratic leadership, including Loftus and Urban Education Committee chair Barbara Notestein. Williams was able to generate considerable Republican support for her initiative. Thompson and Seery nevertheless regarded Williams's plan as a spoiler bill, cutting into support for the MPS plan, even though Williams's bill received more support. WEAC lobbied to defeat both Seery's and Williams's bills. After the votes, the legislature requested that the Legislative Reference Bureau study the issue of parental choice, keeping the topic in the spotlight.[92]

Williams backed parental choice legislation because it would create an alternative to MPS for black students who were not succeeding in MPS schools. At the same time, Williams continued to demand that MPS and the state legislature do more for public school children in predominantly black schools. For example, during the same legislative session that defeated the Williams and Seery parental choice bills, the assembly passed a bill sponsored by Williams to redirect $8 million from Chapter 220 transportation aid to hire paraprofessionals and tutors in 28 predominantly black schools and create a new specialty school on the near-North Side. This bill was passed over the opposition of Loftus, but the Senate's Education Committee rejected it.[93]

Over the summer of 1989, Williams and her staff worked on a new parental choice bill. Representatives of Urban Day School and Harambee helped draft the legislation. This bill was similar to Thompson's early 1989 proposal, except that up to 3,000 MPS students could participate. An important part of this bill was that participating private schools would receive the actual cost of education per student, the same as the inter-district provision of Chapter 220. Her proposal, like Thompson's, was not "revenue neutral"—it required the state to fund participating students at a higher rate than the amount of current state aid per capita to MPS students.

Williams stated that Wisconsin has aided and supported suburban schools through Chapter 220, and the same should be done for independent community schools. "When we go to the state for this program, we will not accept less than was provided suburban schools. And I'm not going to compromise on that point." During the summer and early fall, Williams also lined up assembly and senate support for her proposal. Although Loftus and the Democratic caucus in the assembly declined to support Williams's bill, her office forged a coalition of conservative Democrat, black Democrat, and Republican support. "Only the white liberals fought it," said Williams. In general, liberal Democrats opposed the bill because they believed that vouchers would undermine Wisconsin's public school system.[94]

The Parental Choice Options Bill was introduced by Williams in October 1989, with 46 Democratic and Republican co-sponsors (9 lawmakers also introduced the plan in the senate). It was this bill, in modified form, which Thompson signed into law in April 1990, as the Milwaukee Parental Choice Program. MPS promised a counterproposal, and Urban Education Chair Barbara Notestein agreed to hold the Williams bill in committee until MPS could have a new parental choice bill introduced. By late 1989, Thompson and Norquist switched their support of parental choice from legislation emanating from Peterkin and the Democratic leadership to legislation backed by Williams. On October 26, Thompson visited Harambee Community School as part of a one day fact-finding tour of Milwaukee's Inner Core. Thompson praised Williams's bill, telling Principal Callista Robinson, "If choice passes, you will get state help. It would be a godsend for the school." He concluded from his tour that "The investment has got to be in education. ... The school choice program is badly needed."[95]

In early 1990, Thompson supported Williams's bill at a parental choice conference held by the national Black Women's Network in Milwaukee. At this conference, Bonnie Guiton (special advisor to President Bush) and Joan Davis-Ratteray (president of the Institute for Independent Education in Washington, an organization that supported private, African American schools) spoke in favor of Williams's bill, as did Howard Fuller, State Representatives Spencer Coggs and Gwendolynne Moore, and school board member Jared Johnson. Norquist lent his support while touring Highland Community School with Children's Defense Fund Director Marian Wright Edelman in November 1989. He stated that choice legislation represented a struggle between community supporters and MPS. "It may boil down to an issue of which side wins the battle of control: Will it be MPS or the parents?" But the Milwaukee school superintendent did not resubmit a proposal to the legislature. In a letter to the *Milwaukee Community Journal*, Peterkin expressed skepticism of the success of Williams's proposal because it bypassed MPS. Peterkin also stated that MPS would have to "foot the bill" under the Williams plan, since students already enrolled in private schools could participate. According to MPS official Doug Haselow, the superintendent did not introduce a counter proposal in part because Thompson had previously enlisted Peterkin's help, but then the governor switched to Williams. [96]

Peterkin and other MPS supporters were out-maneuvered by Williams and Thompson beginning in July of 1989. According to Grover, "MPS lost its legislative support. There was no imperative that you be a friend of MPS. The system had no friends in Madison." In addition, WEAC did not apply a "full court press" to oppose the legislation. According to Thompson's educational policy advisor Tom Fonfara, WEAC dropped its opposition when Thompson promised not to use his line-item veto power to expand the program once the legislature passed it. Because of the affiliation between MPS teachers and WEAC, it is somewhat surprising that WEAC did not apply more pressure on elected officials. Not to be discounted, however, was that legislative leaders in the end folded MCPC into the budget bill. This helped remove opponents from the equation, since the budget contained all programs. [97]

Williams also worked the Senate. Her office helped persuade Senator Gary George to support their legislation. Williams and Harwell noticed that Superintendent Peterkin and Senator George did not "get along" and exploited this personality clash. After meeting with community residents and Thompson, George eventually came down on Williams's side. George was persuaded that Williams's proposed legislation would contribute to remedying the "dire educational circumstances affecting low-income minority and majority children in the Milwaukee Public Schools who are not experiencing educational success." His support, as co-chair of the legislature's Joint Finance Committee, was crucial. Williams also gained the support of Marcia Coggs, the only black representative to oppose Williams's earlier bill. Parents, students, and personnel of Harambee and Urban Day testified in favor of parental choice legislation in Milwaukee and Madison. In addition, Williams held meetings in Milwaukee and enlisted the support of other public officials, including all three black members of the common council and one of the three black school board members, Jared Johnson. [98]

The final obstacle to pass MPCP in the assembly was Notestein, who held the bill in committee. Notestein held a community meeting on the choice legislation at the MPS administration building on February 23, 1990, in which most of the speakers favored vouchers. During the three hours of testimony, Notestein "repeatedly ordered the crowd of several hundred people to withhold applause or cries of 'amen.'" Williams and Harwell outlined the bill for the audience. At this time, the bill contained provisions for the state to provide full tuition for participating students and schools, with state funding at MPS reduced by the per capita rate. Williams's legislation was not a "zero-sum" proposal—the state would provide additional funds when state per capita MPS aid fell short of tuition at the participating schools. Howard Fuller urged passage, as did other community leaders. Haselow was the only official to voice opposition to the bill.[99]

Soon after, Notestein released the voucher bill, with modifications from her committee, which reduced the number of participants from 3 percent to 1 percent of MPS enrollment, added academic and attendance requirements for students at participating schools, and included a five year "sunset" provision. The committee limited the per-pupil funding received by participating private schools, from full tuition to "an amount equal to 53 percent of the average per pupil cost for pupils who are enrolled in the school district." Essentially, this provision reduced per pupil funding to participating schools from full tuition to per pupil MPS state aid plus approximately $600. Most significantly, the committee required participating students be currently enrolled in MPS, making students already enrolled in private schools ineligible. By a 7–6 vote, the committee recommended passage, and the Assembly passed it with no further significant modifications by a 62–35 vote. Mostly, liberal white Democrats opposed the measure while Republicans, conservative Democrats, and the assembly's four black representatives supported it.[100]

Less than two weeks before the end of the legislative session, the bill moved to the Senate, where Senator Bob Jauch buried it in the committee on Educational Financing, Higher Education, and Tourism. However, Senator Gary George, who met with Thompson in February to discuss the choice legislation, attached the bill as a rider to the budget adjustment bill. By this time, George became a supporter, due to "guidance" from Polly Williams, and through "numerous focus-group discussions with a broad cross-section of parents and leaders in Milwaukee's African American community." During debate, the Senate removed the provision for 53 percent of per pupil MPS costs (the $600 state grants), amending it with per pupil MPS state aid following the student from MPS to the participating private school. The Senate passed the budget bill on March 22 by a 26–7 vote, and the Assembly passed the budget without debate the same day.[101]

The Milwaukee Common Council voted 11–3 in February to oppose Williams's bill, a resolution that Mayor Norquist vetoed. On March 20, a week after the state assembly passed MCPC, eight members of city council voted to override the veto, three short of the number needed to reverse Norquist. The city council, therefore, did not have a formal position on the bill whereas the mayor became one of the bill's most vocal supporters. Thompson was "elated" that the legislature passed a version of Polly Williams's legislation. He signed the MPCP into law on April 27, 1990, using his line-item veto power to delete the sunset provision. "Once again, Wisconsin is leading the nation," he remarked. "We, as a state, have acknowledged that private schools play an important role and provide an effective option in the education of our children." Two weeks later, Thompson re-enacted the signing at Harambee Community School. At the ceremony, a representative from the federal Department of Education read a message of support from President Bush. Community leaders, including George, Johnson, Spencer Coggs, and Williams also attended. The next month, Bush praised MPCP while campaigning for Thompson in Milwaukee.[102]

Soon after passage, several institutional recipients of Bradley Foundation grants lent support. Williams attended a Brookings Institution conference on parental choice marking the publication of Chubb and Moe's *Politics, Markets, and America's Schools.* The president of the National Center for Neighborhood Enterprise, Robert Woodson, stated he would bring buses of low-income people to Milwaukee to support Williams if needed. William Bennett also lauded MPCP, adding that parental choice was "the next great civil rights arena."[103]

The passage of MPCP received widespread media attention, locally and nationally. Milwaukee's two major dailies, the *Milwaukee Sentinel* and the *Milwaukee Journal,* covered the voucher bills extensively, but did not support MCPC. Milwaukee's two newsweeklies with predominantly black readership, the *Milwaukee Community Journal* and the *Milwaukee Courier,* favored MPCP. *Milwaukee Community Journal* editor Mikel Holt was a strong supporter of the program, and covered parental choice extensively since Thompson's 1988 proposal. The smaller *Courier* did not give the program the same coverage, but greeted the program's passage enthusiastically. At the national level, the *Chicago Tribune, New York Times, Washington Post,* and *Wall Street Journal,* among others, picked up the story. The *Wall Street Journal*'s editorial page repeatedly endorsed the program. The media attention helped heighten expectations within Wisconsin and nationally that school vouchers might help solve the urban school crisis.[104]

From one perspective, it appeared that the compensatory school voucher, one with attributes originally championed by left-liberal policy makers, free-school advocates, and community activists from the 1960s, might have staying power after all. As with voucher proposals pioneered by Christopher Jencks and others, social reform within the Republican Party appeared to serve as midwife. Moreover, vouchers became an issue with which Republicans could appeal to black constituencies that usually voted Democratic. Whereas in the 1960s Republicans often had little more to offer black voters than conservative rhetoric (for example, during a campaign swing to Milwaukee, Richard Nixon promised blacks "a piece of the action"), by the late 1980s vouchers represented a tangible, albeit small, benefit. Governor Thompson ran better in Milwaukee's black wards during his 1990 election campaign (8 percent of the vote in 1986 vs. 25 percent in

1990 and over 40 percent in 1994). Thompson's association with Williams and his support for vouchers contributed to his increased popularity.[105]

But social conservatives of various stripes did not wish to stop at non-sectarian, compensatory vouchers. Religious leaders and other supporters stood on the wings in Milwaukee and elsewhere. Moreover, public school leaders in the teachers unions and elsewhere viewed vouchers plainly as a threat and moved to stop them. But the national showdown over vouchers did not occur in Milwaukee. A new voucher program, one more radical than Milwaukee's 1990 program, took shape in Cleveland, with parochial schooling front-and-center.

Chapter 5

THE CHURCH IN THE CITY

"Research supports the particular effectiveness of the Catholic school in the inner city with those children most at risk of failure," asserted Cleveland Bishop Anthony Pilla in remarks at the Catholic Conference of Ohio's March 20, 1995, Biannual State Legislative Breakfast. "We want to continue our presence and our schools in the neighborhoods of our cities. We want to help families break the cycle of poverty through education." Given that the Ohio Legislature was considering bills that would establish an experimental voucher program in one or more urban school districts, Pilla's remarks were apropos. "It is a matter of distributive justice to parents...to be able to choose a school, public, private, or church-related, and have tax dollars support their choice," he continued. "Our schools are providing a community service." Through the 1980s and 1990s, commentators highlighted with increasing forcefulness the promise of Catholic schools for students from families of modest means. Could the parochial schools help solve the urban school crisis?[1]

Bishop Pilla seemed to think so, and he was not alone. In the years leading up to the enactment of the Cleveland Scholarship and Tutoring Program, academics conducted studies lending credence to the bishop's assertion about the effectiveness of inner-city Catholic schools. The most notable was 1993's *Catholic Schools and the Common Good,* in which Anthony Bryk and his research team at the Harvard Graduate School of Education suggested that the Catholic secondary schools, with their "focused academic curriculum," did a better job educating "disadvantaged students" than at the "laissez-faire" and "highly differentiated" public high schools. To Bryk and his team, the Catholic schools inherited the mantle of the common school ideal—urban public schools no longer provided a common education that lifted poor students out of poverty, but the Catholic schools often did, and as such, "arguments against public support for Catholic schools...seem ungrounded." Bryk's research underscored the important role of inner-city Catholic schools to create positive opportunities for disadvantaged students.[2]

This represented a sea change from perspectives that emerged out of James Coleman's massive 1960s Equality of Educational Opportunity Study, especially Christopher Jencks's *Inequality: A Reassessment of the Effect of Family and Schooling in America.* Jencks and his colleagues argued that while the amount of schooling mattered a great deal, differences in the kind of schooling students received—public or parochial—had little bearing on future occupational status. The findings popularized in *The Catholic Schools and the Common Good* also represented a change from the practical justifications upwardly mobile black parents sometimes used when sending their children to Catholic schools—not so much the superiority of a Catholic education as the promise of maintaining cultural ties to upwardly mobile and politically connected whites. Continuing a trend that began in the 1950s, white Catholics patronized inner-city parochial schools in decreasing numbers; now the Catholic school represented, for African American families, a visible and realistic alternative to the public school system.[3]

More immediate to Ohio, several political and religious heavyweights promoted school vouchers in the 1980s and 1990s, among them Governor George Voinovich, Cincinnati Archbishop Daniel Pilarczyk, Cleveland Bishop Pilla, State Representative Michael Fox, and Akron industrialist and education entrepreneur David Brennan. At critical junctures, these leaders, all of them active in Republican Party circles, were assisted by Democrats supportive of school vouchers, among them Cleveland Mayor Michael White, Cleveland Councilwoman Fannie Lewis, and State Representative Patrick Sweeney. Voucher supporters in Ohio linked ongoing efforts by parochial educators to secure financial support from the state to a new clarion call, that Catholic education could reverse the decline of urban public education. Most of the other voucher advocates, whether supportive because of possible promise for majority-black institutions or because of the potential of the competitive education marketplace to unlock value for students and their parents, supported the idea that religious schools backed with public funds would benefit urban students. While these leaders and advocates supported the 1995 voucher legislation in Ohio, efforts to assist non-public schools with state dollars began long before the 1990 election of George Voinovich as governor.

DEPRESSION-ERA VOUCHERS

Ohio's openness to assist Catholic and other religious schools with public funds was somewhat unusual compared to other states. Unlike the
nearby states of Michigan, Indiana, and Wisconsin, in the decades following the Civil War Ohio did not amend its constitution "to prohibit all aid
to church institutions." For example, state funds could go toward secular
subjects taught in religious schools. Though Ohio considered a constitutional amendment in 1874 prohibiting public funds for parochial schools,
Democrats blocked the measure, in part due to the groundswell of popular opposition to a Republican-backed national civil rights bill that called
for racial integration in the public schools. And although anti-Catholic
rhetoric helped catapult Rutherford B. Hayes to the Ohio governorship
and ultimately to the presidency of the United States, the Protestant backlash to growing Catholic power in the public schools proved to be something of a paper tiger—nationally the Blaine Amendment failed (it sought
to prohibit public funding to parochial schools). In the Buckeye State,
measures to rein in the Catholic schools, such as by taxing church property, also went down to defeat. Ohio was indeed a crossroads state with a
growing urban Catholic population in which the religious divide between
Protestants and Catholics failed to distinguish any clear winners and los-
ers. In the second half of the 19th century, Catholic schooling continued
to expand within a context in which the state legislature refrained from
passing legislation hostile to parochial schools, but it did little to support
them either.[4]

While this equilibrium between church and state was not breached until
World War I (the issue being language policy amid anti-German sentiment
sweeping the nation), the pendulum seemed to be swinging the other way
during the Great Depression. With many school districts facing budget
shortfalls due to declining property tax revenue, Ohio began providing state
aid to local school districts in 1932. In response to this new precedent, supporters of private schools also began to look to the state, since private and
parochial schools also faced financial difficulties. In 1933, Catholic bishops
appointed a committee "to obtain state aid for parochial schools in Ohio."
At the request of Governor George White, a Democrat, lawmakers proposed in an emergency legislative session to include parochial schools as
part of temporary aid to districts and schools under threat of insolvency.
Governor White sought to aid "free tuition elementary schools," and since
most Catholic elementary schools charged no tuition to parishioners, his
mandate centered on Catholic schools. Aid would be based on student enrollment, and in one guise, resulted in $14 per student annually. This bill was

defeated, but not entirely along party lines. Although the bill was considered a Democratic measure, and Democrats held a majority in the House (and a tie in the Senate), some Democrats opposed the measure, as did the overwhelming majority of Republican lawmakers. The assembly reconsidered aid for parochial schools in 1935 and 1937.[5]

In the 1937 version, also controversial, the Senate passed a bill to establish a "parent-child educational fund" to give assistance to children in "schools not supported by state funds." This bill was, essentially, a proposal for school vouchers: parents were to be reimbursed 10 cents per day per child in elementary grades and 15 cents per day for high school, or up to $180 and $270 respectively. The 1937 defeat came down to political machinations—Democrats controlled large majorities in the House and Senate, and while the bill passed in the Senate, a hostile House committee doomed the "Waldvogel Bill." Behind the Statehouse maneuvers, lawmakers remained close to the pulse of their constituents, and in 1930s Ohio, a majority "wanted no tampering with the separation of church and state." The Ohio legislature did not again consider voucher proposals until the 1970s. Republican lawmakers overwhelmingly opposed the 1937 Waldvogel Bill, which they perceived as a Catholic school aid measure, whereas Democrats were divided over the measure. In Ohio, the legislature considered school vouchers long before Milton Friedman and Virgil Bloom popularized them, albeit as part of an emergency measure to head off school closings during an economic downturn.[6]

Moreover, in Ohio, all was not lost regarding state aid to religious schools. The catalyst was the federal government's 1965 Elementary and Secondary Education Act (ESEA), which ushered in a period of cooperation between public and parochial schools in the use of public funds—Ohio delegated local public school districts to implement programs for disadvantaged parochial school students who qualified for ESEA programs. Also in 1965, Ohio passed public bus ride legislation for students in parochial and private schools—requiring school districts that provided public school transportation to also offer it to students in the non-public schools. The Catholic Conference of Ohio was instrumental in generating support for the bus bill from a majority of lawmakers; the Ohio chapter of Virgil Blum's Citizens for Educational Freedom also worked for its passage. Although challenged in the courts, the Ohio Supreme Court upheld the new policy.[7]

By the 1967–1968 school year, through the auspices of the Catholic Conference, Ohio was appropriating $15 million yearly to the non-public schools, approximately $25 per student, to support auxiliary services in speech and hearing, guidance and counseling, and special education programs. The legislature added supplemental payments for lay instructors who taught secular subjects in parochial schools to begin in the 1969–1970 school year, but the U.S. Supreme Court declared a similar law unconstitutional. For the 1971–1972 school year the state legislature enacted a parental reimbursement program of $90 per student in parochial and private schools, but with the *Wolman v. Essex* decision a federal court invalidated it. Governor John Gilligan, a Democrat, also favored state income tax credits for private school tuition, and legislation was enacted in 1972. However, this program, also, was "never implemented," since the same District Court, in *Wolman v. Kosydar,* invalidated the law. In both cases, the Court ruled that the programs violated the establishment clause of the First Amendment, following the 1971 Supreme Court's *Lemon v. Kurtzman* decision. Nonetheless, state support increased in the 1970s. The state added funding per capita for private and parochial school students for administrative costs in 1980.[8]

By the 1990s, state aid ballooned, making Ohio a state with a comparatively high level of taxpayer support for non-public schools. For example, Ohio paid for "approved secular textbooks; speech and hearing diagnostic services; physician, nursing, dental, and optometric services; diagnostic psychological services; guidance and counseling services; remedial services; standardized tests and scoring services; programs for handicapped and gifted children; clerical personnel for the administration of programs; and secular, neutral, and non-ideological computer software and mathematics or science equipment and materials generally used in the public schools." Moreover, the state annually reimbursed most non-public schools for "administrative and clerical costs incurred in preparing, maintaining and filing reports, forms, and records," up to $250 per student by 1996. Table 5.1 shows growth in public spending on Ohio's non-public schools in the 1990s, when the governor and the legislature sharply increased state support.[9]

Table 5.1 Ohio Public Spending on Private Schools, 1994–1998

Year	Auxiliary Services	Growth (percent)	Administrative Cost Reimbursement	Growth (percent)
1994	$77,212,052		$16,776,500	
1995	$80,925,444	4.8	$17,421,610	3.8
1996	$85,500,183	5.6	$30,518,763	75.2
1997	$91,386,921	6.9	$39,837,262	30.5
1998	$95,956,267	5.0	$41,829,125	5.0

Source: "Ohio Leads the Nation in Support of Non-Public Schools," factsheet, box 94, Cleveland Scholarship and Tutoring Program Folder, George V. Voinovich Papers.

CLEVELAND'S URBAN SCHOOL CRISIS

According to the author of a labor-relations report conducted under the auspices of Harvard and MIT in 2002, it appeared that public education in Cleveland was "engaged in the early stages of a renaissance." Some evidence supported this view. In 1996 and again in 2001, Clevelanders voted in new property taxes to support the schools, the former an operating levy, the latter a bond issue for capital improvements, augmented by state matching funds. These were the first to pass since 1983; Cleveland voters last approved tax levies for the schools in 1962 and 1967. The district announced extensive capital improvements resulting from the 2001 vote. Considered the largest building program in the history of Cleveland public schools, it had the ambitious goal of rebuilding or refurbishing 112 schools over the next 10 years. Also with great fanfare, in 1998 the schools hired a promising new superintendent, Barbara Byrd-Bennett. She built her reputation in the New York public schools as an administrator who raised academic achievement rates for students in underperforming schools. In Cleveland, she developed a well-regarded strategic plan, *Educating Cleveland's Children,* which focused on academic standards. She also moved to repair relationships with the teachers union: together with Cleveland Teachers Union President Richard DeColibus she launched an extensive reading program and professional development programs in each school. In 2002, she confidently described it as her job "to keep the business, political, philanthropic, and faith communities, the teachers, administrators, and parents, all marching to the same tune, that of raising the educational achievement of our most cherished citizens." For a few years, it seemed that the school superintendent could accomplish such a task.[10]

The renaissance, however, proved to be short-lived. In 2004, the school board cut $100 million from the district's budget and eliminated 1,400 jobs. And in 2005, Byrd-Bennett was gone—she decided not to renew her contract after Clevelanders voted down new operating levies.[11]

Indeed, the renaissance fit a familiar pattern for the Cleveland Public Schools in the post–World War II era, that of declines in student enrollments, poor student attendance, low standardized test scores and graduation rates, shrinking local funding, inadequate state support, and a curriculum that did not, or could not, lead to full employment of graduates. This overall narrative of decline was punctuated with occasional periods of hopefulness, such as with the arrival of Byrd-Bennett, as district officials rolled out this or that new program. "Crisis" was the watchword when explaining conditions in the Cleveland Public Schools. According to a 1998 exposé that appeared in *Education Week* titled "Cleveland: A Study in Crisis," author Beth Reinhard suggested that "poverty, racism, and poor school management go way back in the city once maligned as the 'mistake on the lake'"—way back to "the late 1960s." Others suggest that the crisis began even earlier, particularly for black students. Here is historian David Tyack on conditions in Cleveland in 1923: "25 percent of the children assigned to 'special classes' for defective children…were black, even though in theory mental retardation was equally common among whites. Likewise, 50 percent of all work permits issued to Negro girls…were marked 're-tarded,' signifying that the students had not 'passed the seventh grade by reason of mental retardation.' By contrast, only 4 percent of native-born white children received 'retarded' work permits."[12]

From 1950 to 2000, Cleveland's population plunged from 914,808 to 478,403. This exodus reduced demand for Cleveland's residential property, so that property values fell relative to growing suburbs. Table 5.2 and Figure 5.1 illustrate changing population demographics in Cleveland. While the city lost population in the post–World War II era, the decline was not evenly distributed by race. White out-migration to the suburbs and elsewhere was commonplace, along with considerable in-migration of blacks from the South. By 2000, a majority of Cleveland residents were African Americans.

In 1960, the Cleveland Public Schools' per-pupil spending ranked lowest in Cuyahoga County. In spite of the population decline, the high birthrates of the baby boom and in-migration from the South increased the student enrollment in the public schools, at least initially, from 99,686 students in 1950 to a peak of 152,000 in 1966. Even though an aggressive school building program to relieve overcrowding commenced in 1962, after passage of a bond program and levy, problems followed in its wake. Not only did the building program exacerbate racial segregation in the schools, which were built in locations that contained black students within predominantly black neighborhoods, but just as the building program hit its stride, the population of the Cleveland Public Schools declined, to 86,565 students by 1980, and down to 73,000 students by 1995. In 30 years, then, from 1966 to 1995, student enrollments declined by more than half. Table 5.3 and

Table 5.2 Cleveland Population Changes, 1970–2000

Year	White	African-American	Hispanic	Others	Total
1970	458,084	287,841	N/A	4,978	750,903
1980	299,970	249,504	17,772	6,576	573,822
1990	242,723	233,860	22,330	6,703	505,616
2000	185,641	241,512	34,728	16,522	478,403

Source: U.S. Census.

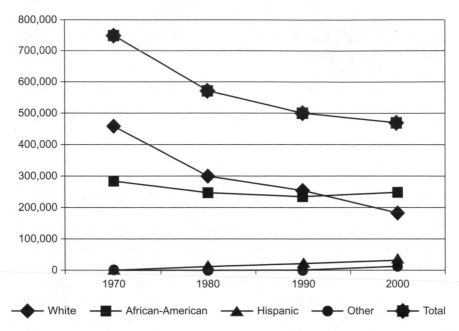

Figure 5.1 Cleveland Population Changes, 1970–2000. (*Source:* U.S. Census.)

Table 5.3 Cleveland Public School Enrollment, 1970–2000

Year	White	African-American	Hispanic	Others	Total
1970	61,340	86,371	N/A	2996	150,707
1980	22,543	54,445	3,001	778	80,767
1990	14,770	49,669	4,439	1141	70,019
2000	14,106	52,626	6,172	1322	74,226

Source: William D. Henderson, "Demography and Segregation in Cleveland Public Schools: Toward a Comprehensive Theory of Educational Failure and Success," *N.Y.U. Review of Law & Social Change* 26, no. 4 (February 2002).

Figure 5.2 highlight changing enrollment patterns in the Cleveland public schools.[13]

Decisions on which schools to close and which programs to eliminate embroiled the school board and a divided population in often-bitter struggles. By 1992, for example, over a 20 year period the numbers of school buildings had only been reduced by 9 percent, whereas student enrollment fell by 49 percent. Many of the buildings had been targets for vandalisms and break-ins since at least the 1950s. According to a 1994 report, the sheer numbers of old and under-utilized buildings resulted in "12,000 new work

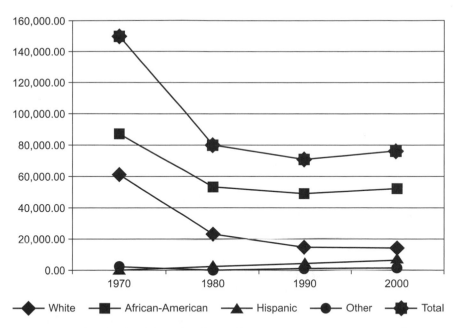

Figure 5.2 Cleveland Public School Enrollment, 1970–2000. (*Source:* William D. Henderson, "Demography and Segregation in Cleveland Public Schools: Toward a Comprehensive Theory of Educational Failure and Success," *N.Y.U. Review of Law and Social Change* [February 2002].)

orders com[ing] into the system each year though there is little chance of acting on most of them." Heightened conflicts over reducing the size of the physical plant and over school desegregation resulted in failed school levies as many whites withdrew their support from Cleveland's public schools. Moreover, funding from the state government did not keep pace with local district needs. The percentage of the state's budget devoted to K–12 education fell from 45.1 percent in 1975 to 38.6 percent in 2003.[14]

In the post–World War II era, Cleveland experienced significant population loss coupled with structural changes to the city's economy beginning in the early 1970s that reduced manufacturing jobs and increased low-wage and high-wage employment in the service sector. At the same time, Cleveland's population became increasingly impoverished. The impact of these changes on the schools was enormous. The high poverty rate in the district increased the need for instructional programs and ancillary services of the highest quality, but at the same time a skeptical public expected more progress reducing the size of the physical plant and payroll to reflect the decline in student enrollment. This contradiction contributed to the high turnover in school superintendents in the city, adding to the perception of schools in crisis. Academic achievement and other measures of student success in the Cleveland Public Schools languished in the postwar years. In the 1991–1992 school year, for example, the district's graduation rate stood at 36 percent. In the mid-1990s, Ohio established statewide standards measured by proficiency tests for students in five academic subjects at five grade levels, together with attendance and graduation rates. For the 1998–1999 school year, Cleveland was "the only school system in the state to fail all twenty-seven standards." Lower rates of achievement compared to other school systems, lack of progress in closing underutilized school buildings, rejection of most school levies beginning in the early 1960s, and shifting state priorities away from K–12 education brought the district to the brink of bankruptcy and to state receivership in the early 1980s, and contributed to a state takeover of the insolvent district again in 1995.[15]

SCHOOL DESEGREGATION AND RESEGREGATION

In school politics, the largest postwar clash by far was the civil rights push and backlash pertaining to educational access for Cleveland's growing black population. Embedded within Cleveland's population loss was significant change in the racial composition of public school students. In 1950, public school enrollment was 74 percent white and 26 percent black, whereas by 2000 the ratio had essentially reversed, with a 19 percent white and 71 percent black enrollment. The Great Migration brought southern blacks to Cleveland beginning at the turn of the 20th century and, after interruption during the Great Depression, migration crested with the economic boom of World War II and lasted into the 1960s. Meanwhile, whites migrated out of Cleveland by the tens of thousands, often settling in the growing suburbs. This out-migration reduced the percentage of middle-class residents living in Cleveland, but many working-class whites also moved out of the city. Black Clevelanders also departed, albeit at lower rates than whites, a reflection of less income and wealth per capita and due to discriminatory housing practices in many suburbs. The postwar era also saw high numbers of Appalachian migrants to Cleveland. By the last decades of the 20th century, the racial and ethnic composition of the schools was diversified by modest levels of immigration from Latin America and Asia. The 2000 enrollment in the public schools included 8 percent Latino and 1 percent Asian students.[16]

The struggle for civil rights in Cleveland's schools began long before 1973, when NAACP lawyers brought suit in Federal District Court. And it continued after the resulting 1976 *Reed v. Rhodes* decision, which held the Cleveland Board of Education and the State Department of Education liable for unconstitutional racial segregation in the Cleveland Public Schools. In the 1920s, for example, black parents complained "when their children had to travel to attend the nearly all-black high school even when other schools were more convenient." And the intransigence of the school board to the 1976 decision, as well as changing demographics in the schools, meant that litigation dragged through the 1990s. While black students and their parents faced several affronts in predominantly black East Side schools in the postwar era—shoddy physical plants, a narrow range of course offerings, poorly prepared teachers with low expectations, inadequate social services, prohibitions on transferring to predominantly white schools, and few black professionals in positions of authority—the one that rankled most was over-crowding.[17]

In 1957, the district instituted double sessions in East Side schools, essentially reducing the student's school day by half. Protests at elementary schools using the double shift became commonplace, and in 1961 parents began picketing school board headquarters, demanding that the district transport their children to schools with extra space—predominantly white schools, mostly on the West Side. By 1963, the protests coalesced around the United Freedom Movement (UFM), a citywide coalition of parents, religious congregations, the NAACP Cleveland Branch, and the Congress of Racial Equality (CORE). 1964 proved the high water mark of direct action to improve educational conditions in black Cleveland. Before the year was out, Cleveland witnessed UFM demonstrations and violent counter-demonstrations at elementary schools in two white East Side enclaves (Murray Hill and Collinwood), a UFM sit-in at district headquarters, a CORE-sponsored rally where Malcolm X delivered "The Ballot or the Bullet" speech, the death of a white minister and CORE activist at a school construction site, and a UFM-sponsored school boycott that involved nearly all black students, who attended some 80 freedom schools instead. In spite of a new school superintendent, Paul Briggs, who came in at the end of the year and took tentative steps to desegregate the teaching staff and to promote blacks to administrative positions, segregated conditions for most students prevailed and, due to the new school superintendent's massive school construction program in black neighborhoods, became even more entrenched. In the few schools that experienced a modicum of racial mixing, such as Collinwood High School, racial violence flared through the 1960s and early 1970s. White students and their parents felt threatened by increasing numbers of black students at erstwhile single-race schools, and lashed out at black students and their defenders. Black students and their parents also felt threatened, but nonviolent protest was no longer the only respectable response to racism—Black Power competed with nonviolence in the civil rights struggle; black students fought back.[18]

After the 1976 ruling, the Board of Education continued to contest and obstruct most federal orders to desegregate. The Board appealed *Reed v. Rhodes* to the Supreme Court (which declined to hear it). Judge Frank

Battisti, the federal district court judge responsible for the ruling, found the Board and certain administrators in civil contempt of court in 1980 and ordered the appointment of a special administrator of desegregation. The next year the Court went as far as to order the school board president and the treasurer to jail for refusing to disburse pay raises for the desegregation staff, which the court-appointed administrator of desegregation had approved against the wishes of the school board (Judge Battisti released the district officials the same day, after paychecks were delivered). Not until 1984 did the school board majority favor desegregation. The most controversial directive in *Reed v. Rhodes* was busing to achieve racial desegregation. The first buses rolled between Cleveland's East and West Sides in 1979; by 1982 busing was fully phased in. Although busing, in the black community, was greeted supportively and with little opposition at least initially, by the early 1990s disillusionment was palpable. And although there were some modest benefits for black students in the 1980s, desegregation had failed to remove most of the underlying obstacles to academic success. In other words, unemployment, poverty, substandard housing, and lack of adequate healthcare—non-school factors that interfered with academic success—continued to stalk Cleveland schoolchildren and their families.[19]

Desegregation as a policy was becoming increasingly unpopular in minority communities by the early 1990s, but the social inequalities that sparked calls for desegregation to begin with remained in place. A new school superintendent, Sammie Campbell Parrish, amplified the viewpoint of many Clevelanders, that desegregation had outlived its usefulness, but what she could not address were the underlying factors—economic, social, political—that made it unlikely that Cleveland's public schools could impart academic achievement at the same levels that students enjoyed in many nearby suburban districts. Parrish came to Cleveland in 1992 with the expectation that her proposed reform plan, developed with input from the wider Cleveland community as part of the mayor's series of education summits, would bring to Cleveland "the schools of the 21st century." Her *Vision 21* plan aligned local reform with the national trend of parental choice in place of desegregation. *Vision 21* signaled the return to segregated neighborhood schools coupled with the expansion of school choice programs. The plan called for the number of magnet schools in the district to double, and in the remaining elementary schools, renamed "community model schools," parents could choose from a number of schools within the region where they lived. Parrish testified in court on the Cleveland desegregation case that she had "grave concern about potential for increased absenteeism and drop in academic achievement among bused students." *Vision 21* commenced in the fall of 1993. "Too long the focus has been on [the wrong] things," School board member Reverend James Lumsden asserted. "The plan would bring high-quality education to Cleveland. The transportation issues which have received so much focus in the past are secondary to the quality of educational opportunities we will provide to all of our students."[20]

Ultimately, *Vision 21* stimulated neither academic improvement, nor urban revitalization, and Superintendent Parrish resigned from the Cleveland schools in early 1995. While the plan produced a number of magnet schools performing better than regular schools in terms of achievement and attainment, those rates continued to languish in the district as a whole. Moreover, the relatively higher performance of magnets was most likely a result of the socioeconomic creaming effect of such schools typical in most urban districts, with potentially adverse effects on the regular public schools. Nonetheless, the expansion of magnet schools in the district increased the amount of school choices for parents of the most academically able students and heightened expectations of residents that, in counterpoint to desegregation policies, school choice would be the royal road to improved public schools.[21]

In the mid-1990s, changes were afoot regarding school desegregation in the city, even though there were modest gains for students during the desegregation years of the 1980s. For example, from 1983 to 1990, reading and math scores in the California Achievement Test steadily increased for both races. Though whites consistently outscored blacks, the rise in black scores narrowed the gap by seven and five units in reading and math respectively. From 1981 to 1990, attendance rates increased from 84 to 88 percent for blacks and from 82 to 84 percent for whites. The retention rate for blacks remained about 2 percent lower than that for whites. The dropout rate for blacks, expressed as a percentage of students in grades 7 through 12, declined from 8.9 percent in 1982 to 6.7 percent in 1986, but increased to 8.8 percent in 1990. The corresponding percentages for whites were 13.1, 10.1, and 12.6. As to attitudes on race relations, in a 1983 survey, 71 percent of black and 63 percent white parents agreed or strongly agreed with the statement that "desegregation made education better for students." The corresponding percentages among students were 76 for blacks and 69 for whites.[22]

Countervailing forces worked against such academic and attainment gains, however. During the 1980s, impoverishment of Cleveland residents continued. Suburbanization was part of the reason for this impoverishment; Clevelanders with children who had options to move to the suburbs often did, and the families that remained were often poorer than the ones that moved. The percentage of white students in the district stood at 41 percent in 1978 but declined to 18 percent in 1992. As the Cleveland public schools became racially isolated, the city experienced unprecedented levels of social and economic decline. Deindustrialization underlay the pattern of low income for blacks in Cleveland. Starting in the late 1960s, most new jobs in the region required high skills and were located either in the prestigious downtown area or the surrounding suburbs, inaccessible to the majority of urban blacks in terms of both qualifications and geography. According to the Cleveland public schools, from 1975 to 1990, the proportion of black students qualifying for free or reduced-price lunch increased from 60 to 94 percent. The adverse effects of this economic hardship were coupled with the declining levels of trust, loyalty, and cooperation in black neighborhoods in the 1980s.[23]

The persistent interaction of racial isolation, joblessness, and neighborhood social disorganization played a major role in the erosion of the double-parent family structure among urban blacks. In Cleveland, the problem became systemic prior to desegregation in early 1970s, reaching chronically high levels in the 1980s. From 1975 to 1990, the proportion of black students in single-parent families rose from 56 to 79 percent, reaching well above 80 percent in the 1990s. Since single-parents in the urban context tended to have low levels of education and occupational status, many children in Cleveland lacked not only economic and social capital, but also parental support.[24] Given these obstacles, by the early 1990s desegregation within the Cleveland school district boundaries became largely irrelevant as a reform that could deliver increased opportunities to most Cleveland public school students. This was not lost on Cleveland residents: "For all it was worth, having my daughter bused no longer makes sense to me," a black parent pointed out in the late 1980s. "I mean we are taking kids out of Black schools and sending them again to majority-Black schools." The validity of such sentiments and the increasing burden of busing on black students would bolster arguments against school desegregation in the 1990s. Overburdening of black students in transportation programs in Cleveland and elsewhere helped trigger resistance to busing among black parents. Moreover, the deleterious effects of growing poverty rates on academic achievement caused residents to question the utility of desegregation, since it did nothing to counteract the non-school factors undermining academic performance. In 1990, for example, school board President Stanley E. Tolliver asserted that "Busing makes no difference since the kids have to be saved before they get to school."[25]

The realities of demographic changes in the school district and city— together with sentiment among parents, business executives, elected officials, and school leaders—motivated the plaintiffs in the *Reed v. Rhodes* decision to enter into a consent decree with the district in 1994, in which *Vision 21* was the centerpiece. The following year, authority in the district unraveled. In spite of the fact that the popular mayor, Michael R. White, and the charismatic superintendent, Sammie Parrish, both had similar viewpoints on Cleveland school desegregation (they wanted to end it), they had a political falling-out following the defeat of two operating levies. "The public has the perception that school officials were not driving the reform of the [school] system," stated Mayor White. "It's time to break glass." Superintendent Parrish, for her part, charged the mayor and school board with political interference. She quit three months later. Moreover, in late 1994 the long-time federal judge that directed school desegregation in Cleveland, Frank Battisti, contracted Rocky Mountain spotted fever and died. His replacement, Judge Robert Krupansky, took a dim view of the political infighting and of the projected $29.5 million shortfall in district's annual budget. On March 3, 1995, he ordered the State Superintendent of Public Instruction to assume administrative and operational control of the Cleveland Public Schools. He also directed the district to close at least fourteen school buildings. After two years of state control, the legislature voted to place Cleveland's public schools under mayoral control. White appointed a new school board and superintendent in 1998.[26]

School desegregation for the Cleveland Public Schools ended as the century drew to a close. In May 1996, Judge Krupansky ended judicial supervision of the assignment of students to schools and ended the requirement of an enrollment at each school reflective of system-wide racial composition within 15 percentage points (this essentially ended busing). In 1998, Judge George W. White concluded that the district had achieved "unitary status" and released the district and the state from nearly all other obligations, with the exception of Judge Krupansky's March 3, 1995, order and Judge Battisti's 1994 Consent Decree, some of which remained in effect until 2000, including guarantees of state funding. For those who believed desegregation policies themselves were what hampered district efforts to educate its students successfully, the Courts removed such obstacles in 1996 and 1998.[27]

Little wonder, then, that with the transfer of school authority from the state department of public instruction to a black mayor, Michael White, the end of school desegregation policies for the Cleveland Public Schools, the arrival of Barbara Byrd-Bennett as CEO, and the passage of the two school levies, things appeared to be looking up for Cleveland's public schools at the end of the century—after three decades of turbulence, Clevelanders believed the public schools might finally have stability and even improved student achievement. Moreover, an important school funding case made its way through the Ohio courts in the 1990s, brought forward by rural school districts that had difficulties meeting educational obligations through primary reliance on local property taxes. In Ohio the wealthiest of the 611 school districts spent more than $12,000 per student, compared to less than $4,000 in the poorest. In 1997, the Ohio Supreme Court ruled in the *DeRolph* case that Ohio's system of financing public education was unconstitutional, and this raised hopes in Cleveland and other low-wealth school districts that the state would direct more money to the schools. Indeed, the state matching funds for new school construction was one of the outcomes of the *DeRolph* cases.[28]

But in the midst of the 1994–1998 meltdown of leadership and change in control of the Cleveland public schools, the state legislature passed school reform laws that had other repercussions for Cleveland. The most controversial was the Cleveland Scholarship and Tutoring Program, which the governor signed into law in June 1995 and which began operations in the fall of 1996.

STATEHOUSE AND CITY HALL POLITICS

A lot changed in statehouse politics since the Depression, making school vouchers possible. One of the most notable developments was that the Republican Party lost its anti-Catholic sensibility. Governor Frank Lausche led the way. This former Cleveland mayor, with his base of Slovenian and other white ethnic voters, was elected Ohio's first Catholic governor in 1944. A Democrat, Lausche had an independent streak as governor in the 1940s and 1950s. To the Republican Party Lausche represented hard evidence that Catholic politicians were not only electable to statewide office, they could also take centrist positions; Catholic votes were to be courted rather than used as a foil to rally Protestant supporters. A generation later, another Catholic, Slovenian, and former Cleveland mayor—George V. Voinovich— would be elected Ohio governor. Regardless of what political party was in power in the House or Senate, beginning in the 1960s lawmakers gradually became more supportive of legislation that benefitted parochial schools. And as Ohio's Republican lawmakers became more supportive of Catholic causes, Democratic lawmakers became increasingly allied with organized labor, especially the teachers unions, whose leadership viewed vouchers as an existential threat. Hence, Republicans were drawn to school vouchers in the 1970s and 1980s as most Democrats, the traditional supporters of school vouchers in the Buckeye State, moved away from them.[29]

Following legislation in the mid-1960s that guaranteed bus service to private school students in districts that provided it to public school students, the legislature began considering other bills to aid students in non-public schools. Some of these pertained to school vouchers and tuition tax credits. For example, in 1971–1972 the assembly considered tax deductions for tuitions and fees paid to schools other than colleges and universities; other bills of this nature were introduced into the legislature periodically. In the 1973–1974 legislative session, a bill to develop a demonstration voucher program was considered; a similar bill was introduced in the 1975–1976 session. These voucher bills, with priority to children from low-income families, suggested that the participating school district contract with the federal government for funding, largely along the lines of what the federal OEO sought. In the 1991–1992 session, Representative Michael Fox and others introduced bills to create a five-year voucher pilot project for students in Ohio's eight largest school districts. While none of these bills became law, private school supporters nevertheless succeeded in persuading the state to increase its aid to non-public schools. Efforts to pass school voucher and tuition tax credit legislation, together with state aid for auxiliary services and administrative cost reimbursements, demonstrated how much the legislature had changed since the Depression: from a system in which one of the two major political parties—the Republican Party—could be counted on to vote against assistance to private and parochial schools, to one in which politicians on both sides of the aisle voted for aid to non-public schools by the 1980s and 1990s.[30]

Black political power had also increased somewhat at the state level, and the Great Migration to Cleveland was essential for this change. In 1947, Clevelander Harry E. Davis became the first black elected to the state senate "in over fifty years," and Clevelander Hazel Mountain Walker "became the first black member of the Ohio Board of Education in 1961." The first black Democrat elected to the Ohio legislature was Carl B. Stokes, in 1962. Elected in an at-large ward, Stokes used his proven ability to appeal to voters on both sides of the color line as a springboard for his campaigns for mayor of Cleveland (he won election in 1967). As a state representative, Stokes was involved in two redistricting controversies: he supported a Republican redistricting plan for the state because the likely result would be three black state representatives from Cleveland's East Side, but he opposed congressional redistricting in 1964 because it would siphon votes from the predominantly black Twenty-First Congressional District. Stokes lost the battle on congressional redistricting but won the war. He sponsored a lawsuit in federal court that challenged the redistricting, and after the Supreme Court ruled in his favor, his older brother, Louis Stokes, was elected to U.S. Congress in 1968.[31]

While Cleveland's first black mayor, Carl Stokes, cut his teeth participating in the civil rights efforts to desegregate the public schools, Cleveland's second black mayor, Michael White, negotiated an end to school desegregation. After Stokes decided not to seek a third term in 1971 (he cited the declining tax base as a reason for leaving office), his black caucus of

Cleveland elected officials returned to the fold of the regular Democratic Party. This ushered in a nearly two-decade period of city politics in which whites were the majority on city council but an African American, George Forbes, was council president and considered Cleveland's most powerful black politician. Black voter registration and participation languished during these years, and black Cleveland was not able to translate the increasing proportion of African Americans in the population to the election of blacks to the mayor's office. Forbes even supported a Republican, George Voinovich, in his mayoral reelection campaign of 1985, and for his part, Voinovich worked to cultivate electoral support in black Cleveland. Voinovich was first elected to Ohio office from Collinwood in 1966, when he opposed the state's fair housing law. Collinwood was undergoing considerable racial turbulence in its neighborhoods and its schools; Voinovich won election even though registered Democrats outnumbered Republicans two to one. Voinovich was first elected mayor in 1979, when he defeated Dennis Kucinich, whose tumultuous mayoralty generated backlash among Cleveland's corporate elites. Voinovich was the beneficiary, but he could not have been elected without the support of black Clevelanders. Hence, as mayor Voinovich did little to offend George Forbes or other black leaders. Since there was little opposition to school desegregation in the black community in the early 1980s, for example, Voinovich did not actively oppose it either. Instead, he appointed blacks to his administration and in the judiciary, and he was supportive of minority contracting.[32]

Michael White was elected to his first term as mayor in 1989. Originally a protégé of Forbes, White had experienced electoral success in his race for the state senate, and when Forbes and White were the only candidates left standing for the Democratic primary run-off election, White was more successful than Forbes in precincts on the West Side (they split the East Side), and this put White over the top. As mayor, White continued trends pioneered by Voinovich, including downtown development with tax abatements that left fewer local public resources for Cleveland's schools and residential neighborhoods. If anything, White was more vocal in his opposition to busing than Voinovich. Both politicians also favored school vouchers, but White, who made the improvement of the Cleveland school system a centerpiece of his mayoral campaigns, only began to support vouchers publicly in 1994, after the efforts by voucher proponents in state government increased the likelihood that Ohio would pass voucher legislation in some form.[33]

CLEVELAND VOUCHER SUPPORTERS

Although the efforts and prestige of Governor George Voinovich was vital for the passage of school vouchers in 1995, he was not a vocal proponent of them while he was mayor of Cleveland in the 1980s. Nor did he place school reform at the top of his agenda. Indeed, Voinovich took the position that mayors usually take—that the elected school board runs the public schools, and "the mayor has no authority whatsoever over school and educational decisions." At a deeper level, however, observers sensed Mayor Voinovich's support for parochial schools at the expense of public schools. For example, as mayor he transferred his children to Catholic schools and favored tax abatements for major construction projects that reduced the tax base of the schools. On his public pronouncements on desegregation, Voinovich urged that the court order be obeyed peaceably, and his criticisms did not go beyond misgivings regarding "four hour bus rides." Moreover, Voinovich avoided the most prominent anti-busing group, the local chapter of the National Association for Neighborhood Schools, which frequently asked for his support. Although Voinovich was more vocal in

Ohio governor George Voinovich in 1994. As Cleveland mayor he avoided education reform, but as governor he and his allies Anthony Pilla and Akron entrepreneur David Brennan secured Ohio's first voucher program in 1995. (AP Photo/Ted Mathias.)

his opposition to court-ordered busing after his 1985 reelection, there were still limits to what he chose to do. He declined, for example, to sign anti-busing petitions.[34]

Privately, however, Voinovich expressed disgust with the Cleveland Public Schools. "This town is absolutely fed up with what is going on," Voinovich told the State Superintendent of Public Instruction in 1989. "I sincerely wish that you folks had taken over the system a long time ago. As far as I am concerned, it has gone from bad to worse." His solution was parental choice. "The evidence of educational failure is everywhere," he remarked to black students at Central Middle School in 1988. "Public education," he continued, "should not be a monopoly, but rather, have a policy of open enrollment—a choice between neighborhood schools, mag-net schools, or a school of choice within a given district." As to private education, Voinovich favored state aid to parochial schools. He was proud of his record of support as a state representative in the 1970s. "Even then," he suggested to a gathering of the Knights of Columbus, "state legislators looked upon Catholic education as a yardstick by which to measure other schools."[35]

In contrast to Voinovich during his mayoral years, Michael White could be very much characterized as an education mayor. Not only did he make conditions in the public schools a campaign issue in 1989, he also convened a series of annual education summits that were meant to turn the public schools around (with the second summit, in 1992, ending court-ordered busing became one of the objectives). Moreover, White had a string of vic-tories when it came to school politics, victories that the business commu-nity applauded. He sponsored a bloc of candidates for school board in 1991, and asserted that the candidates he endorsed would clean house: "There is as much patronage in the Cleveland public schools as there are fish in Lake Erie," White said. When his supporters were elected, giving White a major-ity of supporters on the Board of Education, it paved the way for reforms he favored. Two years later, White's school board candidates defeated his two most outspoken critics. The election of the White-backed candidates also helped stifle calls from Governor Voinovich for putting Cleveland's schools under state control. White's influence brought two promising new school superintendents to Cleveland: Parrish in 1992 and Byrd-Bennett in 1998.[36]

His strong-arm tactics during 1996 contract negotiations—"the inmates will be running the asylum" unless the teachers union compromises on work rules, White remarked—applied pressure that may have averted a teacher strike in 1996, while the schools were under state control. More im-portant, during his tenure, he sought out and received an end to desegrega-tion requirements in Cleveland, particularly those connected with student school assignments. The mayor succeeded in casting himself as a leader of a measured, "controlled" movement to end court-ordered busing, in contrast to anti-busing activists in white Cleveland who wanted desegregation to end immediately. White even turned Judge Krupansky's order placing the schools under state control into victories for the mayor's office, in spite of White's perception of the judge's "hostility" toward him. For example, the federal court ordered an operating levy request on the ballot in 1996. During the successful levy campaign, supported by White, campaigners told "voters repeatedly that now children are able to go to a school in their own neighborhood." And as an alternative to state control, White advocated mayoral control, which the legislature granted him in 1997.[37]

School vouchers were not the main event in Cleveland's education politics during the mid-1990s—that distinction went to the state takeover and the desegregation consent decree that ended court-ordered busing. Moreover, the governor and the assembly had more to do with Cleveland vouchers than the mayor and the city council. Nevertheless, in 1994 Mayor White offered tepid support for school vouchers. It was not always this way. In the early 1990s, the mayor was skeptical of them—his office argued that they would siphon support from the public schools. Furthermore, White's slate of school board candidates unseated two members who were pro-voucher. And in his series of annual education summits, White kept vouchers off the agenda, since it was an issue likely to divide participating leaders from business groups, civic organizations, and public schools. But following the 1994 levy defeat—a campaign that the mayor co-chaired—White urged that the Board of Education consider other strategies to improve the public schools. "For all the African American officials that have come out against vouchers, you will never find my name because I've never said I am against it," he said. "I think we need to embrace any model that could potentially give…the poorest children, black and white, the opportunity for a better education." He added that the district should consider partnering with the Catholic schools, "since they are succeeding and we are failing." This was White's only signal that he favored school vouchers; he did not comment publically as the state legislature prepared to pass them in 1995. But state lawmakers considered the Cleveland mayor an ally in their efforts to bring a voucher pilot project to the Forest City.[38]

White was not the only elected official in Cleveland city government to support vouchers. One of the other prominent supporters was Councilwoman Fanny Lewis, a longtime leader in the Hough neighborhood on the East Side. She was arguably one of Cleveland's most highly regarded politicians, due to her staunch defense of her working-class constituency and her squeaky-clean reputation. As a city councilwoman, Lewis had no formal power in the Statehouse, but her support of vouchers was important nevertheless, because her presence helped demonstrate to the state law-makers that there were black elected officials in Cleveland who favored vouchers and—perhaps more important—that there was demand in Cleveland's black community for them. An outspoken critic of city policies since she first came to public attention in the wake of the 1966 Hough riots, Lewis was first elected to City Council in 1979. She campaigned without the support of George Forbes and the Twenty-First District Caucus, the Democratic organization that slated candidates in the county's predominantly black districts.[39]

Lewis's interest in school vouchers began in the early 1990s, when she made contact with attorney Clink Bolick and the Institute for Justice, a leading voucher advocacy law firm and a successor to Landmark Legal Foundation. Soon Lewis actively supported school vouchers, using her cordial relationships with Governor Voinovich and Bishop Pilla to help make East-Siders pro voucher. Her major argument was that vouchers could create viable alternatives for parents of modest means, the typical parents that Lewis represented. "You've got to have a better plan for your children," argued Lewis. "They can't go to the Cleveland Public Schools because they're just going to mess them up." As with Mayor White, Lewis's supportive stance toward vouchers put her out of step with more traditional viewpoints in black Cleveland, at least initially. Following a 1991 Ohio speech by George H. W. Bush that called for vouchers, for example, the *Call and Post,* an influential African American weekly in Cleveland, opined in 1991 that "unfettered school choice" would damage "the broad-based nature of the schools." The editors believed that "private and parochial schools could take only the best of those students from the public schools while leaving the rest." But once the state established vouchers for Cleveland, in 1995, the editors relaxed their opposition: "The school voucher experiment contained in the budget offers hope to many Cleveland school children—and questions for many others."[40]

Lewis traveled to Milwaukee to learn about the Milwaukee Parental Choice Program, where she met Representative Polly Williams, Bradley Foundation director Michael Joyce, and Milwaukee Public School Superintendent Howard Fuller. Following this trip, Lewis brought Polly Williams to Cleveland in 1994 to explain school vouchers and the legislative process to her Hough constituents, and to help Lewis persuade them on the advantages of school vouchers. (This was the second voucher advocacy trip to Cleveland for Williams—in 1991 she addressed residents through the auspices of the Heartland Institute, a pro-voucher think tank.) In early 1995, Lewis organized some 300 parents and school children to travel to Columbus and lobby lawmakers, delivering letters to every state representative and senator. This visit occurred the same day that the governor proposed vouchers for Cleveland as part of the state's biennial budget. Lewis also began to organize a school for her neighborhood, called Hough Academy, which was slated to begin operations should vouchers come to Cleveland. (Hough Academy never operated, however. Lewis stated that the death of one of her supporters, a longtime educator in Hough, side-tracked the school.) Finally, through the sponsorship of the Institute for Justice, Lewis was present at the U.S. Supreme Court in 2002 during oral arguments for *Zelman v. Simmons-Harris*.[41]

In the mid-1990s, Mayor White and Councilwoman Lewis were in step with prevailing sentiment in the black community favorable to vouch-ers. For example, in a national survey conducted by the Joint Center for Political and Economic Studies, 48 percent of the black population sup-ported vouchers and 44 percent opposed (compared to 43 percent support and 50 percent opposed in the general population). The mayor and the councilwoman were nevertheless latecomers in bringing their support for vouchers to the statehouse debate. Unlike them, politician Patrick Sweeney supported the state's efforts to fund non-public schools through auxiliary School Aid and Administrative Cost Reimbursements, and even though the legislature did not term such aid to the non-public schools as vouch-ers, Sweeney believed that they were, since the state funding followed the child to the private or parochial school. A Clevelander from the heavily Catholic and white West Side, Sweeney was first elected state representative in 1966. Generally, Sweeney favored legislation that benefited individual families, but he was skeptical of legislation that he considered "social en-gineering." Hence, he favored Head Start (in which families had a choice of where to send their children) but opposed court-ordered busing (in which families had no choice in the public school their child must attend). During the decades of Democratic control of the House (1973–1994), he became increasingly influential, rising to chair of the powerful Finance and Appropriations Committee. With Republicans elected to the majority in 1994, Sweeney was stripped of his chairmanship and became house mi-nority leader instead. When Sweeney ran again for minority leader, House Democrats replaced him—Sweeney's support for vouchers was the stum-bling block. He switched to the Senate in 1997 and, when his term ended, he retired from politics.[42]

Sweeney first sponsored voucher legislation in 1973—this co-sponsored bill provided $100 grants to parents in public and non-public schools as reimbursement for the "cost of providing to their children quality educa-tional opportunities." And although this bill "didn't get anywhere," accord-ing to Sweeney, it attracted the ire of the teachers unions and their allies in the AFL-CIO. This made it "dangerous for Democrats to be supportive" of school vouchers, clearing the stage for Republican voucher initiatives, which became more commonplace in the 1980s and early 1990s. Sweeney was one of the few Democratic representatives willing to work with Republican colleagues on vouchers. In 1991, he co-sponsored a bipartisan bill with Michael Fox and others to create a five year voucher pilot program. This bill proposed school vouchers for 3,000 public school students living in families below the federal poverty line "in the amount of the per pupil cost to educate a child in the district where the student is entitled to attend school"—1,000 vouchers for students whose parents apply for vouchers in Ohio's eight largest school districts, 1,000 vouchers for randomly selected students in the eight largest districts, and 1,000 vouchers for students whose parents apply for vouchers in any other district. As Finance and Appropriations Chair, Sweeney helped move a budget bill in 1994 that contained a similar voucher pilot program (it did not survive the Senate). And as House Minority Leader in 1995, Sweeney supported another budget bill that contained the Cleveland Scholarship and Tutoring Program (Voinovich signed this one into law). With Republican majorities in the House and Senate in 1995, conceivably the Cleveland Scholarship and Tutoring Program might have passed even without Sweeney's help. But it is nevertheless significant that there was Democratic support for a school voucher plan that was spearheaded by a representative from Cleveland's West Side. Ten other Democratic representatives from West Side Cleveland and other cities also were supportive of school vouchers and voted for the budget bill.[43]

There were many opponents of school vouchers in the early 1990s. Most of Cleveland's black Democratic lawmakers opposed vouchers, for example. "For the governor of Ohio to exacerbate the condition of education in the Cleveland public schools by instituting a voucher system which would guarantee the total collapse of the public schools," insisted U.S. representative Louis Stokes, "is . . . a declaration of war on our children." Stokes headed the Black Elected Democrats of Cleveland. Other opponents included the Ohio School Boards Association, The Ohio State Board of Education, the Buckeye Association of School Administrators, the Ohio Federation of Teachers, the Ohio Education Association, the Ohio AFL-CIO, and People for the American Way. Together the voucher opponents presented a formidable front, but conservative backers of vouchers in 1994 and 1995 were able to generate enough unity and support to side-step the opponents.[44]

THE CHURCH IN THE CITY

Similar to Milwaukee and other large cities outside of the Sunbelt, since the 1950s the Catholic presence declined in Cleveland while it grew in

Cleveland's suburbs. In 1950, Cleveland's population included 234,786 Catholics in 88 parishes. By 1990, the Catholic population declined to 126,602 in Cleveland, spread over 76 parishes. In contrast, in the same 40-year period the Catholic population in the rest of the county grew from 102,009 to 363,096, and the number of parishes grew from 41 to 65. Cleveland's Catholics were part of a larger trend—the out-migration of people and businesses from the city's core to the suburbs. In his "Church in the City" vision statement, unveiled in November 1993, Cleveland Bishop Anthony Pilla sought to blunt this trend, because it caused "stark separations of people: city vs. suburb, and even suburb vs. suburb." One deleterious consequence of out-migration was that "the poor and minorities have been isolated in concentrations that severely limit opportunities for a decent and secure life." In Pilla's view, all of the diocesan parishes needed to work together in response to out-migration, not just the urban parishes. As important, he believed what was needed was renewed cooperation between the Church and government. "We must recognize and respond to the needs of those, the urban poor, who have been terribly hurt by the out-migration of the non-poor and employers; and we must become engaged in changing the practices of our governments that have contributed to the disastrous situation before us." In this way, not only will the poor be aided in the Cleveland Diocese's largest cities—Lorain, Akron, and Cleveland—but redevelopment at the urban core will also facilitate a healthier economy in all of metropolitan Cleveland. To do otherwise weakens "the fiscal strength of county governments, jeopardizing the region's capacity to compete in the global economy."[45]

Catholic schools were not immune to the effects of out-migration. "Catholic schools in the cities will serve an increasingly poorer population and will face increasing difficulty with financial support," Pilla wrote. To implement his Church in the City vision, a task force recommended school partnerships among urban and suburban Catholic elementary schools and high schools. The task force also called for "resource sharing and restructuring" among the urban and suburban schools. Usually, this took the form of retreats and school-to-school projects that paired inner-city schools and their suburban counterparts. Overall, the task force recommended that the diocese "strengthen our Catholic schools and support our public school systems, recognizing that both Catholic schools and public schools have essential roles within our cities." The 1993 Church in the City vision never mentioned vouchers per se. But Pilla's initiative presented a framework in which Catholics and others in metropolitan Cleveland took notice of the urban Catholic schools and became more receptive to government programs that would assist them. School vouchers fit the Church in the City mission. Praising the Cleveland voucher program one year

Cleveland bishop Anthony Pilla in Washington, D.C., 1995, after being elected president of the National Conference of Catholic Bishops. His support for school vouchers in Cleveland propelled him to national stature. (AP Photo/Charles Tasnadi.)

into its operation, Pilla remarked that the voucher program "strengthens and supports families and...provides a setting for Cleveland to grow and flourish."[46]

It was not self-evident to all Catholic school supporters in the mid-1990s, however, that school vouchers were the best strategy to support Catholic education. Perhaps the biggest obstacle was the Ohio Catholic Conference, the lobbying arm of the state's Catholic bishops, which took a neutral position in the voucher debates. "Although the Conference is committed to the principal of equitable distribution of education tax dollars to public schools and non-public schools alike," read a 1993 Ohio Catholic Conference statement, "we would prefer to pursue this commitment in cooperation with others, including our public school counterparts." School vouchers were not the preferred means to enhance the tax support of the Catholic schools. Rather, the Ohio Catholic Conference preferred to negotiate for increases to auxiliary aid, transportation funding, and administrative cost reimbursements. Unlike school vouchers, in the 1990s these other forms of state aid were less likely to alienate teachers unions and other organizations that supported the public schools. During the run-up to school vouchers in the early 1990s, then, the Catholic Conference of Ohio was largely silent on this issue.[47]

Another hurdle was the concern that with voucher students in attendance, the state might require further regulations of the Catholic schools. One such regulatory obstacle was whether to require that students in non-public schools take state-sponsored exit exams. In 1989, the Ohio legislature voted in the Ninth Grade Proficiency Test as a condition for high school graduation, during Democratic Governor Richard Celeste's second term. In the early 1990s, Governor Voinovich believed that students in private schools receiving state funds should also take the test, as public school students did (public school students began taking the Ohio proficiency test in 1991). Groundwork for parochial school test participation was laid as Governor Voinovich and Akron businessman David Brennan began their push for school vouchers. "I agree with David [Brennan]," Voinovich informed the bishop, "that our non-public schools should participate in the proficiency examinations given by the State of Ohio." Pilla replied that the Catholic schools "have been avoiding [proficiency testing].... But, with the voucher initiative, I think we need to rethink our position." Testing for graduation began in the private schools in 1995. There was an additional, albeit minor worry that some Catholic school supporters had with vouchers—parents concerned that the presence of children in attendance through vouchers would lower educational quality. Vouchers "could hurt the quality of education I am willing to pay for without vouchers," remarked one parent. "The large influx of students resulting from such a program could cause many problems parish schools have struggled to avoid."[48]

Looking at Catholic efforts in the 1990s to bring school vouchers to the Buckeye State, Bishop Pilla was something of an exception—while other bishops stood on the sidelines, he lobbied for them publicly, perhaps inspired by his own Church in the City pastoral. Moreover, Pilla faced significant fiscal challenges in keeping afloat Catholic schools that served children in Cleveland's poorest neighborhoods. In the mid-1990s, the Cleveland diocese compiled statistics on eight schools (seven elementary, one secondary) deemed to serve the "inner city." The seven elementary schools enrolled 2,823 students, of which 84 percent were minorities and 74 percent were non-Catholic. Half the students belonged to families with incomes below the federal poverty line. Most tellingly, the average cost per pupil was $1,920 whereas the average tuition and fees per pupil were $1,230. The

Diocese subsidized the schools and also raised external funds for their support. In the late 1980s, Pilla established an Inner-City School Fund raising five million dollars from corporations and individuals to subsidize the schools during the years 1988–1990. He sought another five million dollars to continue to support the inner-city schools through 1993. The Inner-City School Fund was quasi-independent of the diocese: funds were deposited in an account affiliated with the Greater Cleveland Growth Association, a business group. Despite support from this fund, some of the inner-city Catholic schools closed in the 1990s nonetheless, from 13 schools in 1992–1993 to 8 schools five years later. To maintain the operations of its inner-city schools, the Inner-City School Fund was not enough. The bishop explored "other alternative long-range funding solutions," calling a meeting in early 1992 "of a select group of business leaders to strategize on ways and means of building a broader base of public and private support for the inner-city schools." School vouchers were an alternative that Pilla sought that would help to stabilize Catholic schools in the inner city.[49]

But the most important efforts to bring vouchers to Cleveland emanated from two Catholics who were not part of the Church hierarchy—Governor Voinovich and one of his staunchest campaign contributors, David Brennan.

THE GOVERNOR AND THE ENTREPRENEUR

As Cleveland's mayor, there was good political reason for George Voinovich to avoid school vouchers. His support would have risked alienating black Clevelanders, an important part of the electoral coalition that propelled Voinovich to the mayor's office for two terms. Such political expediency was not required for election to statewide office, however. Once in the governor's office, Voinovich used a heavier touch when it came to Cleveland's schools. For example, he proposed legislation in 1991 that would allow Cleveland voters to "put their troubled school district into state receivership." And Voinovich's interest in education reform extended beyond the Cleveland public schools. He sought comprehensive improvements statewide, and during his first campaign he picked up endorsements from some important public school constituencies, including the Ohio Federation of Teachers. Voinovich positively embraced education politics during his two terms as governor, promising to fix Ohio's public schools during his 1990 campaign and, once reelected in 1994, he pushed a vouchers pilot program through the legislature.[50]

Voinovich's school reform efforts in Ohio used President George H. W. Bush's *America 2000* initiative as a foundation, but as his plan for schools in the Buckeye State emerged, it was clear that Voinovich intended school reform to be even more comprehensive. The governor favored accountability measures that would measure and reward the academic achievement of students and the instructional efforts of teachers. He also intended to bring sounder management to Ohio's extensive system of public schools. Moreover, he sought to revamp the state's funding system in ways that would reduce the differences in what relatively wealthy and poor local school districts provided their students. "All your efforts to bring good management to state government...are important only in that they will allow us to do more for education and for others who need our help," confided his lieutenant governor, Mike DeWine. "You need to be like the preacher who shows the congregation Hell before he takes them up on the mountaintop and shows them heaven....People must understand how bad things are and how immoral it is that there is such a discrepancy between rich and poor school districts." In his first term Voinovich moved quickly to establish his agenda for the public and private schools. "I want to be the education governor," Voinovich said. "And I want Ohio to be the education state." Although he was sincere in his efforts to improve the schools for each child in Ohio, the governor was most successful in the areas of education management, accountability, and choice. Ending funding inequalities among local school districts proved considerably more intractable.[51]

Voinovich created his Governor's Education Management (GEM) Council in 1991. The governor served as its chair. Charged with recommending ways that Ohio's public schools could improve student outcomes through better management and targeted funding, GEM was comprised of business leaders and heads of some of the established education advocacy organizations. Among its members were representatives of the Ohio Business Roundtable, other business organizations, private foundations, state legislators, the Ohio Department of Education, the Ohio Board of Regents, teacher organizations, and education associations. With Voinovich's blessing, business representatives wielded the most influence. Indeed, William H. Kolberg, President of the National Alliance of Business, viewed Voinovich's initiative as "perhaps the best example in the country of a public-private partnership." At the national level the Business Roundtable "made a ten-year commitment to improve the elementary and secondary education system." Encouraged by the national organization, representatives of major Ohio companies within the Business Roundtable were keen to join the GEM Council. At this time, the Business Roundtable's positions on education remained supportive of public education—almost a belief that business leaders would support increased funding to schools, provided that, in Voinovich's words, "they see results coming from the money they are already investing in their local school systems." There was considerable sentiment in the business community that American public education needed an upgrade, so that American businesses could compete more effectively on the world stage. In the 1990s, American business groups were open to spending money to improve the schools, in part because they recognized that business groups in other developed nations were doing the same. In the words of a director of McKinsey and Company, the global management consulting firm, John Banham of the United Kingdom stated that "increased investment in the teaching of science and innovation is vital," that "we can afford it," and that "business, collectively, has a key role to play."[52]

Several new policies and laws emerged from GEM deliberations. GEM helped select a new State Superintendent of Public Instruction, Ted Sanders, in 1991. It influenced the legislature to decrease the size of the State Board of Education. GEM helped to "change the focus" of the Ohio Department of Education from one of regulation to one of providing local school districts with "service, support, and technical assistance." It recommended ways of achieving the national goals contained in President Bush's *America 2000*. By 1993, GEM-supported legislation included student accountability measures such as grade-level proficiency tests for public and private schools, although the legislature did not pass another GEM recommendation— teacher accountability through periodic evaluations. In terms of educational equity, the legislature earmarked funds for an educational technology equity program, expanded early childhood programs such as Head Start, and increased the "Jobs for Ohio Graduates" program for at-risk youth. One third of the new $463 million in state education funding went to further subsidies for Ohio's lowest wealth school districts. Interestingly, the equity provisions of the GEM recommendations represented a compromise—some of the members wanted to sponsor a statewide referendum for a tax increase, a political risk that the governor was unwilling to take.[53]

The GEM Council and its supporters divided over the question of school vouchers. According to State Superintendent Ted Sanders, "Every education organization, except those representing private schools, draws the line on this issue. If it's in they're out." For example, Ronald Marec of the Ohio Federation of Teachers warned Voinovich that vouchers were "a divisive issue that could explode any chance of building a statewide consensus." If vouchers become linked to the mainstream of Education Reform," he continued, "we will have serious trouble." Some members of the business community tended to agree. Procter and Gamble's R. L. Wehling, for example, believed that Voinovich's public support for vouchers "will serve to splinter the broad [reform] coalition." The Business Roundtable staked out a moderate position on school choice, viewing it as "one part of a broader reform effort," but the organization was also "skeptical" of education reform "that treats school choice as a panacea." Its national director, Chris Cross, warned the Ohio governor's office that "Indiana is in a mess because of bitterness over this issue." Yet, other CEOs in Ohio were "very supportive of choice." The governor, for his part, decided to insulate his GEM Council from the potential divisiveness of school choice. He nevertheless wanted school vouchers in some form, even though he was sure to lose the endorsement of the Ohio Federation of Teachers. In 1992, he established a separate group, the Governor's Commission on Educational Choice, composed, in the governor's words, "of hard-headed business leaders...familiar with both the public and non-public school systems."[54]

Considerable care went into the timing and composition of the choice commission. The governor wanted to present his commission as a group that merely considered "one more alternative on the smorgasbord of education reform." Choice would be "one of many" initiatives that his "administration has undertaken." More important, Governor Voinovich sought to avoid the perception that his choice committee was a Catholic initiative to garner state funding for parochial schools. In 1991 Voinovich solicited the help of Cincinnati Archbishop Daniel Pilarczyk in identifying possible committee members, those in the private sector with favorable dispositions towards school choice. But the archbishop's assistance was to be behind the scenes. "Quite frankly," Voinovich wrote to Pilarczyk, "I would like the majority of the committee to be made up of people who are not Catholic." Pilarczyk obliged with a list of names—"Some of these persons are Catholic, but most are not." For the same reason, Voinovich kept the head of the Cleveland Catholic Inner City School Fund, Paul Schloemer, off the Choice Commission. The governor's strategy was a simple one: first he would go forward with the reforms recommended by the GEM Council. He would also establish a separate committee to compose recommendations on school choice. Voinovich would then work with the legislative leadership to shepherd a "choice" bill through the house and senate. "Once we get the report from the Choice Commission, it can be evaluated, the [GEM] Council will probably not be as responsive as I would like them to be," wrote Voinovich. "Then it's a question of my working to implement the recommendations with legislative leadership."[55]

A year before the governor announced the creation of the Choice Commission through a 1992 executive order, he had someone in mind to appoint as chair—David Brennan, an Akron tax attorney, entrepreneur, and industrialist. Outspoken and with a penchant for white Stetson cowboy hats, Brennan made money in Ohio and Florida real estate. He also bought up manufacturing concerns—among them an Alabama steel mill—returned them to profitability, and resold them. In the mid-1980s he began to focus on the Rubber City, using tax subsidies and private capital to become a major redeveloper of the Akron downtown. Paralleling this shift in business strategy, Brennan increased his donations to political campaigns. Brennan was a member of President Bush's "$100,000 Club" of prominent contributors—the president even appeared at a fundraiser at Brennan's Akron home. Also in attendance was George Voinovich, running for governor. Brennan "gave the 1990 Voinovich campaign $89,000," according to the *Akron Beacon Journal*. And in 1994 Brennan's donations helped the GOP win a majority of seats in the Ohio House.[56]

From his days running factories with his business partners, Brennan became interested in the education of his employees. "We weren't utilizing our employees as we could have," he said. "We found at our South Carolina plant with 600 employees that half were functionally illiterate and innumerate." Brennan established a learning center at that plant and then others in the 1980s. In 1990 he spun the learning centers into a separate company, Brenlin Learning Centers, headed by his daughter, Nancy Brennan (eventually the company was renamed Brennan Learning Services). Brennan became convinced of the power of computer assisted learning to improve his workers' literacy, and he believed computers could raise achievement in elementary and secondary schools also. In the late 1980s a foundation that he controlled provided computers at a public and a private school in Akron and according to Brennan, test scores improved in both schools.[57]

Brennan's ideas for education, meanwhile, began to embrace school vouchers. His wife, Ann Brennan, returned from a workshop on school choice at the Heritage Foundation in Washington, D.C., "in 1989 or 1990" and this inspired her husband to favor privatization of the public schools. He also found Milton Friedman's positions on school vouchers to be influential. In November 1990, he announced to the *Akron Beacon Journal* editorial board that "he has decided to lead a crusade to reform education." As he immersed himself in Ohio school politics the aura of confidence that served Brennan so well in his business dealings extended to his plans for education. "Our biggest resource in the country is our innovative spirit," he said in 1997. "American innovation will solve the education problem in a matter of four years if we open it up." In comments he made in 1992, Brennan was careful that his efforts for vouchers "not be identified as a Catholic movement." He nonetheless believed that religion needed to be restored to public education. "Not our religion, but a religion," he said. "Let the parents choose to give values back to the kids."[58]

Brennan had an exclusive position in the genesis of education vouchers, one that combined public service with private entrepreneurship. On the one hand, his ties to the governor as a friend and campaign contributor positioned him to lead the governor's efforts to bring school vouchers to Ohio. On the other hand, his learning centers gave him experience as an education entrepreneur, motivating him to establish schools in Ohio that could benefit from any legislation that might emerge from the governor's Commission on Educational Choice. Brennan recognized he had competition. For example, Governor Voinovich asked him to comment on businessman Chris Whittle's Edison Project, in which he and former Yale University president Benno Schmidt proposed a network of 1,000 schools nationwide, a network that could benefit from President Bush's voucher proposal. Brennan advised the governor that Whittle's business model of $5,500 tuition per student was "very unrealistic," when it was possible to run schools with variable costs of $1,500 per elementary school and $3,000 per high school. And unlike the man with the white hat, Whittle lacked the state public service appointment that might have ensured him vouchers at an amount that matched his expectations. The Edison Project floundered, whereas Brennan's public-private school ventures mostly succeeded in Ohio.[59]

The first school that Brennan created in anticipation of vouchers was Interfaith Family Elementary School, established 1993 in Akron, at the site of the former St. Bernard parish school, and operated by his daughter's company. The school was poised to take advantage of voucher legislation emerging from the Choice Commission. Two years later Brennan created Hope for Cleveland's Children, which established private schools in Cleveland. As it turned out, Brennan was too far ahead of the legislation when he created Interfaith Family, since the legislature declined to pass a voucher system that would benefit students in the Akron area. Not so with Hope for Cleveland's Children. When the Cleveland Scholarship and Tutoring Program went into effect in the 1996–1997 school year, Brennan's two Hope Academies represented nearly all the non-sectarian enrollment for the voucher program. "We started two schools within two weeks," he said. "Starting a school is easy, it is not difficult."[60]

Brennan's positions on school vouchers evolved over the course of the early 1990s. At first, he focused on tuition tax credits, looking to model them on a Minnesota program that included credits for public school expenses also (the U.S. Supreme Court upheld the program in 1983). The Brenlin Foundation, one he co-founded, commissioned a poll in 1990 on Ohio citizen's views on tuition tax credits. The University of Akron published the results in 1991—only 23 percent of those polled had heard of tuition tax credits, while a majority cited "lack of financial support" as the biggest challenge. In spite of these findings, the report recommended that Ohio forge ahead with tuition tax credit legislation. However, State Superintendent Sanders advised Voinovich to be leery of tax credits, and Brennan was also persuaded to avoid this strategy.[61]

Voinovich gave Brennan wide latitude in composing and leading the Choice Commission. While Brennan used some of the names that Archbishop Pilarczyk suggested, he shaped the commission largely by himself, and Voinovich had "no problems with the additional members" Brennan selected. In the end, the choice commission consisted of business people from across the state, rounded out with school superintendents, teachers, a university provost, and a pastor. The commission began meeting in 1992, hoping to take advantage of federal funding for state and local school voucher programs that President Bush had unveiled in his "GI Bill for Children." By the time the Commission had its bill prepared, however, the GI Bill for Children was gone, along with its sponsor—both were casualties of the 1992 election. As it emerged in the state legislature, the commission's proposal consisted of two options for interested school districts. First, by school board decision or ballot issue, a school district could establish a voucher program in grades one through twelve. Second, a school district could establish a voucher program that would be phased in, grade level by grade level. Twenty percent of places in private schools accepting vouchers would be reserved for students from low-income families, and the voucher would be worth approximately 45 percent of the school district's per capita cost.[62]

In the Democratic-controlled House, the bill languished and died, since the chair of the House Education Committee, Ronald Gerberry, was hostile to school vouchers. Lawmakers' opposition to vouchers was not the only stumbling block. The unveiling of the commission's proposal was greeted with newspaper reports that pointed out that the "sweeping" program "could move 340,000 children from public to private schools and eliminate the jobs of 20,000 public school teachers." In addition, it was not self-evident that district boards of education would choose vouchers if given the option, or that residents of school districts would elect to create local voucher programs. Also, the Ohio Catholic Conference declined to support the proposal, due to "significant constitutional concerns." The lesson that Brennan probably drew from this experience was that a voucher program would have to begin more modestly and in a form that the Catholic Conference could support, since parochial schools made up the majority of non-public schools. And school district sponsorship, either through board of education decisions or through a popular vote, might have to be bypassed. While he favored a statewide system, political realism dictated that vouchers would begin as a pilot program.[63]

Voinovich sought to secure the neutrality of the Catholic Conference of Ohio on a possible Education Choice Commission voucher plan that the state assembly might consider. Archbishop Pilarczyk wrote to Voinovich in March 1994 and expressed disappointment that additional non-public school aid would not be forthcoming in the spring legislative cycle. Pilarczyk mentioned an October 29, 1993, telephone conversation between him and the governor in which the governor wanted the Conference to "take a neutral position" on vouchers. In return, Pilarczyk recalled, "You indicated a willingness to consider additional assistance for our students." The Catholic Conference made three requests: an increase to Administrative Cost Reimbursement per pupil from $78 to $124, Auxiliary Services "increased at the same rate as the overall increase in state funding for Education," and funding for wiring and technology "to connect to the Ohio Education Computer Network." And in December 1994 the executive director of the Catholic Conference wrote to Voinovich's executive assistant, reminding him that "our Bishops are expecting to see in a new budget bill" increases to non-public schools that the bishops requested at a June "luncheon with the governor." Voinovich's proposed budget, unveiled in January 1995, contained increased aid to non-public schools in the three areas that the Catholic Conference had identified.[64]

THE CLEVELAND SCHOLARSHIP AND TUTORING PROGRAM

Similar to electoral politics at the federal level, the 1994 election changed the equation in favor of the Republican Party in Ohio. Even though the 1992 election had been a setback for school vouchers at the federal level, it appeared, as Republicans took control of the House of Representatives in Washington, that the political climate would again favor school reforms that stressed privatization. The national Republican Party's "Contract with America" included provisions for child tax credits, for example, as part of a proposed "American Dream Restoration Act." In the Buckeye State, Republicans had occupied the governor's office since 1990, and Republican lawmakers also had the majority in the Senate. In 1994, a Republican majority came to the House, Republican control of the Senate widened, and Governor Voinovich won reelection in a landslide. Representative Gerberry lost the chairmanship of the Education Committee, and longtime Representative Vern Riffe lost his post as House Speaker. David Brennan did his part to make the 1994 election outcome possible. He convinced major contributors to the GOP from Cincinnati, Dick Farmer and Carl Lindner, to help raise $2 million. "We will select 14 or 15 races and we will take back the House," he wrote. "And that's what we did." One of the immediate benefits of a Republican majority in the House was the elevation of Representative Michael Fox as chair of the Education Committee. Fox was a recipient of campaign contributions from Brennan; he was also a long-time advocate of school vouchers.[65]

Michael Fox served in the House since 1975 and he favored school vouchers from the beginning. A former teacher, he was endorsed by the teachers union in his first campaign. School vouchers were "far off the chart as a viable political issue," Fox recalled. "It wasn't even considered an issue worth worrying about," as far as the teachers unions were concerned, something that changed over the next two decades, as more lawmakers began to consider them. In Fox's view, several preconditions made vouchers possible in 1995—the policy debates triggered by publication of the federal "A Nation at Risk" report in 1983, the better data on academic achievement generated by enactment of state exams beginning in 1989, and the more conservative political climate—beginning with the election of Ronald Reagan—that stressed "the whole idea of empowering individual parents." To Fox, the support of David Brennan was especially important, because his campaign contributions provided "protection" to voucher supporters from the efforts of the public school lobby to unseat them. Brennan was also insistent, when he and Fox drafted legislation, to use the term "scholarship" instead of "voucher." According to Fox, "when you ask, do you support vouchers, people don't know what you're talking about or they don't like it.... If you use the word scholarship, everyone supports scholarships."[66]

After the 1994 election, voucher proponents redrafted legislation and tried again. One bill for Cleveland emerged from Fox's Education Committee, and the governor included different language in the biennial budget bill he presented to the House. David Brennan continued to be influential—it was on his suggestion, for example, that vouchers for tutoring became part of the proposal. Voinovich and Brennan were already skeptical that school vouchers could emerge from Columbus as a statewide program, and Michael Fox agreed. In Fox's view, on the one hand there were Republican lawmakers from suburban districts who "did not want a fight with their local superintendents and school boards." There were also Republicans in vulnerable districts who wanted to be reelected. Voucher programs in their districts would present problems. On the other hand, the largest school district in the state—Cleveland—was in the public eye. "The school district was a mess, it was impossible to defend it," Fox said. It was not only the low test scores and high school graduation rates. Finances were questionable, negotiations over the desegregation consent decree were contentious, and, in March 1995, the federal court bypassed the school board and put the district under state control. This event most likely convinced lawmakers outside of Cleveland with ambivalent views on school vouchers that the proposed program would be helpful to students in the Cleveland Public Schools.[67]

In the House Education Committee, Michael Fox introduced a voucher bill, held hearings, and helped to line up lawmakers to support the new pilot voucher program for Cleveland. As the legislative session drew to a close in June 1995, the House did not consider vouchers in a stand-alone bill, however. Early in 1995, the governor included a voucher proposal for Cleveland in the biennial budget bill he presented to the House. In its lobbying efforts that spring, the Catholic Conference of Ohio called on pastors and school principals to encourage their constituencies to urge their lawmakers to approve increases to administrative cost reimbursements and auxiliary services. "We hope that the legislators will approve the voucher proposal," Director Timothy Luckhaupt informed Catholic school principals. "But not at the expense of the [other] increases.... [that] benefit all children, not just a small percentage of the pupils attending non-public schools." While parents at various Catholic schools in Cleveland became quite vocal in support of school vouchers, the Conference maintained a low profile.[68]

Action on the budget bill heated up in June. According to Brennan, Voinovich telephoned conservative lawmaker Bill Batchelder with his concern that school voucher language "created no difficulties with the First Amendment." The drafting team—Michael Fox, Representative William Batchelder, and David Young, a lawyer who represented the Ohio Catholic Conference—came back with language for a Cleveland pilot program designed to pass constitutional muster. As the House considered the budget, Representative C. J. Prentiss (D-Cleveland) sought to remove the voucher program by amending the bill, but her amendment was defeated, in part due to Representative Patrick Sweeney's influence with other Democrats. In the Senate, lawmakers stripped the voucher provisions from its version. With such a large bill in play, the budget moved to reconciliation, a meeting among the governor and two members of the majority party from each chamber. The voucher program survived the horse-trading of budget reconciliation, most likely because of Governor Voinovich's insistence (another school reform that the governor favored, performance reviews of teachers, did not survive the meeting). Voinovich signed the budget into law on June 30. Meanwhile, in the same month, Wisconsin's legislature voted to expand the Milwaukee Parental Choice Program to include religious schools.[69]

The contours of the Cleveland Scholarship and Tutoring Program were as follows: Set to begin with the 1996–1997 school year, children entering kindergarten through second grade who resided within the boundaries of the Cleveland school district were eligible for scholarships that would remain through the eighth grade. Scholarships amounts were either 75 percent or 90 percent of private school tuition, with the larger scholarships going to students from families with incomes below 200 percent of the federal poverty level (families above 200 percent would receive the smaller scholarship and be expected to contribute more). The difference between the scholarship and the full tuition (up to $250 or up to $625) would be made up based on arrangements between families and non-public schools. The maximum scholarship in the first year was $2,250 (90 percent of $2,500). Non-public schools within school district boundaries could apply to participate, as could all public school districts surrounding Cleveland. Scholarships were to be awarded by lottery, with priority going to low-income families. The tutoring program was similar to the scholarship program, but students had to be enrolled in the Cleveland public schools, kindergarten through third grade, and the maximum tutoring award was $450. Anyone with a valid Ohio teaching certificate could apply to become a tutor. The Cleveland Scholarship and Tutoring Program was revenue-neutral—the legislation set the initial cost of the program at $5.25 million, to be paid through the Cleveland schools' share of Ohio's Disadvantaged Pupil Impact Aid. As to passing constitutional muster, several of the provisions could be construed as evidence for upholding the Establishment Clause of the First Amendment—any non-public school could participate (religious or not), any or all of the eleven public school districts abutting Cleveland could participate, and children enrolled in the Cleveland public schools could apply for tutoring vouchers. Whether the program advanced religion was a question for the courts.[70]

In 1995, the Ohio legislature enacted other provisions that also benefit-ted non-public schools, as part of the budget bill. Administrative cost reimbursements doubled, non-public schools were included in a new program to ensure that buildings were wired for the most up-to-date educational technology, and funding for auxiliary services increased. Ohio's Catholic bishops, including Pilarczyk and Pilla, wrote to Voinovich expressing gratitude for the governor's "gentle nudging" of lawmakers. "Everything we asked you to do was included in your budget as introduced." Speaking shortly after its passage, Michael Fox was "convinced that market forces and parental empowerment" were the keys to better education for students in Cleveland. To David Brennan, the benefit of the program was simple: "This does nothing more than give parents the power to decide the quality of education for their child," he said a few months later. And to George Voinovich, writing in a letter to the *Toledo Blade* as the program went into operation in the fall of 1996, he boasted that "Our Cleveland pilot program has become a model for the country, because it is the first to include the choice of parochial, nonpublic schools." He added that the program will "encourage all Cleveland schools—public, private, and parochial—to improve the quality of education."[71]

Opponents didn't see it this way. In January 1996, teachers groups (the Cleveland Teachers Union, the Ohio Education Association) and civil liberties groups (Americans United for Separation of Church and State, the American Civil Liberties Union of Ohio, and People for the American Way) filed lawsuits challenging the Cleveland Scholarship and Tutoring Program. Plaintiffs claimed that the program violated the federal and state constitutions' separation of church and state. They also challenged the program as a violation of the Ohio constitution's one subject requirement for legislation. Thus began a six year saga that culminated in the U.S. Supreme Court. Voinovich was unfazed. "And for the life of me, I cannot understand why the education lobby is fighting our scholarship program in the Cleveland Public Schools," he remarked in his State of the State address. "To those who would stand in the way, I say: 'Give those parents a choice.'"[72]

State Superintendent of Public Instruction John Goff assured Voinovich that he and Cleveland School Superintendent Richard Boyd were "committed to making this opportunity for Cleveland's students a success." David Brennan was not convinced, however. Among his criticisms, the Ohio Department of Education delayed hiring a director and establishing an administrative budget, "made an internal decision to limit the maximum tuition to $2,000," failed to notify private schools, and limited the scholarships to "students at or below the poverty line." By law, half of the total number of participating students could attend private schools already, but Goff limited the private school students to 25 percent. Brennan's complaints ended the stonewalling, and the Department of Education hired a former Cleveland School Principal, Bert Holt, to direct the program in November 1995. She ensured that parents and schools received the necessary information and organized lotteries that began in January 1996, open to students from families with incomes up to twice the federal poverty level. Families at or below poverty level received priority, however. In the summer of 1996, state courts denied requests for restraining orders, and the legal clouds overhanging the program appeared to be lifting.[73]

In spite of the lawsuits and the foot-dragging at the Ohio Department of Education, the Scholarship and Tutoring Program was launched as scheduled in the fall of 1996. Fifty-two private schools in Cleveland participated in the first year, most of them Catholic, and dispersed throughout the city. Two additional schools opened in August 1996—Hope Central Academy and Hope Ohio City Academy. Brennan launched the schools to provide places for approximately 350 students who were not admitted to the other participating schools. Start-up costs for the Hope Academies were underwritten by $500,000 grants from the Brennan Family Foundation and the Walton Family Foundation. Interestingly, given Brennan's motivation to restore religion in public education, the Hope Academies were non-sectarian. They enrolled nearly all of the voucher students who did not attend a religious school. In the first year, 1943 students participated in the Scholarship

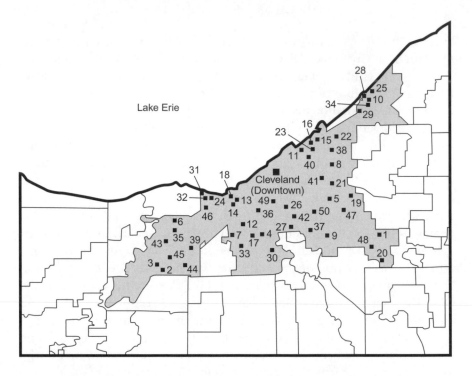

Lake Erie

Cleveland
(Downtown)

1. Archbishop James P. Lyke – St. Henry	26. Saint John Cantius
2. Ascension School	27. Saint John Nepomucene
3. Birchwood Elementary School	28. Saint John Nottingham Lutheran
4. Blessed Sacrament School	29. Saint Joseph Collinwood
5. Calvary Center Academy	30. Saint Leo The Great
6. Cleveland Community Islamic School	31. Saint Mark Catholic
7. Corpus Christi Elementary School	32. Saint Mark Lutheran
8. Covenant Kindergarten School	33. Saint Mary Byzantine
9. Holy Name Elementary School	34. Saint Mary Collinwood
10. Holy Redeemer	35. Saint Mel
11. Immaculate Conception	36. Saint Rocco
12. Luther Memorial School	37. Saint Stanislaus
13. Metro Catholic Parish (St. Boniface)	38. Saint Thomas Aquinas – Saint Philip
14. Metro Catholic Parish (St. Stephen)	39. Saint Vincent De Paul
15. Ministerial Full Day Kindergarten	40. Saint Vitus
16. Montessori School – Holy Rosary	41. Second New Hope Christian Academy
17. Our Lady of Good Counsel	42. Villa Montessori Center
18. Our Lady of Mount Carmel	43. West Park Lutheran – Holy Cross
19. Our Lady of Peace	44. West Park Lutheran – Mount Calvary
20. Ramah Junior Academy	45. West Park Lutheran – Bethany
21. Saint Adalbert	46. Westside Baptist Christian School
22. Saint Agatha – Saint Aloysius	47. Archbishop James P. Lyke – St. Catherine
23. Saint Francis	48. Archbishop James P. Lyke – St. Timothy
24. Saint Ignatius Elementary	49. Hope Ohio City Academy
25. Saint Jerome	50. Hope Central Academy

Map 5.1 Distribution of Participating Schools, Cleveland Scholarship and Tutoring Program. (*Source:* Cleveland Scholarship and Tutoring Program, Member Schools, 1996.)

Program, with 76.8 percent of the students attending religious schools. The demographic breakdown of participating students tended to mirror the city as a whole—approximately 50 percent of the participating students were African American, and working-class and middle-class families were both represented. Participating private schools were evenly distributed throughout Cleveland, as Map 5.1 shows. However, there was some evidence that black students traveled greater distances to attend.[74]

One private elementary school that did not participate in the Scholarship Program, at least not initially, was Urban Community School. Founded in 1968 as a merger of three schools, this near-West Side ecumenical school had origins and mission similar to Milwaukee's network of community schools, with the distinction that the school maintained ties to the church—the parishes maintained the school building, but the school, with philanthropic support, was responsible for paying the teachers. Although Brennan pushed for Urban Community School to participate in the voucher program, after months of debate the school declined for a variety of reasons: tuition was sliding scale, there was legal uncertainty, and accepting vouchers might send the wrong message to donors (contributions represented 75 percent of revenues). But Urban Community School was the exception. Nearly all non-public elementary schools located in Cleveland elected to participate. At the same time, none of the public school districts sharing borders with Cleveland elected to accept students living within the borders of the Cleveland Public Schools.[75]

By 1996, two voucher programs were up-and-running in the United States—the Milwaukee Parental Choice Program (poised to expand to 15,000 students who could attend religious schools) and the smaller Cleveland Scholarship and Tutoring Program (also open to students in religious schools). In the case of Ohio, parochial school advocates—especially the governor and his Cleveland bishop—provided the core support. They were aided by an influential campaign contributor who framed his agenda as one of restoring parental rights to public education. But the linchpin for passing school vouchers in the Buckeye State was linking these efforts to the rise of urban education as a policy problem. Once parochial education and parental rights could be associated with reversing the decline of urban public schools, the logic of school vouchers seemed unstoppable. But first, the Cleveland program, and the one in Milwaukee, weathered challenges from opponents in state and federal courts.

Chapter 6

FIXING SCHOOL VOUCHERS

During the periods of litigation, 1990–2002, the rhetoric surrounding school vouchers—inside and outside of the courtrooms—was highly charged. Urban education was akin to a prison for the students, according to voucher advocates. Milwaukee was bad enough, but the center of the gulag was Cleveland, Ohio. The Cleveland Public Schools had "indisputably failed." Students didn't attend the public schools; it was a "sentencing." Vouchers were the only way that students could "escape." Voucher opponents sometimes matched the supporters in their exaggerations: vouchers were part of a "long-term strategy to defund all government institutions and programs," insisted president of the Cleveland Teachers Union Richard DeColibus. Voucher opponents also magnified instances of voucher mismanagement and voucher school closings that periodically emerged. Inside the courtrooms the language was sometimes more measured. Voucher advocates emphasized that the programs were all about giving underprivileged children better educational opportunities than the public schools could provide, while opponents stressed constitutional limitations—while it was admirable for parents to choose religious education for their children, it was not constitutional to do so with public money. But sometimes judges added to the hyperbolic rhetoric. Milwaukee public school students were "doomed," according to Wisconsin Supreme Court Justice Louis Ceci. Parental choice was their salvation—"a life preserver" thrown to "children caught in the cruel riptide...of poverty, status-quo thinking, and despair."[1]

THE LEGAL CHALLENGES

Immediately after Wisconsin Governor Tommy Thompson signed the Milwaukee Parental Choice Program (MPCP) into law in the spring of 1990, State Superintendent Herbert Grover expressed opposition and even publicly encouraged teachers unions and civil rights organizations to take him to court. On May 30, a coalition of opponents did just that—the Wisconsin Education Association, the Wisconsin Federation of Teachers, the Association of Wisconsin School Administrators, the Wisconsin Congress of Parents and Teachers, and the Milwaukee Administrators and Supervisors Council petitioned the Wisconsin Supreme Court for an immediate ruling on the program's constitutionality. These groups, all with connections to public education, argued that the program circumvented collective bargaining and district authority. The NAACP-Milwaukee Branch soon joined the plaintiffs, opposing the measure on grounds that it did nothing for the 60,000 black school children in the Milwaukee Public Schools (MPS). According to branch president Felmers Chaney, reform efforts were better directed toward the public schools. "We are out of our cotton-picking minds," he stated, "to be talking about choice for a thousand students when we need to put the brakes on Milwaukee public schools and the teachers union and say, either you teach our children—all of them—or we might as well close the schools." The plaintiffs hired a law firm whose lead attorney, Robert Friebert, also headed the Democratic Party of Wisconsin.[2]

Superintendent Grover imposed regulations on the participating private schools that went beyond the law's provisions—he required that the participating schools meet stringent building codes, agree to state audits, and provide for handicapped children. His regulations sparked a lawsuit by participating schools and parents. Plaintiffs alleged that Grover's requirements had "the potential to cripple the schools financially." Their lawsuit, *Davis v. Grover,* was filed in Dane County District Court on June 25, 1990.

Representative Williams organized the plaintiffs through her office and appointed Clint Bolick to represent them. Bolick was director of the Landmark Legal Center for Civil Rights in Washington, D.C., a conservative law firm. The Bradley Foundation covered his fees. According to Larry Harwell, Williams's policy director, "We hired Clint Bolick because he would do what we wanted." He added, "I know that they [Michael Joyce and the Bradley Foundation] helped us reach our goals; they didn't dictate to us." Bolick went on to found a new libertarian law firm, the Institute for Justice, in 1991, but he worked under Landmark for the duration of the *Davis v. Grover* appeals.[3]

The day after *Davis v. Grover* was filed, the Wisconsin Supreme Court, in a 4–3 ruling, dismissed the opponents' lawsuit without comment. Rather than filing a new lawsuit, the Court allowed opponents to join the *Davis v. Grover* suit as intervenors. The intervenors sought to block the program on state constitutional grounds whereas the plaintiffs sought to limit the Department of Public Instruction's authority in implementing the program. The defendant, State Superintendent Grover, filed an amicus brief opposing the program on constitutional grounds, but the Attorney General's Office, which represented the state (and Grover), defended the program. It was an ambiguous position for the state—the Attorney General defended the constitutionality of MPCP as well as the regulations promulgated by Grover.[4]

District Judge Susan Steingass, a Madison, Wisconsin judge with a liberal reputation, considered several issues: Did State Superintendent Grover overstep his bounds by leveling additional requirements on the participating schools? Since MPCP was passed as part of a budget adjustment bill, did this violate the constitutional provision that "no private bill which may be passed by the legislature shall embrace more than one subject"? Did MPCP violate the uniformity clause, that the state establishes school districts that are "as nearly uniform as practicable"? Does the states' funding of private schools in MPCP serve a public purpose? Oral arguments were heard on Saturday, July 28, 1990, with community school students and parents in attendance. At the hearing Friebert, for the opposition, defended the common school ideal whereas Bolick, for the MPCP advocates, argued along the lines of parental choice—a matter of underprivileged children exercising the same options as more affluent children to attend public or private schools. At one point, Bolick surprised the opposing attorneys by presenting a letter from the U.S. Department of Education that granted federal waivers for MPCP. According to eyewitnesses Bolick presented the more persuasive and emotional argument, and most of the spectators supported him. Many of the spectators at this and subsequent judicial hearings in Wisconsin and Ohio were school children who had been awarded vouchers, their parents, and educators at the participating schools.[5]

During the summer of 1990 conservative writers and the Bush administration sparred with Grover. On June 27, the *Wall Street Journal* editorial page deemed Grover an enemy of civil rights, comparing him to prominent segregationists of the 1950s and 1960s. He stood accused of "blocking the schoolhouse door" like Alabama Governor George Wallace. For good measure, the editorial also compared Grover to Arkansas Governor Orval Faubus during the Little Rock crisis. In September, Vice President Dan Quayle stated that "the education establishment" has put public schools "behind a 'Berlin Wall'... of rules and regulations that stifle ingenuity and limit competition." Finally, Secretary of Education Lauro Cavazos toured Bruce Guadelupe Community School but visited no public schools during a visit to Milwaukee the same month. For his part, Grover denied that Bush was the "Education President," stating that Bush was "preppy by background. He wouldn't recognize a common school if we built it across from the White House." He named Cavazos "the Secretary of Private Education." Characterizing the George Wallace comparison as "unfair," Grover stated that he was "trying to keep the students in the schools, Wallace was trying to keep them out."[6]

On August 6, 1990, Judge Steingass upheld the program on constitutional grounds and found that Grover "exceeded his authority by imposing requirements under the Education for the Handicapped Act." To Steingass, the public purpose was obvious: "quality education." MPCP opponents appealed the decision four days later. Wisconsin Court of Appeals denied the intervenors "relief pending appeal" on August 20, the date of oral argument. This removed the last legal obstacle to the commencement of MPCP at the start of the 1990–1991 school year. The three-judge Appeals Court overturned the District Court ruling on November 13, 1990, after MPCP had been up and running with 397 students. Judges ruled unanimously that MPCP was "'private or local' legislation that could not constitutionally be passed as part of a bill which embraces more than one subject." The Court of Appeals did not address the other constitutional issues. MPCP was allowed to operate under the shadow of the appeals court decision for 15 months, until the Wisconsin Supreme Court ruled. The Wisconsin Supreme Court was much slower in reaching its decision on the constitutionality of MPCP than the District and Appeals Courts had been. According to Bolick, he and his clients "took our sweet time" appealing to the final level. The Supreme Court heard oral arguments on October 4, 1991, and decided the case on March 3, 1992. In its 4–3 decision, the court upheld the program. The justices ruled that MPCP was not a private or local bill, did not violate the uniform school districts provision, and did not violate the public purpose doctrine. Rather, the program was an experiment that could enable Wisconsin to "engender educational success competition between the public and private educational sectors for students of low-income families."[7]

MPCP grew modestly at first, beginning in 1993. With Representative Polly Williams's support, lawmakers raised the cap on the number of students from 1 percent to 1.5 percent of MPS enrollment, and participating non-sectarian schools could enroll 65 percent of their students through vouchers (up from 49 percent). The passage of a greatly expanded Milwaukee program in 1995 added the constitutional dimension of religion, since the expanded program enabled parents to use vouchers to enroll their children in religious schools. Hence, court-watchers predicted that the U.S. Supreme Court would determine the program's survival. And since the Ohio legislature enacted the Cleveland program at the same time, it was anybody's guess which lawsuit—the one challenging the Milwaukee or the Cleveland program—would reach the Supreme Court first.[8]

The expansion to include Milwaukee's religious schools was an outgrowth of a private voucher program that began in 1992, in which underprivileged students attended Milwaukee parochial and private schools on vouchers up to $1,000. The program, entitled Partners Advancing Values in Education (PAVE) was entirely funded through private dollars. PAVE was an extension of the Milwaukee Archdiocesan Education Foundation, a Catholic charity that made "high quality educational materials and opportunities available to the students enrolled in the primary and secondary schools in the Archdiocese of Milwaukee." In 1992, this foundation was renamed PAVE to "convene corporations and foundations as partners." The Bradley Foundation donated $306,290 to PAVE in its first year of operation, while the DeRance Foundation, a Catholic philanthropy with roots in the Miller Brewing Company, was the biggest contributor ($1.2 million in the first year).[9]

As a result of the 1994 midterm elections, Republican lawmakers secured majorities in both of Wisconsin's legislative chambers, which increased the likelihood of an expanded program even without the support of black Democratic lawmakers, a group that was essential to the passage of the original program. According to Bolick, the Bradley Foundation encouraged business support for public vouchers to Milwaukee parochial schools. Bradley's goal was to win public funding for PAVE, and participating parents in the private voucher program were "highly motivated" to lobby for expansion of MPCP. A coalition took shape—Republican Governor Tommy Thompson and Democratic Milwaukee Mayor John Norquist were the most high-profile politicians, but there were other supporters, including civil rights activist and former Milwaukee school superintendent Howard Fuller. Bradley Foundation Director Michael Joyce urged Milwaukee corporations to donate to PAVE with the understanding that their influence would help convince the legislature to expand public vouchers to Milwaukee's religious schools. Milwaukee's business community, organized as the Metropolitan Milwaukee Association of Commerce, soon "adopted expansion of school choice as its top legislative priority." Williams provided tepid support for the expansion, but after it was passed, she "very quickly changed her mind, and began attacking the business-run coalition." Most other black lawmakers who had supported the original program in 1990 opposed its expansion. For example, Representative Spencer Coggs informed his assembly committee that "a church elder (this one from the South) told me that he feared this program would be a forerunner to nationwide religious school choice that would hearken back to segregated academies in the South." But the combination of support from the Milwaukee Archdiocese, the governor, state lawmakers in a Republican-dominated assembly, and a handful of Democratic supporters put the expansion over the top. As part of a budget bill, the reinvigorated program provided vouchers for up to 15,000 students in Milwaukee, subjected to family income restrictions, redeemable at any private elementary or secondary school within the city. The legislation also removed the limit on the percentage of voucher students private schools could enroll.[10]

The legal battle that followed included two State Supreme Court rulings in addition to decisions in the lower courts; the U.S. Supreme Court declined to hear an appeal. Meanwhile, Polly Williams went as far as introducing a bill in 1996 "to rescind the 1995 changes and go back to the 1993 law." The National Education Association (NEA) and the American Federation of Teachers (AFT) filed lawsuits in Dane County Circuit Court that summer. Joining the NEA were several prominent civil liberties organizations, including the ACLU, the NAACP, Americans United for the Separation of Church and State, and People for the American Way (NEA and AFT lawsuits were soon consolidated). The lead attorney was Robert Chanin, the NEA's general counsel. At a strategy meeting convened by Michael Joyce in Milwaukee, attended by Governor Thompson and others, voucher advocates assembled a legal team headed by former U.S. Solicitor General Kenneth Starr, the recently appointed Whitewater Special Prosecutor who led the congressional investigation of the Clinton administration. Governor Thompson replaced his Attorney General James Doyle, a Democrat, with Starr for the defense of the program, and the Bradley Foundation agreed to reimburse the state for appointing Starr. Clint Bolick played a supporting role. The plaintiff's case rested on the same state constitutional issues as the original challenge to MPCP, with the addition of the prohibition of state support for religion under state and federal constitutions. In the summer of 1995 the Circuit Court issued a preliminary injunction of the 1995 expansion. For reasons that remain murky, both sides requested removal of the case from the Circuit Court to the Wisconsin Supreme Court, which agreed to hear the case while enjoining the state from expanding the program. According to Bolick, the state's legal team was confident that the State Supreme Court would support the expanded program. Starr presented oral arguments for the defense; Robert Chanin for the plaintiffs. In a surprise ruling in the spring of 1996, however, the Court deadlocked three to three (one of the justices "recused herself because she had received campaign money from the state teachers association"). Nevertheless, the court enjoined the expansion, and as a result of the deadlock, the case was remanded to district court.[11]

In Dane County Circuit Court the defense "attempted but failed" to remove Judge Paul Higginbotham from the case, "charging he was biased against choice." For his part, the judge immediately lifted the injunction for non-sectarian schools, allowing them to admit more voucher students. Among the witnesses Bolick called during the evidentiary hearing before Judge Higginbotham was Harvard University political scientist Paul Peterson, whose research on the academic effectiveness of MPCP was at odds with the researcher that the state had assigned to analyze the first five years of the voucher program, University of Wisconsin political scientist John Witte. Using substantially the same data, Peterson found that the program boosted student test scores, unlike Witte, who argued that MPCP made little difference in this area. Peterson also circulated his findings to the Wisconsin state legislature, and charged that "the real Mr. Witte, 'the unabashed critic' of vouchers, hides behind the facades of an objective social scientist and a friend of voucher schools." Witte shot back and soon their disagreement was the topic of a 1996 *Wall Street Journal* article that demonstrated the ambiguities of educational research. Neither researcher was able to determine, once and for all, whether vouchers raised academic achievement. Plaintiff lawyers also called an expert witness, the University of Wisconsin-Milwaukee's Alex Molnar, a well-known opponent of school vouchers, who testified that vouchers were "snake-oil." Judge Higginbotham ruled in January 1997 that the inclusion of religious schools was unconstitutional in Wisconsin and under the First Amendment, and that the legislation violated the state's public purpose doctrine and the article prohibiting local or private bills. In spite of this, Higginbotham allowed the modifications to continue for non-sectarian schools. In August 1997 the Court of Appeals ruled that the expanded program was unconstitutional "because it directed payments of money from the state treasury for the benefit of religious societies," in violation of the Wisconsin Constitution. Once again, MPCP was argued before the Wisconsin Supreme Court.[12]

This time the court obliged voucher advocates. In a 4–2 decision in June 1998, the Wisconsin Supreme Court ruled that expansion to religious schools was permissible under the Wisconsin Constitution. Moreover, the Court found that the Establishment Clause of the U.S. Constitution permitted such legislation, since, following *Lemon v. Kurtzman,* "it has a secular purpose, it will not have the primary effect of advancing religion and it will not lead to excessive entanglement between the state and participating sectarian private schools." Moreover, the court found that the program "places on an equal footing options of public and private school choice, and vests power in the parents to choose where to direct the funds allocated for their children's benefit." As a result of this decision, MPCP quadrupled in size: when the 1998–1999 school year began, enrollment jumped from 1,545 students in 23 non-sectarian schools to 6,085 students in 83 sectarian and non-sectarian schools. Given the direct reference to the U.S. Supreme Court through the three-pronged *Lemon* test, it was all but certain that the Milwaukee program would end up at the High Court. But in an 8–1 decision later in the year, the U.S. Supreme Court declined, without comment, to hear the case. Eyes turned to Ohio.[13]

Legal challenges to the Cleveland program began in early 1996. The Ohio Federation of Teachers, joined by a spokesperson for the Ohio Parent Teacher Association and others, filed suit against State Superintendent John Goff and the State of Ohio in Franklin District Court, seeking an injunction on grounds that the program was religious in nature and therefore violated Ohio and federal constitutions. Plaintiffs also alleged that Cleveland Scholarship and Tutoring Program (CSTP) violated the Ohio constitutional requirement of "uniformity," since the law only applied to Cleveland. A second lawsuit challenging the program was filed a few days later. It added that CSTP violated the state constitutional requirement of "a thorough and efficient system of common schools throughout the state." The second lawsuit also argued that the program violated the "one subject" constitutional requirement, since CSTP was enacted as part of a budget bill. The district court consolidated the lawsuits and also allowed others to intervene as defendants—David Brennan's Hope for Cleveland Children and Fanny Lewis's Hough Academy for Higher Learning (two organizations that did not yet have schools up-and-running), and a group of seven established private schools. Plaintiffs' lawyers included Robert Chanin (representing the NEA) and Marvin Frankel (a retired federal judge who represented the AFT). Ohio Solicitor General Jeffrey Sutton defended the program; he was joined by Clint Bolick (representing Brennan's and Lewis's organizations) and David Young (an Ohio Catholic Conference lawyer representing the Hanna Perkins group of private schools). Twenty-five organizations and individuals filed amicus briefs in support of, or in opposition to vouchers; one of the supporting organizations was the Citizens for Educational Freedom. Unlike the Milwaukee case, in Ohio the local NAACP branch did not join the plaintiffs.[14]

Franklin County Court of Common Pleas ruled on July 1, 1996, that CSTP was constitutional and violated neither the Ohio nor the U.S. Constitutions. Judge Lisa Sadler found the Cleveland program permissible under the First Amendment, because "the decision about which particular school to attend, and whether that school will be sectarian or non-sectarian, is made entirely, and independently, by the parents." In other words, the program met the requirements for the second prong of the Lemon test, that it was religiously neutral. Moreover, she ruled that CSTP did not violate the uniformity clause of the Ohio Constitution because of its status as a pilot project, since "Presumably the General Assembly will at some point decide either to expand the program to every school district in the state, or to end the program." As to the "thorough and efficient clause," Sadler wrote that "it is simply impossible at this point to say whether the effect of the scholarship program will be to deprive those students who do remain in the public schools of a fair educational opportunity." And finally, the judge found that CSTP did not violate the single subject requirement because, as part of a comprehensive biennial budget bill that directs funding to all state programs, "this court cannot say" that it constitutes "a gross and fraudulent violation of the single subject requirement." This decision cleared the way for students to attend private schools with vouchers for the 1996–1997 school year.[15]

In May 1997, Ohio's Tenth District Court of Appeals overturned Sadler's decision, ruling unanimously that the program was unconstitutional and violated religious separations of the U.S. and Ohio constitutions as well as the "Uniformity Clause" of the Ohio Constitution. More so than the trail court, Judge John C. Young's opinion focused heavily on a U.S. Supreme Court's decision, *Committee for Public Education and Religious Liberty v. Nyquist* (1973), in which the High Court struck down a New York program that provided tuition aid to parents whose children attended private schools, "practically all of which were sectarian in nature." Because of this, the *Nyquist* ruling found that "the grants were not available to parents on a religiously neutral basis." Moreover, the appeals court noted that in the *Nyquist* ruling, the tuition grants "amounted to direct subsidies [to religious schools] even though they were paid directly to parents rather than to the schools." The Appeals court was not persuaded by the state's argument that the CSTP was neutral regarding religion because the law permitted neighboring public school districts to enroll Cleveland Public School students: "we cannot ignore the fact that not a single public school chose to participate in the program." It also rejected the state's contention that the tutoring grants, available to parents in the public schools, added to religious neutrality: benefits to parents at the private schools (mostly religious) are "of a much greater value" than the tutoring grants, tilting the program toward religious schools, and "to hold otherwise would permit the state to provide massive subsidies to religious institutions simply by creating companion programs which provide sole benefit, no matter how meager, to the religious institutions' secular counterparts." Judge Young also found that CSTP did not comport to Ohio's uniformity clause, since the program was limited to the city of Cleveland. Attorney General Betty Montgomery filed a motion for a stay, which the Ohio Supreme Court granted, allowing CSTP to continue pending the state's appeal.[16]

Meanwhile, Ohio enacted legislation establishing charter schools in 1997. The charter schools program (called "community schools" in Ohio) was

established as a pilot for Lucas County and expanded to Ohio's eight largest school districts the same year. Charter schools were similar to voucher
schools in that public funding followed the student from the traditional
public school, and public regulations were lighter. Sectarian charter schools
were not permitted, however. Charter schools received the same per-pupil
foundation payments from the state that would have gone to the public
school district. Hence, funding for Ohio community schools was significantly higher than the public funding Ohio provided to voucher students.
This difference was not lost on charter school supporter David Brennan.
In June 1998 his management company converted the schools that he established and operated in Cleveland from voucher schools to community
schools since, in Brennan's words, "the State would pay for each child at
least double the amount that it would pay if they selected to scholarship."
Essentially, this conversion removed most secular options for students in
CSTP. More important, from a national perspective, charter schools represented a new form of publicly funded but privately operated schooling that
overshadowed school vouchers.[17]

In a four-to-three decision in May 1999, the Ohio Supreme Court reversed the lower court on the most important dimension—religion—but
nevertheless struck down the program as a violation of the single-subject
rule, since CSTP had been enacted as part of the biennial budget rather
than as a stand-alone bill. The court applied the three-pronged *Lemon* test,
but unlike the appeals court, the justices did not hold *Nyquist* as the prevailing case. "The *Nyquist* holding has been undermined by subsequent
case law," Justice Pfeifer wrote. Instead, the court emphasized *Agostini v.
Felton,* a more recent U.S. Supreme Court decision (1997). In *Agostini,* the
High Court ruled that "placing full-time [public] employees on parochial
school campuses does not as a matter of law have the impermissible effect
of advancing religion through indoctrination." This case had reversed a
1985 Supreme Court ruling that required public school specialists to work
in trailers or other off-site locations if they provided public services to students enrolled in sectarian schools. *Agostini* used different criteria than
Nyquist or *Lemon* "to evaluate whether government aid has the effect of
advancing religion." The *Agostini* criteria were "(1) whether the program
results in governmental indoctrination, (2) whether the program's recipients are defined by reference to religion, and (3) whether the program cre-
ates excessive entanglement between government and religion." The Ohio
Supreme Court found no religious indoctrination and no excessive entanglement. It did find, however, that one category of students with priority
for receiving vouchers—"students whose parents are affiliated with any organization that provides financial support to the school"—defined recipients with reference to religion, and therefore, the court required the state

to alter this part of the program. As a result, voucher supporters David Brennan, Secretary of State Kenneth Blackwell, and others worked with Governor Bob Taft to draft a stand-alone bill that omitted the religious reference, which the legislature passed in June 1999.[18]

Voucher opponents filed a new lawsuit on First Amendment grounds, this time in federal district court in Cleveland, Judge Solomon Oliver presiding. They also sought an injunction. Clint Bolick wanted to press for a different judge, since Judge Oliver was a member of the NAACP, an organization that had opposed vouchers in Milwaukee, but he was overruled by Attorney General Betty Montgomery. To the consternation of voucher advocates, and to the surprise of even the opponents, Oliver granted the injunction on August 24, at the point when "a few voucher schools had already opened for the fall and many more were to open the next day." CSTP, according to Judge Oliver, had "the primary effect of advancing religion." However, Oliver soon backpedaled on his injunction—daily newspapers across the state responded negatively, and, moreover, the Bradley Foundation and the Friedman Foundation (established by Milton and Rose Friedman in 1996), along with conservative philanthropists John Walton and Peter Flanagan, pledged $6 million to pay for students to enroll in the participating schools. Attorney General Montgomery challenged the injunction immediately. Three days later Oliver lifted the injunction for all but the "587 first time participants. Past participants could remain in private schools through the end of the semester." This was not enough for Montgomery. She filed suit on August 30 requesting a stay with the Sixth Circuit Court of Appeals and, when the appeals court did not respond, filed suit with the U.S. Supreme Court in October. The Supreme Court Justice who supervised the Sixth Circuit, John Paul Stevens, was not considered an ally of voucher supporters; he could have decided on his own whether to bypass the circuit court. Instead, he requested that the entire Supreme Court review the injunction. In a five to four order on November 5, the Supreme Court lifted Oliver's injunction pending his decision in U.S. District Court. In a portent of the Supreme Court's 2002 decision, the majority was comprised of Chief Justice William Rehnquist and Justices Anthony Kennedy, Sandra Day O'Connor, Antonin Scalia, and Clarence Thomas. In dissent were Justices Stephen Breyer, Ruth Bader Ginsburg, John Paul Stevens, and David Souter. Judge Oliver got the Supreme Court's message. In December 1999, as expected, he ruled CSTP unconstitutional, but at the same time, he allowed the program to continue pending appeal. Oliver followed the *Agostini* ruling, but unlike the Ohio Supreme Court, he found that CSTP resulted in "religious indoctrination." Oliver noted that the overwhelming majority of participating schools were sectarian, and he was persuaded that the mission statements of the religious schools proved indoctrination.[19]

In January 2000, voucher supporters sought tighter oversight of the Cleveland voucher program. Since the beginning, CPST had been hobbled by management oversights, transportation cost overruns, and, most important, fraudulent practices at a few of the participating schools, which usually took the form of enrolling phantom students or an inability to meet payroll. Referring to the fraud at one school, Ohio School Choice Committee Chair David Zanotti stated, "We are absolutely sick and tired of this kind of distraction." The advocates backed a bill seeking to transfer oversight from the Department of Education to the Ohio Auditor. This bill went nowhere, but the School Choice Committee arranged for unnamed private sources to compensate the state for an $86,940 debt owed by one of the schools. Voucher opponents also sought to end the fraud. They passed a bill with "near-unanimous support" that closed the loophole of allowing participating schools to apply for exemptions from Ohio regulations that governed its non-public schools.[20]

Voucher supporters appealed to the Sixth Circuit on January 12, 2000; the court handed down its two-to-one decision on December 11, finding the voucher program unconstitutional. Writing for the majority, Judge Eric Clay argued that the case most "on point with the matter at hand" was *Nyquist,* the Supreme Court ruling on the New York State tuition grant program for parents enrolling their children in private schools. In the Circuit Court's view, "The [Cleveland] school voucher program is not neutral in that it discourages the participation by schools not funded by religious institutions." The court noted that 82 percent of the participating schools were sectarian when CSTP began in 1996, rising to 96 percent in 1999. "Therefore," Clay wrote, "the program clearly has the impermissible effect of promoting sectarian schools." Judge James Ryan in his dissent disagreed that CSTP was similar to the New York program that was the focus of *Nyquist,* because the New York program had the express purpose and effect of providing "financial help to New York's financially troubled *private schools*... [whereas] the purpose of the Ohio statute, on the other hand, is to provide financial help to poverty-level students attending the *public schools* in Cleveland." He added that the circuit court, "in striking down this statute today... perpetuates the long history of lower federal court hostility to educational choice." Although voucher supporters lost in the Circuit Court, they were nevertheless confident that the Supreme Court would review the case. And since the appeals court ordered an extension of the stay of the injunction pending a decision in U.S. Supreme Court, a review was all but guaranteed.[21]

On May 23, 2001, Montgomery appealed to the Supreme Court. She was joined a month later by Solicitor General Theodore Olson, who filed an amicus brief on behalf of the United States urging review. Montgomery designated one of her assistant attorneys general, Judith French, to lead Ohio's legal team; she also brought in Kenneth Starr. David Young and Clint Bolick played supporting roles, something that Bolick accepted only after a brief public spat with Montgomery over her assignment of French. When the Supreme Court agreed to review CSTP September 25, 2001, victory for voucher supporters was all-but-assured. Justice Sandra Day O'Connor was long considered a swing vote on religious issues, but her vote with the majority to stay Oliver's injunction in 1999 made it less likely she would oppose the Cleveland program. Moreover, the drift of Supreme Court rulings over the past decade seemed to "welcome religion into the public sphere." Once the Supreme Court agreed to review the case, a blizzard of friend of the court briefs followed, most in favor of school vouchers. Some of the signatories had celebrity status, such as New York City mayor Rudolph Giuliani. Several states submitted briefs in support of vouchers, and national organizations included the Freidman Foundation, Focus on the Family, the Black Alliance for Educational Options, the National Association of Independent Schools, the Union of Orthodox Jewish Congregations of America, and the U.S. Conference of Bishops. Opponents included the NAACP, the National Committee for Public Education and Religious Liberty, and the American Jewish Committee. Altogether, 38 individuals and organizations filed amicus briefs, and in terms of religion and ethnicity, supporters and detractors could be found on both sides.[22]

The Supreme Court heard oral arguments on February 20, 2002, and handed down its decision on June 27. As expected, the High Court found the Cleveland program constitutional, in a five-to-four decision that broke down the same way as its 1999 order that stayed Judge Oliver's injunction. Justice O'Connor remained with the 1999 majority. Chief Justice Rehnquist penned the decision. In overturning the Sixth Circuit Court opinion, Rehnquist set the case against the backdrop of a school system in crisis— "The program challenged here was enacted for the valid secular purpose of providing educational assistance to poor children in a demonstrably failing public school system." Rehnquist found that the Ohio program was "neutral in all respects toward religion" since the "program permits the participation of *all* schools within the district, religious or nonreligious" and since the program "confers educational assistance directly to a broad class of individuals defined without reference to religion." Scholarships go to parents, "who, in turn, direct government aid to religious schools wholly as a result of their own genuine and independent private choice." Moreover, the High Court considered CSTP within the context of other alternative programs available for students in the Cleveland Public Schools. "Cleveland schoolchildren enjoy a range of educational choices," Rehnquist wrote. "They may remain in public school as before, remain in public school with publicly funded tutoring aid, obtain a scholarship and choose a religious school, obtain a scholarship and choose a non-religious private school, enroll in a community school, or enroll in a magnet school." That a majority of the participating schools were sectarian was "irrelevant." Finally, the High Court rejected the argument that *Nyquist* remained the controlling case. "*Nyquist* does not govern neutral educational assistance programs that, like the program here, offer aid directly to a broad class of individual recipients defined without regard to religion." [23]

In his concurring opinion, Justice Thomas invoked the Fourteenth Amendment in his consideration of school choice as a means of providing quality education to minority children in urban schools: "School choice programs that involve religious schools appear unconstitutional only to those who would twist the Fourteenth Amendment against itself by expansively incorporating the Establishment Clause." Justice Souter's lengthy dissent began with the 1947 *Everson* decision, one the Supreme Court never repudiated: "No tax in any amount... can be levied to support any religious activities or institutions, whatever they may be called, or whatever form they may adopt to teach or practice religion." For Souter, the overriding consideration was the preponderance of religious schools participating in the voucher program. "In the city of Cleveland the overwhelming proportion of large appropriations for voucher money must be spent on religious schools if it is to be spent at all." While Souter was persuaded that religious schools receiving "96.6 percent" of voucher funding violated the Establishment Clause, the Supreme Court majority was not.[24]

SCHOOL VOUCHERS IN PERSPECTIVE

School vouchers are the most radical form of what in recent years has been called "school choice." Voucher policies separate public school funding from public school provision. While the state retains its responsibility of funding elementary and secondary schools and, to some degree, retains its governance of them, it steps back from its role of furnishing schools of its own. Instead, private entities fill in, whether they are pre-established private sectarian and non-sectarian schools or new schools established by organizations of entrepreneurs, educators, and parents that expect to attract voucher students to their schools and educate them more effectively than traditional public schools.

The pursuit of various conceptions of freedom was the overriding cultural goal that voucher supporters had in common. Freedom took many forms. First was freedom for parents to have their children associate with whom parents choose. Freedom of association took shape as a response to school desegregation, first in the form of white supremacy in Louisiana and other southern states, as a means to continue the tradition of racially separate and unequal public schools. Later, in Wisconsin and Ohio, freedom of association also motivated racial minorities who were disillusioned with the outcomes of urban school desegregation and sought public funding to attend schools with which they could better identify. Second was freedom of religion. Here, the leaders of religious denominations in New Hampshire, Ohio, and Wisconsin—spearheaded by Catholics—sought to educate the children of their co-religionists and sometimes others according to sectarian principles and beliefs. While the U.S. Constitution prohibited states from establishing religious schools, voucher supporters believed that the state could support their free exercise of religion by helping them support schools of their own, free of the requirement that parents pay for both traditional public schools and private school tuition. Third was economic freedom—in an open educational marketplace supported with public funds, such as the one envisioned for New Hampshire, individuals and organizations with promising educational visions could create schools and attract students. Fourth, and perhaps the form of freedom paramount in the views of voucher advocates, was freedom from the public schools themselves. In Louisiana and other southern states proponents viewed the desegregating public schools as a repressive and unjustified exercise of federal power. As vouchers grew in popularity outside of the South, advocates also viewed the public schools as ineffective, remote, secular, and—similar to views of southern architects of grants-in-aid programs—pointlessly engaged in social engineering. All of these public school characteristics, in the eyes of voucher supporters, were detrimental to the proper education of children and youth. While considerable support for public school systems remained in many suburban and rural areas, over the last two generations the stature of urban public schools declined. Vouchers promoted alternatives in Milwaukee and Cleveland to public schools that voucher advocates deemed ineffectual.

The introduction highlighted two ways of interpreting the growth of school vouchers in the second half of the 20th century. The first, and in my view the most judicious way of making sense of the evidence, is to suggest that vouchers are the product of an evolving American conservatism set within a contradictory welfare state. The second, less satisfying way to interpret school vouchers is to consider them as a policy tool—a funding mechanism—that served many masters in the postwar United States. Before turning to evolving American conservatism, the latter interpretation deserves more comment.

Here, the idea of "fixing" school vouchers to particular times and places is a useful metaphor. Fix, in this sense, means to situate and make stable, as in fixing a picture to a frame or fixing a gaze on an object. In a far different context, geographer David Harvey conceptualized the "spatial-temporal fix," a concept he used to explain patterns of imperialism within capitalist economic systems. To Harvey, the spatial-temporal fix had a dual meaning. It referred to capital that is "literally fixed in and on the land in some physical form for a relatively long period of time." Examples here are harbor facilities, power stations, factories, airports, highways, and railroads, on the one hand, but also long-term "social expenditures" that take the form of schools, hospitals, and houses, on the other. His spatial-temporal fix also has a metaphorical meaning: the fix is a "solution to capitalist crises through temporal deferral and geographical expansion." In other words, one solution to the over-accumulation of capital and to falling rates of profit is to redeploy in a different land and on a larger scale. Sociologist Giovanni Arrighi extended this concept to describe the shifting center of capitalist development since the 16th century, in which the Holland succeeded the Italian city-states in the 17th century, Britain succeeded Holland in the 18th century, and the United States succeeded Britain in the 20th century. Harvey and Arrighi suggest that in the 21st century, the spatial-temporal fix may entail China succeeding the United States.[25]

To be sure, school vouchers in the educational marketplace are not the equivalent of the global circulation of financial and industrial capital. But the spatial-temporal fix, shorn of its teleological assumption of redeployment on ever-grander scale, is nevertheless a useful concept for making sense of school vouchers. The vouchers concept has always been relatively straightforward—governments transfer taxes to parents for payments to schools where their children are enrolled, thus inflating demand for schools that private sources organize and provide. Here, the voucher is something akin to financial capital whose owners seek to deploy it in profitable ways. Both are highly liquid; both are real only to the extent that they are converted to a tangible form, be it a diploma, a school, a factory, or a freeway. Politicians applied school vouchers to particular places and times just as financial managers deployed capital to different regions of the world at different times. With vouchers, historical actors "fixed" them to spatial-temporal ends such as massive resistance to the civil rights movement, opposition to the welfare state, the survival of urban parochial schools amid Catholic out-migration, and the enhancement of educational opportunities for racial minorities. Put another way, voucher supporters had specific goals in mind—continued racial segregation, tax support for parochial schools, aid to urban community schools, or opening up the public school sector to private management companies. The voucher was the tool that fixed various ideas of freedom to these spatial-temporal ends.

Vouchers also fixed themselves to two important postwar trends that made them appealing to wider constituencies. They emerged as a social policy in an era in which the New Deal consensus came unhinged. In the American South, this New Deal consensus unraveled in the 1950s, since the federal government, beginning with *Brown,* moved the American political culture from "racial nationalism" to "civic nationalism," to use historian Gary Gerstle's framework. The boundaries of national belonging were no longer limited to the descendents of European immigrants; in the 1950s and 1960s they expanded to include African, Asian, Latin American, and First Nations descendents. School vouchers in the American South were short-lived, however. Federal authorities did not allow them to be used to maintain civic nationalism. A consequence of backlash to the civil rights movement in the South—and the federal government's insistence on schooling based on civic nationalism—was withdrawn support for public education generally, symptomatic of a less-robust welfare state in this region in the latter half of the 20th century.[26]

Outside of the South, other states that enacted vouchers also did so within the context of an unraveling New Deal consensus. As a social policy, school vouchers had the potential to broaden the state's role by extending public funds to tuition assistance at private elementary and secondary schools, an expansion of the welfare state. But voucher programs in Wisconsin and Ohio were, for the most part, revenue-neutral. Rather than expanding public resources to include private schools, the states shifted public funding from public schooling to private schooling in two of their largest cities. Moreover, the rhetoric that surrounded vouchers in Wisconsin and Ohio was far from welfare statist—rather than stressing the public obligation of governments to educate all of its children and youth, the rhetoric emphasized freedom of choice. What remained of the rhetoric of the common school ideal was couched in the language of public obligation to provide educational alternatives to students enrolled in urban schools.

In the expansion of educational provision in the postwar era, the school voucher also straddled the contradictory forces of centralization and decentralization in American education. On the one hand, primary and secondary schools since the 1990s were marked by increasing regulations that emanated from state and federal governments—curriculum standards, mandatory testing, focused teacher preparation, and so forth. In terms of the academic outcomes that states increasingly required of their students, and of the curricula that states mandated for their schools, the American education system centralized. On the other hand, vouchers were but one form of widening policies of school choice, which took the form of public school open enrollment, the rise of alternative types of public schools within local school districts, the emergence of charter schools, and the

growth of home schooling. Through school choice, the American education system decentralized further. While the education voucher was a reform squarely in the decentralizing camp, leaders presented vouchers at
the same time that governments centralized the curriculum and tightened
academic standards. Recall, for example, that Ohio began requiring private
schools to administer achievement and graduation tests at the same time it
enacted vouchers redeemable at Cleveland private schools.

In Harvey's and Arrighi's concept, the spatial-temporal fix is a metaphor
for a solution to the real-world problem endemic to capitalism—the ten-
dency of overproduction as more capitalists compete in the most profitable sectors. So too, were vouchers a solution to the real-world problem
endemic to American conservatism—how to expand and wield power in
a democracy in which the welfare state seemed destined for permanence.
The growth of school vouchers in the United States, then, is best understood as a quintessential social policy in the evolution of conservatism.

At the midpoint of the 20th century, American conservatism was on
its heels. The Great Depression put American business culture into disrepute; conservatives had no effective solution to the economic crisis. Into
the breach stepped liberals with Keynesian economic policy, forging a
New Deal accord that seemed iron clad. Not only had liberalism captured
the Democratic Party, it was also paradigmatic in the Republican Party.
National political candidates vied over who could manage the welfare state
more efficiently, rather than one representing party trying to expand the
welfare state and the other trying to roll it back. American conservatism
was weak for another reason as well. The shift to civic nationalism in the
aftermath of World War II drove a wedge through the conservative movement. While most conservatives outside of the South acquiesced to civic
nationalism, at least in principle, southern conservatives continued to embrace racial nationalism; they remained wedded to Jim Crow. Moreover,
until the mid-1960s they remained wedded to a divided Democratic Party
in which liberalism held the most sway. About the only topic that united
conservatives was anti-communism with its vigorous prosecution of the
Cold War. But this was a position that conservatives had in common with
liberals as well, at least until the late 1960s.

In this context, the social movement for school vouchers in the 1950s
and early 1960s was overwhelmingly sectional. Southern grants-in-aid programs represented conservative social policy in the classical sense—school
vouchers helped conserve traditional racial practices in education. While
conservatives outside of the South sometimes expressed sympathy toward
massive resistance to the civil rights movement and its allies in the federal
government—witness the denunciation of federal intervention in the Little
Rock crisis featured in the *Manchester Union Leader*—for the most part

southern and northern conservatives did not cross-pollinate at this time. In the South conservatives were slow to embrace free-market justifications for school vouchers. They kept Milton Friedman at arm's length in the 1950s and early 1960s. They were also loath to include Catholic schools in the voucher programs they set up to counter *Brown*. They kept Virgil Blum at arm's length also. In putting a stop to grants-in-aid, the federal government removed the South as a site for voucher programs for a generation or more.

The Republican Party was the premier political site whereby southern and non-southern conservative interests re-congealed, as southern whites bid adieu to the Democrats in the wake of President Johnson's civil rights and Great Society initiatives. Moreover, southern conservatives got their wish: as school desegregation moved outside of the South, many white voters in the rest of the nation began to reassess civic nationalism, heretofore a bulwark of the New Deal consensus. One result of this reassessment was rolling back school desegregation with the election of President Nixon, his appointments to the Supreme Court, and anti-busing legislation in Congress. Another result was to reunify conservatives inside and outside of the South.

But to win greater popular support conservatives established social policies of their own. They could not solely be perceived as purveyors of backlash to social policies created elsewhere. In the words of political scientists John Micklethwait and Adrian Wooldridge, "the Republicans ever since the 1960s have played the populist card." As innovations, conservative policies cluster into three areas, those that enhance individual freedoms, those that bolster traditional morality, and those that back a strong military projected around the world. Noticeably, policies in all three areas arise within a welfare state that grew even larger in the second half of the 20th century, no matter who occupied the White House. Leaving aside military growth and brawny foreign policy (which by definition increased the size of the state), conservative social policies stressed privatization as a means of straddling the other two areas. For example, proposals to privatize social security, from a conservative viewpoint, gave control to individuals to manage their own pensions but still allowed older Americans to live out their retirement years in dignity.[27]

School vouchers evolved as a social policy quintessential for conservatives and indeed for the resurgent Republican Party beginning in the late 1960s. It started with the election of Richard Nixon, who successfully courted southern voters with his opposition to school desegregation. After his administration took charge of the OEO, the new leadership focused on school vouchers to the exclusion of other initiatives inherited from the Johnson Administration. As to Head Start, the education initiative that was emblematic of Johnson's War on Poverty, Nixon transferred it to the Department of Housing and Urban Development. During the first four years, voucher supporters labored under a New Deal Consensus that remained powerful—OEO hired a liberal social scientist, Christopher Jencks, to conduct the feasibility study, which recommended compensatory vouchers indexed to family income. Liberalism only went so far when it came to school vouchers, however. No urban school districts elected to adopt vouchers that included private schools. That most cities tended to vote Democratic, but Republicans spearheaded vouchers, contributed to big-city school boards being leery of them. That teachers' unions opposed them also, and in a period of public-sector union militancy, this also fed the skepticism.

Nevertheless the OEO was able to convince a state government to embrace vouchers in the early 1970s—the administration of the ultra-conservative New Hampshire governor, Meldrim Thomson. In the end, however, Thomson was out of step with his conservative-leaning state when it came to education policy. Voters in school districts were not ready for "pure" vouchers, ones that were seen as tax-supported tuition reimbursements that would most benefit families that could already afford private schools. It didn't help, of course, that supporters proposed New Hampshire's voucher program at the same time federal courts were most opposed to public dollars going to sectarian schools, which excluded from participation the largest bloc of schools in the private sector, the parochial schools. What emerged from the New Hampshire voucher set-back was that states with Republican governors presented conservatives with the best opportunities, that it was unlikely that local public school districts would adopt vouchers on their own, that lawmakers viewed compensatory vouchers more empathetically than pure ones, and that demand remained for vouchers among supporters of religious schools, Catholic or otherwise.

When vouchers finally came to fruition outside the South in 1990, most of these conditions were met: a popular Republican governor backed vouchers for Milwaukee, the program emerged from the state legislature instead of the local school district, lawmakers supported a program in which vouchers were limited to families of modest means, and the private schools at the center of the program had previous ties to the Catholic Church. That Governor Tommy Thompson was able to move vouchers through a Democratic-controlled legislature points to other factors unique to Wisconsin: to a large degree, the Milwaukee-based Bradley Foundation was able to shape the public debate over vouchers, and Wisconsin's Progressive tradition opened lawmakers to experimental social policies. Moreover, vouchers had a formidable spokesperson in State Representative Polly Williams, who generated grass-roots support among African Americans and convinced other black Democrats in the legislature to support the program. For Governor Thompson, vouchers became an issue with which

Republicans could attract black voters; during his gubernatorial years he garnered an increasing percentage of voters in Milwaukee's North Side. Indeed, school vouchers became a staple of Republican politics on the national level, helping the party distinguish itself from the Democrats. And in Wisconsin, after the Republican landside of 1994 tipped the legislature to a Republican majority, expanding the Milwaukee program to include religious schools was a relatively easy task.

A factor that Milwaukee had in common with other large cities was the condition of urban public school systems. Academic achievement was lower in the large urban school districts than it was in most suburbs, and sentiment grew among working-class and minority residents that school desegregation no longer held promise of educational improvements. As desegregation receded, school vouchers, along with other forms of educational privatization and choice, moved into the space. Conservative school reforms began to shape the terrain of urban education whereas liberal reforms—equalization of school funding among districts, smaller class sizes, expanded early childhood education, compensatory programming— while still significant, had less traction in state legislatures. Cleveland, Ohio, was a case in point.

Conservatives in the Statehouse, with the support of Governor George Voinovich, used urban education as an opportunity to showcase their reforms, some of which stressed raising academic standards, and others that stressed school choice, especially vouchers. Indeed, vouchers became a moral issue for many conservatives—a means to improve the educational opportunities of disadvantaged urban children and youth. Some of Ohio's resources for Cleveland, in the form of Disadvantaged Pupil Impact Aid, could be diverted to vouchers for deserving families. While there were students in Cleveland who received vouchers whose families would most likely have enrolled their children in private schools regardless, the perception among conservatives remained that Cleveland vouchers were compensatory in purpose. And indeed, this voucher program, enacted in 1995, remained focused on Cleveland. The legislature, under a new Republican governor, created a separate program for the rest of the state, but it, too, limited participation to students enrolled in public schools that the state identified as failing. Moreover, the legislature and the governor enacted Cleveland vouchers at the same time the federal court with oversight of school desegregation ordered the state to take control from the Cleveland Board of Education, and vouchers arrived at a time when this court halted school desegregation there. In Cleveland, much like the program that expanded in Milwaukee in 1995, Republican lawmakers enacted vouchers without the significant support of black elected officials, even though black students would be most affected by the change. Behind-the-scenes support from Ohio's Catholic bishops, in contrast, helped to move plans forward for vouchers in Cleveland.

The 1995 voucher legislation in Milwaukee and Cleveland included religious schools, and large majorities of participating schools in both cities were Catholic. Just as conservatives had mended the sectional fence that separated them over racial politics—inside and outside of the South, conservatives accepted a degree of civic nationalism—so too were religious distinctions among conservatives less of an obstacle to unity. By the 1990s Virgil Blum's goal of uniting conservatives across religions on the basis of Catholic freedom was realized. Catholic, Protestant, and Jewish organizations expressed support for vouchers as the Cleveland program made its way through the courts, although other, less conservative Protestant and Jewish organizations opposed them. Conservative voucher advocates embraced Catholic education by the 1980s and 1990s, a significant change from the earlier era, when grants-in-aid programs in Louisiana and elsewhere excluded Catholic schools. In their use of vouchers to provide greater access to religious schools, conservatives revitalized their support among many voters whose identities were strongly religious.

In terms of education, by the 1990s conservatives were no longer content lamenting the passing of an earlier, idealized time of strict discipline in traditional public schools. Instead, vouchers held up conservatives as educational innovators intent on solving the problems of the urban schools and presenting working-class and minority parents with alternatives for their children that included religious schools. In Republican circles, vouchers became both a shibboleth to distinguish Republicans from Democrats, and a magnet to attract new constituencies of supporters.

PROSPECTS FOR SCHOOL VOUCHERS

With *Zelman v. Simmons-Harris,* it seemed that school vouchers were destined for expansion in other cities and states, and that vouchers would enable religious schools to flourish. This has not happened, at least not in the short run. While Congress enacted a voucher program that provided tuition scholarships for approximately 2,000 students in Washington, D.C., in 2004, this was an exception, and in 2009 Congress voted to phase out the scholarships. The federal government also provided vouchers for students affected by Hurricane Katrina. In 2008 Louisiana established a voucher program of its own for New Orleans, with provisions similar to the Cleveland, Ohio, program. Most other publicly funded voucher programs are specialized. For example, Arizona provides vouchers for children in foster care and for students with disabilities. Utah, Georgia, and Florida have programs for students with disabilities as well. Utah enacted a state-wide voucher program in 2007, but in a state referendum later that year voters defeated it. Florida enacted a statewide voucher program in 1999—a much larger program than those operating in Cleveland, Milwaukee, and Washington, D.C.—but the Florida Supreme Court declared it unconstitutional in 2006, a violation of the state's requirement of a uniform system of public schools. And Ohio established its second voucher program in 2005, available to public school students who attend schools that the state deemed ineffective for two out of three years.[28]

Part of the reason that the growth of school vouchers has been anemic since 2002 was the brisk growth of charter schools beginning in 1991. In this public-private hybrid, state or local education authorities contract with private companies and directors to establish non-sectarian schools free of some of the regulations under which public schools operate. Public funding is based on charter school enrollment, and in this sense, charter schools are similar to private schools accepting vouchers, in that public funding follows the student. As of 2010 charter schools operated in 40 states plus the District of Columbia, enrolling nearly 2 million students. States with the largest numbers of students in charter schools were, in descending order, California, Florida, Arizona, Texas, Ohio, and Michigan. Although charter school provisions vary, states generally fund charter schools at higher rates per-capita than in voucher programs. As we have seen, in Ohio the most prominent advocate of vouchers, David Brennan, who had established two non-sectarian schools in Cleveland to attract vouchers, reconstituted them as charter schools to take advantage of the higher funding. In the first decade of the new century, state legislatures and voters were more attracted to charter schools than they were to voucher programs, perhaps because charter schools avoided church-state entanglements. An exception to this is in Milwaukee, where vouchers have thrived in spite of a competing charter school program in Wisconsin. Milwaukee enrolled over 20,000 students in private and parochial schools in 2010, whereas the Cleveland voucher program enrolled slightly more than 5,000 students. And Ohio's more recent voucher program enrolled nearly 12,000 students in 2010 (its vouchers have higher value than Cleveland's). Despite some growth in voucher programs nationally, charter school reforms enrolled the lion's share of the students—2 million of them.[29]

In the long run, in spite of the presence of charter schools that have stolen the thunder from school vouchers over the past decade, it is inevitable that voucher programs will multiply—in Ohio, they already have—and the largest programs will be ones that allow religious schools to participate. Since school vouchers are here to stay in the United States, I conclude with thoughts about "fixing" them, this time, in the sense of repairing.

Over the last two decades, the American education system has stressed higher standards, so that students are exposed to a more rigorous academic curriculum, one that prepares them—whether or not they matriculate to universities—to succeed in a national workforce that is more competitive and productive in the global marketplace. To ensure that students master this curriculum, states have established, with the blessing of federal authorities, mandatory examination systems. The new emphasis on testing is a way of promoting and graduating students based on their academic achievement. Public education has moved away from social promotions: to progress through the grade levels and to graduate from high schools, states require students to demonstrate academic merit. In a voucher system of schools, it is incumbent on states to rely on more than just testing systems, if they are to ensure that higher percentages of students perform well. A robust set of academic regulations for private schools is also necessary. In this way, more students can be guaranteed exposure to well-prepared teachers, well-equipped schools, and an academic curriculum that is comprehensive and challenging.

Voucher advocates argue that the market will take care of this all by itself—that the best schools will attract ever more students and the worst schools will close. That a competitive market will ensure quality schools in unpersuasive, however. There are too many schools that devote resources for marketing while neglecting their far more important educational role. Holding schools accountable through a thoughtful set of regulations, backed by school inspections if necessary, is one way of fixing school vouchers so that students are guaranteed exposure to education of the highest quality.

Second, increasing the numbers of schools to which voucher students apply is also necessary. The best way to do this is to open vouchers to schools that are located outside city boundaries. Frequently, private and public schools with the highest rates of academic achievement are located in relatively affluent suburbs. A spur for higher academic achievement is to provide students access to schools with high-achieving peers, many of whom enroll in suburban schools, public and private. As a condition of access to public funds, states could require such schools to enroll small percentages of voucher students.

In 1970, Christopher Jencks recommended that vouchers for students from low-income households be assigned a higher value than vouchers assigned to children from households of greater affluence. Such a reform of voucher systems would make students with fewer economic resources more attractive to schools with the highest rates of academic achievement. In this way, the rhetoric would come closer to the reality of providing students of modest means with the same educational opportunities as those enjoyed by children from more abundant means. High-achieving public and private suburban schools would be required to accept voucher students; awarding higher-value vouchers to low-income families would enable schools to do so with less coercion. In a nutshell, then, fixing school vouchers entails rigorous government oversight of public and private schools, opening up the education market in the suburbs, and indexing voucher amounts to family income—the smaller the income, the larger the voucher.

Of course, such reforms would cost; they would not be revenue-neutral. Moreover, these reforms would have more efficacy if a variety of factors outside of the schools changed too. But full-employment, higher wages, safer housing, better healthcare, etc., take us beyond the scope of school vouchers. Yet, if school vouchers can be fashioned to contribute a small piece to the puzzle of raising academic achievement across the board, then improvements in non-school factors that correlate to academic achievement are of the highest importance.[30]

Perhaps more than any other education reform, school vouchers are an example of a social policy emanating from conservative circles. To increase academic achievement across-the-board, rather than accepting it as a zero-sum game in which those students with the most acquisitive parents (regardless of income) have greater chances of access to high-quality schools, school vouchers would benefit from reforms that hold participating schools to high standards and unlock their compensatory potential.

NOTES

CHAPTER 1: FREEDOM

1. Knabb, Rhome, and Brown, "Tropical Cyclone Report"; Hurricane Katrina Deceased-Victims List.

2. Hoff, "More Openings Scheduled," *Education Week,* September 21, 2005, p. 18; Hearing before the United States Senate Subcommittee on Education and Early Childhood Development, p. 19; Tomsho, "After Katrina, School Choice Gains New Fans," *New York Times,* November 16, 2005, p. B1.

3. U.S. Department of Education, "New Support for Families"; Bolick, *Voucher Wars;* Bolick, "Vouching for Children: Grinches Are an Obstacle to Constructive Education Aid," *National Review Online,* October 4, 2005; National Education Association News Release, September 16, 2005.

4. *Poindexter v. Louisiana* 275 F. Supp. 833 (1967) in La Noue, ed., *Educational Vouchers* (New York: Teachers College Press, 1972), pp. 30–45.

5. Paine, *Rights of Man;* Baker, *The Life of William H. Seward,* pp. 212–213.

6. McAffe, *Religion, Race, and Reconstruction.* See also Justice, "Thomas Nast and the Public Schools of the 1870s" and Justice, *The War That Wasn't.*

7. Goldin and Katz, *The Race Between Education and Technology,* p. 186; Beadie, "Education and the Creation of Capital," pp. 1–29; Beadie, *Education and the Creation of Capital in the Early American Republic.*

8. O'Brien, "Private School Tuition Vouchers"; *Zelman v. Simmons-Harris* 536 U.S. 639 (2002).

9. Ignatiev, *How the Irish Became White,* p. 70.

10. See Floden, ed., "Policy Tools for Improving Education." There are other, histrionic interpretations: some view *Zelman v. Simmons-Harris* as the completion of the civil rights revolution, whereas others see in vouchers the dismantling of public education.

11. See, for example, Brighouse, *School Choice and Social Justice.*

12. See, for example, Jefferson, "Notes on the State of Virginia," in Peterson, ed., *Thomas Jefferson: Writings;* Mill, *On Liberty;* and Rawls, *A Theory of Justice.*

13. Brinkley, *The End of Reform,* pp. 9–10.

14. Friedman, *Capitalism and Freedom,* pp. 2–4.

15. Kruse, *White Flight,* p. 9; Clark, "Alternative Public School Systems," Mecklenburger and Hostrop, eds., *Education Vouchers,* p. 23; Sizer, "The Case for a Free Market," in Mecklenburger and Hostrop, eds., *Education Vouchers,* pp. 26–29.

16. Sizer, "The Case for a Free Market"; McGreevy, *Catholicism and American Freedom,* p. 206.

17. Constitution of the State of Ohio, Article 6, section 2, 1851; Constitution of the State of Louisiana, Article 8, Section 1, 1974; Constitution of the State of New Hampshire, Article 83, 1783.

18. Herrington and Fowler, "Rethinking the Role of States," in Boyd and Miretzky, eds., *American Educational Governance on Trial,* p. 278; Hochschild and Scovronick, *The American Dream and the Public Schools,* p. 69; *DeRolph v. State* (2001) 91 Ohio St. 3d 1274.

19. Hochschild and Scovronick, *The American Dream and the Public Schools,* p. 21. Another exception: the State of Hawaii has one school district.

20. Ravitch, *The Troubled Crusade,* p. 5.

21. National Commission on Excellence in Education, "A Nation at Risk," pp. 5–6.

22. Kolko, *The Triumph of Conservatism;* Weinstein, *The Corporate Ideal in the Liberal State;* Brinkley, "The New Deal and the Idea of the State," in Fraser and Gerstle, eds., *The Rise and Fall of the New Deal Order,* pp. 85–121; Fraser, *Every Man a Speculator,* p. 474; Offe, *Contradictions of the Welfare State,* p. 153.

23. Labaree, *How to Succeed in School Without Really Learning,* p. 18; Tyack, *Seeking Common Ground,* p. 182.

24. Armstrong, Glyn, and Harrison, *Capitalism since World War II,* pp. 167–320; Thurow, *The Future of Capitalism,* pp. 20–42. A memoir by Ronald Reagan's budget director famously illustrates the difficulties of shrinking the welfare state: Congress and cabinet officers supported tax cuts but opposed reductions to federal programs. Stockman, *The Triumph of Politics.*

25. See, for example, McGuinn, *No Child Left Behind.*

26. Dudziak, *Cold War Civil Rights.* Hirschman, *Exit, Voice, and Loyalty,* pp. 16–17.

27. Micklethwait and Wooldridge, *The Right Nation,* p. 11; Friedman, *Capitalism and Freedom,* pp. 5–6. For a seminal overview of American conservatism, which divides it into economic and social wings, see Brinkley, "The Problem of American Conservatism," pp. 409–429.

28. Micklethwait and Wooldridge, *The Right Nation;* Patterson, *Grand Expectations;* Hayek, *The Road to Serfdom;* Weaver, *Ideas Have Consequences;* Judt, *Ill Fares the Land.*

29. Phillips-Fein, *Invisible Hands;* McGirr, *Suburban Warriors;* Zimmerman, *Whose America?;* Perlstein, *Nixonland;* Wilentz, *The Age of Reagan.*

30. Friedman, "The Role of Government in Education," in Solo, ed., *Economics and the Public Interest,* pp. 123–144; Friedman, *Capitalism and Freedom,* pp. 85–98;

Friedman and Friedman, *Free to Choose;* Allen, ed., *Bright Promises Dismal Performance;* Letter from Friedman to Author, November 21, 2005, in Author's possession; Friedman Telephone Interview with Author, December 2, 2005. *Bright Promises Dismal Performance* is a collection of Friedman's *Playboy* interview and columns from *Newsweek, U.S. News and World Report,* and the *Wall Street Journal* that originally appeared in the 1970s and early 1980s.

31. Friedman, "Free to Choose," *Wall Street Journal,* June 9, 2005. Quotes are from this opinion piece, with the exception of the quote on vouchers and the one limiting the role of government, which are from Friedman, *The Role of Government in Education,* 1955, p. 127.

32. Gerstle, *American Crucible,* p. 4.

33. Goldfield, *The Color of Politics;* Carnoy, *Faded Dreams,* p. 13.

34. *Green v. School Board of New Kent County* 391 U.S. 430 (1968); Clotfelter, *After* Brown, p. 8; Henig, *Spin Cycle;* Witte, *The Market Approach to Education;* Hanauer, "Cleveland School Vouchers."

CHAPTER 2: TUITION GRANTS

1. Leflar and Davis, "Segregation in the Public Schools," pp. 404–407.

2. Address by Dekalb County Representative James A. MacKay, "Crisis in the Public Schools," Emory University, November 3, 1958, box 1, folder 18, Save Our Schools Collection (hereafter Save Our Schools Papers); O'Brien, "Private School Tuition Vouchers," pp. 384–5. Harris's article followed the filing of an NAACP school segregation suit in federal district court in Atlanta, *Aaron v. Cook,* Civ. Act.3923 (N.D. Ga. May 16, 1956).

3. Leflar and Davis, "Segregation in the Public Schools," p. 405; O'Brien, "Private School Tuition Vouchers," p. 305; Brady, *Black Monday,* pp. 94–98. Brady quoted approvingly from an article Frank Chodorov wrote for the May 19, 1954, issue of *Human Events.* "The public school is a socialized institution, and suffers from weakness inherent in all monopolies," he wrote. Chodorov proposed that the public schools be put "into competition with free enterprise schools, so they can prove their worth" (63).

4. *Green v. School Board of New Kent County,* 391 U.S. 430 (1968); Clotfelter, *After* Brown, p. 103; Laats, "Forging a Fundamentalist 'One Best System,'" pp. 55–83.

5. Devore and Logsdon, *Crescent City Schools,* p. 235; Fairclough, *Race and Democracy,* p. 167. Sokol, *There Goes My Everything,* p. 48.

6. McCarrick, "Louisiana's Official Resistance to Desegregation," p. 30; Sokol, *There Goes My Everything,* p. 47.

7. William Rainach to Col. Charles S. Hooks, June 17 1955, box 2, folder 19, William Rainach Papers, Archives and Special Collections, Noel Memorial Library, Louisiana State University-Shreveport (hereafter Rainach Papers).

8. Letter to L. H. Perez from W. M. Rainach, July 31, 1954, box 1, Segregation folder, Leander H. Perez Papers, Louisiana Collection, New Orleans Public Library (hereafter Perez Papers); McMillan, *The Citizens' Council.*

9. Jeansonne, "Segregation Forever," ed. Charles Vincent, *The Louisiana Purchase Bicentennial Series in Louisiana History V. XI*, p. 417.

10. Handwritten memo, "Re: $100,000 Segregation Suit, etc., Nov 3, 1955" and handwritten memo, "Re: Action Against NAACP, Nov 29, 1955," both in box 1, folder 9, Rainach Papers; Fairclough, *Race and Democracy*, pp. 196–233.

11. Fairclough, *Race and Democracy*, pp. 196–264.

12. "Explanation of Segregation Bills Passed by Louisiana Legislature," General Session, 1954, July 23, 1954, pp. 1–2, box 1, Segregation Joint Legislative Committee folder, Perez Papers. Letter from William Rainach to Eastland School Faculty, August 17, 1954, box 2, folder 16, Rainach Papers.

13. "Explanation of Segregation Bills Passed by Louisiana Legislature," General Session, 1954, July 23, 1954, pp. 1–2, box 1, Segregation Joint Legislative Committee folder, Perez Papers. See also McCarrick, "Louisiana's Official Resistance," p. 32. Letter from William Rainach to Louisiana School Principals, October 20, 1954, box 2, folder 25, Rainach Papers.

14. "Explanation of Segregation Bills Passed by Louisiana Legislature," General Session, 1954, July 23, 1954, pp. 1–2, box 1, Segregation Joint Legislative Committee folder, Perez Papers. See also McCarrick, "Louisiana's Official Resistance," p. 32; Fairclough, *Race and Democracy*, 170.

15. McCarrick, *Louisiana's Official Resistance*, p. 38; "The Answers to Anti-Segregation," n.d., box 1, Segregation General file folder, Perez Papers; Fairclough, *Race and Democracy*, pp. 186–187; Rainach to Rev. Ardis Smith, District Five Baptist Convention of Louisiana, July 22, 1954, box 1, Segregation Joint Legislative Committee folder, Perez Papers.

16. Memo to William Rainach from Willis Jarrel, October 8, 1954, box 1, folder 19; Letter to Governor Robert F. Kennon from Charles F. Cooper, September 17, 1954, box 1, folder 24, both in Rainach Papers.

17. Letter to William Rainach from P. G. Borron, November 21, 1955, box 1, folder 10; Letter to William Rainach from Paul G. Borron, August 3, 1954, box 3, folder 31; Letter to William Rainach from W. Scott Wilkinson, June 25, 1954, box 3, folder 31; Letter to P. G. Borron from William Rainach, November 26, 1954, box 1, folder 10, all in Rainach Papers. Fairclough, *Race and Democracy*, p. 193.

18. Jacoway, *Turn Away Thy Son*, pp. 211–212.

19. Jacoway, *Turn Away Thy Son*, p. 278; *Cooper v. Aaron* 358 U.S. 1 (1958).

20. Resolution of the Joint Legislative Committee, October 5, 1957, box 8, folder 8, Rainach Papers; McCarrick, "Louisiana's Official Resistance," p. 76; William Rainach to Governor Earl K. Long, October 5, 1957, box 8, folder 85, Rainach Papers.

21. State of Louisiana, *Acts of the Legislature*, pp. 831, 834, 843. For Virginia and Georgia, see, for example, Patterson, *Brown v. Board of Education*, p. 99; Kruse, *White Flight*, p. 132.

22. State of Louisiana, *Acts of the Legislature*, pp. 850–855; Fairclough, *Race and Democracy*, p. 172.

23. McCarrick, "Louisiana's Official Resistance," p. 70; Donald Ross Green and Warren E. Gauerke, "If the Schools are Closed: A Critical Analysis of the Private

School Plan," (Pamphlet), Atlanta: Southern Regional Council, 1959, in box 1, folder 19, Save Our Schools Papers.

24. NAACP Petition to the Orleans Parish School Board, May 13, 1949, box 28, folder 191, NAACP Orleans Branch Collection, Earl K. Long Library, University of New Orleans (hereafter NAACP New Orleans Papers); State Department of Education of Louisiana Bulletin 640, "An Organizational and School-Building Survey of the Public Schools of Orleans Parish," October 1947, pp. 148–149, box 3, folder 27, Orleans Parish School Board Collection, Earl K. Long Library, University of New Orleans (hereafter OPSB Papers); Devore and Logsdon, *Crescent City Schools,* pp. 224–225.

25. *Aubert v. Orleans Parish School Board* Civil Action no. 215 (E.D. La. 1948); NAACP Petition to the Orleans Parish School Board, May 13, 1949, box 28, folder 191, NAACP New Orleans Papers; Muller, "New Orleans Public School Desegregation," in Charles Vincent, ed., *The African American Experience in Louisiana, Part B,* p. 336.

26. Sokol, *There Goes My Everything,* p. 127; "School Enrollment for Orleans Parish," in letter from J. Berton Gremillion of the Louisiana Department of Education to State Rep. E. O. Gravolet, July 2, 1954, box 1, segregation folder, Perez Papers; Muller, "New Orleans Public School Desegregation," p. 340.

27. Wieder, "The New Orleans School Crisis of 1960," p. 124; *Bush v. Orleans Parish School Board* 138 F. Supp. (1956); Fairclough, *Race and Democracy,* p. 162.

28. *Orleans Parish School Board v. Bush* 365 U.S. 569 (1961); Jeansonne, *Leander Perez.*

29. Hubert Humphreys, Interview of William M. Rainach, Oct. 7, 1977, Louisiana State University Oral History Collection, Number 17, Noel Memorial Library, Louisiana State University-Shreveport (Hereafter Humphreys Interview).

30. School Board Minutes, June 20, 1960, p. 117, OPSB Papers; School Board Minutes, November 10, 1960, pp. 390–396, OPSB Papers. Reasons are listed from greatest to fewest numbers of students. The 1960 election was something of a referendum on school desegregation. In the Ninth Ward, Eisenhower's Vice President "won just 18 percent" of the vote, behind Kennedy and the States' Rights Party candidate, who garnered 50 percent and 32 percent of the vote, respectively. According to historian Jason Sokol, "Ninth Ward whites cast ballots against integration" (pp. 127–128).

31. Landphair, "'The Forgotten People of New Orleans,'" p. 839; Sokol, *There Goes My Everything,* p. 127.

32. Jeansonne, *Leander Perez,* p. 253; School Board Minutes, June 20, 1960, p. 164, OPSB Papers; "Board Gives Davis Task of Halting School Mix," *States-Item,* June 21, 1960, Desegregation Files, box 3, folder 28, OPSB Papers. Letter from Armand J. Duvio to Jimmy H. Davis, September 13, 1960, box 60–1, Integration 1960 folder, De Lesseps S. Morrison Collection, New Orleans Public Library (hereafter Morrison Papers). See also Wieder, "The New Orleans School Crisis," p. 129. It is an open question why the school board located its first desegregated schools in a working-class area of the city, where resistance among whites would be fierce. Indeed, some middle-class residents had suggested that white schools with a more

affluent clientele be the first to admit black students. Perhaps the school board majority believed that sharper resistance would cause the federal government to back down; perhaps the school board took what it believed was the path of least resistance—better to upset working-class whites than those of their own class.

33. "Private School Plans Urged by Rittiner," *States-Item,* June 27, 1960, box 4, folder 31, OPSB Papers. Although the entire school board supported segregation, not all favored private schools. "Integration of the public schools is inevitable," Board member Louis G. Reicke told the New Orleans Junior Chamber of Commerce. A private, segregated system would be "a makeshift arrangement at best." "Dislikes Private School Proposal, *States-Item,* July 21, 1960, box 4, folder 32, OPSB papers.

34. Jeansonne, *Leander Perez,* p. 258; Muller, "New Orleans Public School Desegregation," p. 346.

35. Louisiana State Advisory Committee on Civil Rights, *The New Orleans School Crisis,* p. 14; Fairclough, *Race and Democracy,* p. 244; Sokol, *There Goes My Everything,* p. 129; Inger, *Politics and Reality in an American City,* p. 56.

36. Steinbeck, *Travels with Charley,* pp. 931 and 936.

37. Patterson, *Brown v. Board,* p. 107–108; Inez Robb, "The Harpies OK New Orleans," *Chicago Daily News,* December 7, 1960, box 60–2, folder 2; Letter from Johnny W. Hamlet to Chep Morrison, November 30, 1960, box 60–2, folder 4, both in Morrison Papers; George Singlemann and Cullen Vetter Interview, November 15, 1978, Rogers-Stevens Oral History Collection, Amistad Research Center (hereafter Rogers-Stevens Collection); Betty Wisdom Interview, November 17, 1978, Rogers-Stevens Collection. Singlemann was Perez's top assistant on the Citizens' Council; Wisdom worked for Save Our Schools.

38. Jeansonne, "Segregation Forever," in Charles Vincent, ed., *The African American Experience in Louisiana, Part B,* pp. 428, 433.

39. "Old Gambling Hall will be Private School," *Times-Picayune,* December 3, 1960, p. 1; Singlemann and Vetter Interview; Jeansonne, *Leander Perez,* p. 261; George Singlemann Interview by Jeansonne, p. 11; Crain and Inger, "School Desegregation in New Orleans," p. 51; "Private School Plans Advance," *Times-Picayune,* December 4, 1960, p. 1; "Pupils Signing at Arabi Building," *Times-Picayune,* December 12, 1960, p. 3. Vetter's store was located across the street from McDonogh 19. He later claimed in his 1978 interview that desegregation at McDonogh caused him to go out of business: "The white people quit dealing with me."

40. Walter J. Brown Media Archives and Peabody Awards Collection, clip wsbn 44811, December 1960; "School Readied for 400 Pupils," *Times-Picayune,* December 7, 1960, p. 2.

41. "School Annex Well Equipped," *Times-Picayune,* December 8, 1960, p. 13; "School Readied for 400 Pupils," *Times-Picayune,* December 7, 1960, p. 2.

42. "Arabi School Annex Gleams," *Times-Picayune,* December 9, 1960, p. 5; Wieder, *Race and Education,* pp. 101–102.

43. "Arabi School Annex Gleams," *Times-Picayune,* December 9, 1960, p. 5; "Enrollment 212 in Arabi School," *Times-Picayune,* December 10, 1960; "Dr. Redmond

Reports on New Orleans Pupils," *States-Item,* January 18, 1961, folder 34, box 4, Desegregation Files, OPSB Papers; "Suit Dismissal Plea Pondered," *Times-Picayune,* December 14, 1961, box 2, folder 2, Save Our Schools Papers; "Private School Plans Advance," *Times-Picayune,* December 30, 1960, p. 2.

44. "Mixed School Parents Begin Fund Campaign," *States-Item,* April 7, 1961, box 4, folder 37, OPSB Papers; Ninth Ward Private School Association, "Dispossessed!" flyer, Segregation file, Louisiana Collection, New Orleans Public Library (hereafter Louisiana Collection).

45. Armand Duvio, "Private School Leader Says 'Boycott' Not Proper Term," *Southern School News,* August 1961, p. 3; "State and Parish Agree to Permit Federal Inspection," *Southern School News,* October 1961, p. 2, both in box 5, OPSB Papers.

46. "Community Action: Perez Speaks at Dedication," *Southern School News,* December 1961, box 5; "Name Wagner Head of Private School Board," *Times Picayune,* April 19, 1961, box 4, folder 37, both in OPSB Papers.

47. State Legislature Resolution, *States-Item,* December 5, 1960, in box 2, folder 1, Save Our Schools Papers; Fairclough, *Race and Democracy,* p. 247; Rainach Interview, August 19, 1977.

48. Leander Perez Interview, box 1, folder 21, Save Our Schools Papers.

49. McCarrick, "Louisiana's Official Resistance," p. 204; "House OK's Plan of Grants-In-Aid," *Times Picayune,* December 3, 1960, p. 4; State of Louisiana, *Acts of the Legislature,* pp. 54–55.

50. "Louisiana's Grant-In-Aid Program, *PAR Analysis,* October 1963, p. 2, box 71, folder 20; Complaint, *Poindexter v. Louisiana Financial Assistance Commission,* June 29, 1964, p. 7, box 69, folder 19; Louisiana's Grant-In-Aid Program, p. 2, box 71, folder 20; all in Alexander Pierre Tureaud Papers, Amistad Research Center, New Orleans (hereafter Tureaud Papers).

51. Complaint, *Poindexter v. Louisiana Financial Assistance Commission,* p. 6, Tureaud Papers; State of Louisiana, *Acts of the Legislature,* p. 338.

52. McCarrick, "Louisiana's Official Resistance to Desegregation," p. 205.

53. Commission Exhibit Number 1, Brief on Behalf of the Defendant-Interveners, *Poindexter v. Louisiana Financial Assistance Corporation,* April 28, 1967, box 69, folder 20, Tureaud Papers.

54. Complaint, *Poindexter v. Louisiana Financial Assistance Commission,* June 29, 1964, p. 6, box 69, folder 19, Tureaud Papers; John Curtis Christian School Advertisement, *States-Item,* August 10, 1962, box 3, folder 3, Save Our Schools Papers.

55. "Newman Since 1903," Isadore Newman School.

56. "Private School Group Applies for Grant-in-Aid Funds," *Southern School News,* December 1961, p. 9, box 5, OPSB Papers; Letter from A. P. Tureaud to Armand Duvio, January 24, 1964; Letter from Duvio to Tureaud, February 7, 1964; Letter from Tureaud to Director of Carrollton Private School, May 22, 1964; Letter from Tureaud to Director of Garden District Academy, May 22, 1964; all in box 69, folder 17, Tureaud Papers. Since the Louisiana Financial Assistance Commission distributed funds to parents at segregated private schools, however, it is unlikely that Tureaud would have supported the law even if Catholic schools had been included.

57. Transcript, *Poindexter v. Louisiana Financial Assistance Commission,* March 19, 1965, p. 39, box 70, folder 9, Tureaud Papers.

58. Complaint, *Poindexter v. Louisiana Financial Assistance Commission,* June 29, 1964, p. 1, box 69, folder 19; James D. Fountain deposition, August 28, 1967, box 70, folder 14, both in Tureaud Papers; *Poindexter v. Louisiana Financial Assistance Commission* 296 F. Supp. 686 (1968).

59. Deposition of Robert Duvio, Sr., December 12, 1966, box 70, folder 5, Tureaud Papers; Letter from Robert Duvio to Simmons, September 28, 1970; Letter from Simmons to Robert Duvio, October 3, 1970, box 19, folder 204, both in Rainach Papers.

60. Alan Wieder, *Race and Education,* p. 91.

61. Wisdom Interview.

62. "Willie Rainach Today Still a Segregationist," *Shreveport Times,* September 15, 1974, C1–3, fieldnotes folder, Rainach Papers.

63. Claiborne Parish School Board Proposed Decree, School Desegregation, February 1966, box 19, folder 204, Rainach Papers; *Green v. School Board of New Kent County* 391 U.S. 430 (1968); "The Citizen's Report," October 1969, p. 2, box 21, folder 233, Rainach Papers.

64. Letter from Claiborne Academy Foundation to parents, August 25, 1969, box 32, folder 386; Letter from T. M. Deas, MD to Claiborne Parish School Board, June 10, 1970, box 32, folder 382, both in Rainach Papers.

65. Annual School Report, Homer Academy, 1969–1970 session, box 32, folder 386; Proceedings of the Southern Independent School Association meeting, Acapulco, Mexico, November 20–21, 1970, both in Rainach Papers.

66. "About Claiborne Academy."

67. Friedman, "The Role of Government in Education." In R. Solo, Ed., *Economics and the Public Interest,* p. 131; Friedman, *Capitalism and Freedom;* Friedman, Telephone Interview.

68. Letter from Rabbi Leo A. Bergman, Touro Synagogue of New Orleans to Albert Vorspan, Union of American Hebrew Congregations, December 6, 1960, Morrison Papers; "Here is Proof that NAACP is an alien-controlled Organization" leaflet, Box 230, Correspondence folder, Sutherland Series, OPSB Papers.

69. Jencks, "Who Should Control Public Education?" pp. 161–162. See also Jencks, "Is the Public School Obsolete?" pp. 18–27; Friedman, *Capitalism and Freedom;* Friedman, "The Voucher Idea," *New York Times,* September 23, 1973, p. 65.

70. Kruse, *White Flight.*

71. William Rainach to Gov. Earl K. Long, October 5, 1957, box 8, folder 85; William Rainach to Sue Hefley, May 4, 1955, box 2, folder 19, Rainach Papers; Sokol, *There Goes My Everything,* p. 15.

72. William Rainach to M. W. Bagwell, Jr., State Democratic Committee, Sept. 21, 1959, box 3, folder 35, Rainach Papers; Rainach Interview, October 7, 1977; William Rainach to Kenner Howard, Briarfield Academy, June 30, 1971, box 14, folder 136, Rainach Papers.

73. T. W. Holloman to William Rainach, September 7, 1955, box 1, folder 11; William Rainach to P. G. Borron, November 21, 1955, box 1, folder 10, both in Rainach Papers.

CHAPTER 3: DETOUR

1. Nixon, "Second Inaugural Address;" Micklethwait and Wooldridge, *The Right Nation;* Rieder, "The Rise of the 'Silent Majority,'" in Fraser and Gerstle, eds., *The Rise and Fall of the New Deal Order,* pp. 243–268.

2. Kozol, *Free Schools.* According to Kozol, free schools enabled urban students of color, their parents, community activists, and radical educators to participate in small schools free from the oppressiveness and bureaucracy of the public schools. Jenkins, "Stand by for Vouchers," pp. 7–9. Richard Nixon, Lyndon Johnson, and Hubert Humphrey used the phrase "a piece of the action" frequently in the context of the black struggle for civil rights. See, for example, Nixon's 1968 presidential acceptance speech or Johnson speaking to Humphrey in 1964.

3. Most primary sources for this chapter come from the New Hampshire Education Voucher Project Records at the New Hampshire Records and Archives in Concord, New Hampshire (hereafter, the Voucher Project Records). According to the manifest letter to Frank Mever, New Hampshire State Archivist, from Marylene Altieri, Special Collections Librarian at the Gutman Library at the Harvard Graduate School of Education, David K. Cohen compiled and donated the records. He previously taught at the Harvard Graduate School of Education and directed the Center for the Study of Public Policy, the principal consulting agency for the New Hampshire Vouchers Project. Cohen did not respond to requests for an interview. I also draw upon the Governor Meldrim Thomson Papers at the New Hampshire Records and Archives, as well as records from the New Hampshire Department of Education.

4. Kozol, *Free Schools;* Lyndon B. Johnson, *Public Papers of U.S. Presidents, Lyndon B. Johnson, 1963–4;* Doyle Telephone Interview. Doyle was an assistant director at the OEO beginning in 1972 and from 1973 at the National Institute of Education where he helped coordinate the New Hampshire Voucher Project. Levine, *The Poor Ye Need Not Have With You,* p. 227; Lawrence Feinberg, "Tax Credit on Tuition Is Favored by Shriver," *Washington Post,* September 7, 1972, p. A7; Hochschild and Scovronick, *The American Dream and the Public Schools.* In my examination of OEO records at the Johnson Presidential Library, I turned up no evidence of staffers encouraging school vouchers.

5. Joan Didion, "Cheney: The Fatal Touch," *New York Review of Books,* October 5, 2006, pp. 51–56; Morris, "The Undertaker's Tally" 2006; John Herbers, "Rumsfeld Hopes to Speak for Poor," *New York Times,* May 2, 1969; Paul Delaney, "Poverty Agency Replaces 'Inefficient' Rights Unit," *New York Times,* October 2, 1969; J. MacKenzie, "Poverty Lawyers Plan Protest to Rumsfeld," *Washington Post,* November 26, 1970; Stanley, "President's Page," p. 1529.

6. Jack Rosenthal, "O.E.O. to Test Plan to Aid Education," *New York Times,* May 15, 1970, p. 9. Incentives included trading stamps, prizes, and—presumably for teachers and contractors—cash. See also "A Student Aid Plan Runs into a Fight," *U.S. News and World Report,* August 9, 1971, in, box 10766, Press Clippings folder Voucher Project Records.

7. Center for the Study of Public Policy, *Education Vouchers;* Jencks, "Is the Public School Obsolete?" pp. 18–27; Jencks, "Who should control public education?" pp. 161–162.

8. Christopher Jencks, "Private schools for black children," *New York Times.* November 3, 1968, quote at 280; Center for the Study of Public Policy, *Education Vouchers;* Jencks, Telephone Interview.

9. Center for the Study of Public Policy, *Education Vouchers;* Doyle Telephone Interview; E. Wentworth, "OEO to Give Vouchers in School Choice Test," *Washington Post,* May 23, 1970, p. A3; Areen and Jencks, "Education Vouchers," pp. 327–335. The Center avoided urban districts in the South that were under desegregation orders. Most big city school boards, superintendents, and teachers unions opposed the OEO initiative. For example, New York City Public Schools Chancellor Harvey Scribner told a congressional committee that the "market-place has never been known as a friend of the poor or unsophisticated." "Scribner Opposes Voucher System," *New York Times,* May 5, 1971.

10. Lukas, *Night-mare.*

11. Patterson, *Grand Expectations;* Phillips, Telephone Interview; Ambrose, *Nixon,* pp. 62–63.

12. Welsh, "The New Hampshire Voucher Caper," pp. 16–17; Phillips Telephone Interview.

13. Minutes of State Board of Education, April 18, 1973, p. 2415, New Hampshire Department of Education Records, Concord, NH; Donaldson, *Education Vouchers in New Hampshire;* Phillips Telephone Interview; Letter from Bittenbender to Thomson, August 2, 1973, box 54066, Education folder, Meldrim Thomson Papers; Letter from Paul Goldsmith, member of the NH Education Voucher Advisory Board, to Lawrence Uzzell, Voucher Project Coordinator, OEO, June 18, 1973, box 10766, Advisory Board Members folder, Voucher Project Records; Letter from Jack Kemp and fifteen other Congressmen to President's Counselor Melvin Laird, July 25, 1973, box 10766, Gov. Meldrim Thomson Correspondence folder, Voucher Project Records; Welsh, "The New Hampshire Voucher Caper."

14. Menge, "The Evaluation of the New Hampshire Plan," in Hakim, Seidenstat, and Bowman, eds., *Privatizing Education and Educational Choice,* pp. 163–182; Donaldson, *Education Vouchers in New Hampshire;* Doyle Telephone Interview.

15. Letter from Milton Friedman to Author, November 21, 2005, in author's possession; Goldwater, *The Conscience of a Conservative;* Ebenstein, *Milton Friedman;* Friedman, "Why Not a Volunteer Army?" in Tax, ed., *The Draft,* pp. 200–207; Bailey, "The Army and the Marketplace," pp. 47–74.

16. Friedman, "The Role of Government in Education," in Solo, ed., *Economics and the Public Interest,* p. 130; Milton Friedman, "The Voucher Idea," *New York Times,* September 23, 1973, p. 65; Letter from Milton Friedman to Henry Levin, October 24, 1968, p. 2. I am grateful to Henry Levin for sharing this correspondence.

17. Census of the Population, 1970, p. 31–30; Donaldson, *Education Vouchers in New Hampshire,* p. 26; Center for the Study of Public Policy, *Education Vouchers,* p. 31.

18. Benveniste, Carnoy, and Rothstein, *All Else Equal;* Levin, "The Failure of the Public Schools," pp. 32–37; Havinghurst, "The Unknown Good: Education Vouchers," in Mecklenburger and Hostrop, eds., *Education Vouchers,* p. 49; Sowell, *Black Education: Myths and Tragedies,* pp. 242–250; Coons and Sugarman, "Family Choice in Education"; Doyle Telephone Interview.

19. Friedman, "The Voucher Idea." Friedman's *Newsweek* columns and *Playboy* interview were reprinted in Friedman, *Bright Promises Dismal Performance,* ed. William R. Allen.

20. Friedman and Friedman, *Two Lucky People,* p. 168; Letter from Meldrim Thomson to William Bittenbender, May 22, 1973, box 54006, Voucher System folder, Governor Meldrim Thomson Papers, NH State Records and Archives (hereafter, Thomson Papers).

21. "NHEA Position on Vouchers Clarified," pp. 1–2; Pearl Rock Kane, *An Interview with Milton Friedman on Education;* Friedman Telephone Interview; Phillips Telephone Interview. John A. Menge was a Democrat from Lyme who served in the New Hampshire General Court (the legislature) in the 1971 session. His assistance helped give the Voucher Project a bipartisan tenor; Minutes of the New Hampshire State Board of Education, February 21, 1973, p. 2391 and August 14, 1973, p. 2461, New Hampshire Department of Education, Concord, NH.

22. Haraven and Langenback, *Amoskeag.*

23. President's Panel on Nonpublic Education, *Nonpublic Education and the Public Good;* New Hampshire State Board of Education, "Report of the Nonpublic School Study Commission," Concord, NH, June 1974, p. 7, in box 10766, Report of the Nonpublic School Study Commission folder, Voucher Project Records; Section 193:1-a, Title XV Education, NH Revised Statutes Online; *Americans United for Separation of Church and State v. Paire,* 359 F. Supp. 505 (1973) at 510.

24. Fillion, "The State System of School Finance in New Hampshire"; Menge, "The Evaluation of the New Hampshire Plan," pp. 166–167.

25. Friedman and Friedman, *Two Lucky People,* p. 168; McIntyre, *The Fear Brokers,* pp. 215, 246–248, 273.

26. "Brotherhood by Bayonet," Reprinted from the *Manchester Union Leader,* September 26, 1957; Perlstein, *Nixonland,* p. 543; Letter to Virginia Governor Linwood Holton from Meldrim Thomson, April 11, 1973, School Busing folder, Thomson Papers.

27. Areen and Jencks, "Education Vouchers," p. 332; Opinion from Attorney General Warren Rudman to William Bittenbender, December 12, 1973, Choice folder, Office of Legislation and Hearings Records, New Hampshire Department of Education; "An Act Providing for the Test of Education Vouchers Programs," HB 867, April 30, 1975, in box 10765, Legal folder, Education Voucher Project.

28. *Sloan v. Lemon* 413 U.S. 825 (1973); *Committee for Public Education and Religious Liberty v. Nyquist* 413 U.S. 756 (1973); *Lemon v. Kurtzman* 403 U.S. 602 (1971); Nord, *Religion and American Education,* pp. 188–189; Pollack, "Parochiad: End of the Line?" p. 96; F. Norris, "Districts Sought for Voucher Plan," *Concord Monitor,* January 16, 1974, copy in box 10766, Press Clippings folder, Voucher Project Records.

29. Address by William Bittenbender to the Conference on Educational Alternatives, Jefferson New Hampshire, June 25, 1974, box 10767, Public Information folder, Voucher Project Records.

30. New Hampshire Citizens for a Pure Voucher System pamphlet, box 10767, Support Groups folder, Voucher Project Records; *The Voucher* vol. 1, no. 1, April

1974, in box 10766, Newspaper Insert folder, Voucher Project Records. The Diocese of Manchester encompassed the whole state.

31. *The Voucher*, vol. 1, no. 1, April 1974, in box 10766, Newspaper Insert folder, Voucher Project Records. Voucher Project officials prevented other opponents—the PTA, National School Boards Association, New Hampshire Council of Churches, and National Association of State Boards of Education, from publishing statements in the insert. Letter from Donald Murphy of the New Hampshire Education Association to James Leonard, Director of the Voucher Project, April 12, 1974, NHEA folder, Voucher Project Records; "Informed Consent: A Chronological Discussion," p. 4, in Newell Paire, "A Proposal to Fund the Study and Planning of the Education Voucher System in New Hampshire, July 12, 1974, box 10765, Voucher Project Records.

32. Letters from Jack Menge to William Milne, Voucher Project Director, October 2, 1974 and from Menge to Newell Paire, Commissioner of State Department of Education, August 2, 1974, both in box 10765, Professor Menge Correspondence folder, Voucher Project Records.

33. Donaldson, *Education Vouchers in New Hampshire;* "Informed Consent: A Chronological Discussion, pp. 7–8, in Newell Paire, "A Proposal to Fund the Study and Planning of the Education Voucher System in New Hampshire," July 12, 1974, box 10765, Voucher Project Records.

34. Cambridge Survey Research, "A Preliminary Report on the Attitudes Toward the Voucher Program in the State of New Hampshire," July 1973, p. 26, Appendix to New Hampshire Educational Voucher Project Feasibility Study, August 14, 1973, box 10765, Voucher Project Records; Since the Supreme Court ruled to restrict aid to parochial schools after the survey had begun, parents with children already in parochial schools or who had "announced an intention to transfer them there under the voucher plan" were re-contacted (p. 4). Cambridge Survey Research, "A Preliminary Report."

35. "A school district shall be considered to have demonstrated informed con-sent if and only if" details of the plan have been publicized prior to the meeting, voters and the school board agree to participate, the district is aware of undesirable side effects, and there is evidence the district is aware of a range of models from more to less regulated." "Informed Consent: A Chronological Discussion," p. 1, in Newell Paire, "A Proposal to Fund the Study and Planning of the Education Voucher System in New Hampshire," July 12, 1974, box 10765, Voucher Project Records; Legislative Study Committee to Examine Choice in Education, "Final Report of the Committee to Study Choice in Education (House Bill 1175-FN, Chapter 82, Laws of 1990)," December 1990, p. 5, New Hampshire Department of Education Records.

36. "Informed Consent: A Chronological Discussion," p. 2; Letter from Dover Supt. Bernard Ryder to Ron Tenney, Sept. 14, 1973, box 10766, Responses from School Districts folder, Voucher Project Records. Ryder was a prominent local supporter of vouchers and Superintendent in one of three cities in New Hampshire where vouchers were brought to a vote. Letter from Seth O'Shea, Concord Superintendent of Schools to Ron Tenney, September 14, 1973. See also Letter from

Lillian Page, Peterborough Superintendent of Schools, to Newell Paire, February 8, 1974 and Letter from William Baston, Andover Superintendent of Schools to Bittenbender, January 17, 1974; all in box 10766, Responses from School Districts folder, Voucher Project Records.

37. Memo from Bernard Ryder, Superintendent of Dover schools, March 28, 1974, box 10766, NH Superintendents folder; *The Voucher*, April 1974, Box 10766, both in Voucher Project Records.

38. National Education Association, *Addresses and Proceedings*, quotes at pp. 107, 550, 770; J Rosenthal, "Nixon Aide Scores Teachers' Groups," *New York Times*, September 24, 1970, p. 27; Lambert, "After All," p. 64.

39. Letter from James Leonard, Director of the New Hampshire Education Vouchers Project, to Donald Murphy, President of the NHEA, April 2, 1974, box 10766, NHEA folder; Letter from Donald Murphy to James Leonard, April 12, 1974, box 10766, NHEA folder, Voucher Project Records; Thomas Adams, "N. H. Education Association Opposes Vouchers," *The Voucher*, April 1974, p. 7, box 10766, Voucher Project Records.

40. This motto was affixed to city letterhead. Nadeau, *Berlin*, p. 8.

41. Letter from Rev. Michael J. Griffen, Chair of the Berlin Regional Schools, May 9, 1973, box 10766, Berlin folder; Letter from Superintendent Lawrence Dwyer to William Bittenbender, May 17, 1973, box 10766, Berlin folder; "Cooperation Profile of Public and Private Educational Systems in Berlin, NH," May 17, 1973, box 10766, Berlin folder, all in Voucher Project Records. At the elementary school level, approximately 1,340 students enrolled in public schools and 950 in Catholic schools; Letter from Mayor Sylvio J. Croteau to William Bittenbender, June 15, 1973, box 10766, Berlin folder, Voucher Project Records.

42. John Vezina, "Will the Berlin Community Regain Control of Its Public Schools?" n.d., in box 10766, Berlin folder, Voucher Project Records.

43. "Informed Consent: A Chronological Discussion," pp. 6–9, in Newell Paire, "A Proposal to Fund the Study and Planning of the Education Voucher System in New Hampshire," July 12, 1974, box 10765, Voucher Project Records.

44. 1970 Census; New Hampshire Department of Education, "New Hampshire Education Voucher Project: A Summary," August 4, 1975, box 10765, Voucher Project Records; Donaldson, *Education vouchers in New Hampshire*, pp. 21–24.

45. "School Vouchers Rejected in Test," *New York Times*, April 11, 1976; "Response Negative at Voucher Meeting," *Concord Monitor*, February 11, 1976; Tom Borden, "Fear of Unknown Scuttled School Voucher Program," *Lowell Sun*, April 7, 1976; all in box 10766, 1976 Press Clippings folder, Voucher Project Records. See also Donaldson, "Education Vouchers in New Hampshire"; Street, "The Annihilation," pp. 1–2; Friedman, "Free to Choose," *Wall Street Journal*, June 9, 2005, p. A16.

46. Kahlenberg, *Tough Liberal*.

47. Nixon, *RN*, p. 439; Ehrlichman, *Witness to Power*, p. 234; McAndrews, *The Era of Education*, pp. 93–103; McGuinn, *No Child Left Behind*, p. 41.

48. "Informed Consent: A Chronological Discussion," p. 8, and Letter from Henriette Girard, Clerk of Allenstown School District, to Gerard Croteau, Assistant

Superintendent of Supervisory Union no. 53, April 24, 1974, both in Newell Paire, "A Proposal to Fund the Study and Planning of the Education Voucher System in New Hampshire," July 12, 1974, box 10765, Voucher Project Records.

49. Witte, *The Market Approach to Education;* Haffey, "Tax-supported School Vouchers."

50. Carl, "Unusual Allies"; Bodwell, "Grassroots, Inc."

51. *Zelman v. Simmons-Harris.* 536 U.S. 639 (2002).

CHAPTER 4: THE URBAN SCHOOL CRISIS

1. "Lawmaker, MCJ Editor call Choice 'Grass Roots Solution,'" *Milwaukee Community Journal,* pp. 1, 16.

2. Conant, *Slums and Suburbs,* pp. 2–5; Tyack, *The One Best System,* p. 11.

3. Virgil Blum, "Choice Education Programs Suppress Rights of Parents," *Arlington Catholic Herald,* March 9, 1989, Writings and Manuscript Series, box 1, Rev. Virgil C. Blum, S.J., Papers, Department of Special Collections and University Archives, Marquette University (hereafter Blum Papers). In 1995, lawmakers amended the Milwaukee Parental Choice Program to include religious schools, and with a favorable Wisconsin Supreme Court ruling, students began receiving vouchers to attend parochial schools beginning in 1998. Witte, "The Milwaukee Voucher Experiment," in Rury, ed., *Urban Education in the United States,* p. 312.

4. Letter from Blum to Father Provincial, November 4, 1954, and Letter from Blum to James M. O'Neill, March 19, 1952; both in Personal Correspondence Series, box 1, 1952–1954 folder, Blum Papers.

5. Letter from Blum to Father Provincial, November 4, 1954, box 1, 1952–1954 Folder; Letter from Blum to William McManus, National Catholic Welfare Conference, May 28, 1956, box 1 National Catholic Welfare Correspondence 1955–1956 folder; Letter from Blum to Father Provincial, March 17, 1955, box 1, 1955 folder; all in Blum Papers. Blum was referring to *West Virginia State Board of Education v. Barnette* 319 U.S. 624 (1943) and *Brown v. Board of Education* 347 U.S. 483 (1954).

6. Zimmerman, *Whose America?,* p. 138; Herberg, *Protestant-Catholic-Jew;* Blum, *Freedom of Choice in Education,* pp. 1, 67, 96.

7. Blum, *Freedom of Choice,* pp. 19–20. The two publications, in obscure outlets, are Friedman, "The Role of Government in Education," in Solo, ed., *Economics and the Public Interest;* and Thomson, "Educational News and Editorial Comments"; Blum, *Freedom of Choice,* pp. 78, 105. On the Cold War obsession with juvenile delinquency, see Gilbert, *A Cycle of Outrage.*

8. Patterson, *Grand Expectations;* Judt, *Ill Fares the Land;* Blum, "Educational Benefits without Enforced Conformity"; "The Educational Battleground," *Wall Street Journal,* August 25, 1959, p. 8.

9. Lassiter and Lewis, *The Moderates' Dilemma;* Save Our Schools, "Our Stake in New Orleans Schools," August 1, 1960, p. 10, in Matthew Sutherland Collection, box 230, folder 9, Louisiana and Special Collections, Earl K. Long Library, University of New Orleans; Leon Dure, "Dure Presents Plan to Meet State's Crisis

in Education," *The Daily Progress,* December 12, 1958, p. 4, box 3, Correspondence D–F folder, Blum Papers.

10. Letter to Blum from Dure, June 23, 1959, box 3, Correspondence D–F folder, Blum Papers; Letter to Dure from Blum, December 12, 1961, Citizens for Educational Freedom Series, box 1, September 1961–August 1962 folder, Blum Papers; Letter to Blum from Dure, December 21, 1961, box 3, Correspondence D–F folder, Blum Papers.

11. Letter to John Donovan from Blum, October 23, 1961, box 1, September 1961–August 1962 D folder; Letter to Blum from Donovan, May 12, 1961, box 1, September 1961–August 1962 folder; Letter to Blum from Dure, December 21, 1961, box 3, Correspondence D–F folder; all in Blum Papers. In the context of early 1960s Virginia, "desegregated" meant a public school that was so designated, but in reality whites boycotted, leaving blacks to attend without whites.

12. Ravitch, *The Troubled Crusade,* p. 28; Kaestle, "Federal Education Policy and the Changing National Polity," in Kaestle and Lodewick, eds., *To Educate a Nation,* p. 22; Letter from Blum to Monsignor William McManus, May 28, 1956, box 5, National Catholic Welfare Correspondence 1955–1956 folder, Blum Papers; Memo from George Reed to Monsignor Carroll, November 9, 1956, NCWC-OGS Collection, box 33, folder 10, National Catholic Welfare Conference Papers, The American Catholic History Research Center, Washington, D.C.; Letter from Blum to Monsignor William McManus, May 28, 1956, box 5, National Catholic Welfare Correspondence 1955–1956 folder, Blum Papers; Memo from George Reed to Monsignor Carroll, November 9, 1956, NCWC-OGS Collection, box 33, folder 10, National Catholic Welfare Conference Papers, The American Catholic History Research Center, Washington, D.C. Over the next 10 years, relations between Blum and NCWC thawed somewhat.

13. See, for example, letter from Karl Alter, Archbishop of Cincinnati to Blum October 8, 1968, box 6, September 1968 A–D folder, Blum Papers; "Brave Man," *St. Louis Register,* February 17, 1961; Letter from Milton Friedman to Blum, December 19, 1968, box 6, CEF Correspondence 1968 E–M folder, Blum Papers. This and a November 26, 1968, letter from Blum to Friedman was the only private exchange in the Blum Papers.

14. Letter from Blum to Archbishop Joseph Ritter, March 15, 1954, box 23, Archbishop Joseph Ritter folder, Blum Papers.

15. "Private-School-Aid Advocates Turn to Political Action," *CQ Fact Sheet on School Aid Pressure Groups,* December 5, 1962, box 28, CEF Background folder, Blum Papers; Letter to Mae and Martin Duggan from Blum, May 13, 1959; "Citizens for Educational Freedom Formed Here," *St. Louis Dispatch,* August 9, 1959; both in box 19, Duggan 1958–1972 folder, Blum Papers. Both Catholics, Mae Duggan was a mother of six children; Martin Duggan was a news editor at the *St. Louis Globe-Democrat.* Mae Duggan telephone interview

16. Letter to Blum from Mae and Martin Duggan, December 11, 1959, box 19, Duggan 1958–1972 folder, Blum Papers.

17. "Get the Picture, Congressman?" *Fair Share News,* June 1961, p. 1, box 26, Fair Share News 1959–1961 folder, Blum Papers. For desegregation in the Catholic

schools of St. Louis see Hodges, "Moral Persuasion and Episcopal Fiat." For de-segregation in the Kinloch district and the St. Louis public schools, see Monti, *A Semblance of Justice.*

18. Martin Duggan, "Mad Mutiny in Milwaukee," *Davenport Catholic Messenger,* October 28, 1965, box 19, Duggan 1958–1972 folder, Blum Papers. See also Jones, *The Selma of the North.*

19. Testimony of Mrs. Martin L. Duggan, National Secretary of Citizens for Educational Freedom, before the House Subcommittee on Labor, Washington, D.C., March 16, 1961, box 19, Duggan 1958–1972 folder, Blum Papers; *Engel v. Vitale* 370 U.S. 421 (1962) and *Abington v. Schempp* 374 U.S. 203 (1963); Eugene Kelly, "CEF Sparks a Revolution in Educational Choice, unknown publication, 1965, in box 28, CEF Background folder. By the late 1960s CEF had a "35 man board of Jews, Protestants, Catholics, and non-believers." Letter from E. E. Bleck to Evertt Cahill, October 19, 1970, box 6, September 1968 A–D folder, Blum Papers.

20. "Is CEF Truly Non-Denominational?" Fact Sheet, June 1, 1964, box 28, CEF Background folder, Blum Papers; Lacy Fosburgh, "Rabbis Favor Aid for All Schools, *New York Times,* January 28, 1971, Education Reform Subject Files, box 2, CEF Correspondence Agudath Israel of America folder, Blum Papers; Letter to Blum from Joseph Kaminetsky, Director, National Society for Hebrew Day School, June 16, 1967; Letter to Jeremiah Buckley, CEF from Rabbi Morris Sherer, Agudath Israel of America, January 3, 1967; both in box 2, CEF Correspondence Agudath Israel of America folder, Blum Papers; *Church and State,* March 1962, p. 5, box 27 Clippings 1961–1962 folder, Blum Papers. The *Congressional Quarterly* Fact Sheet of December 5, 1962 characterized CEF as "more militant that that of the National Catholic Welfare Conference." box 28, CEF Background folder, Blum Papers.

21. Letter from Mae Duggan to Blum, October 2, 1962; Letter from Blum to Mae Duggan, July 10, 1963; both in box 19, Duggan 1958–1972 folder, Blum Papers; Letter from William Consedine to Mr. Cody, January 6, 1972, box 3, Catholic Conference folder, Blum Papers.

22. Letter from Mae Duggan to Blum, August 31, 1965, box 19, Duggan 1958–1972 folder, Blum Papers.

23. Duggan to Blum, August 31, 1965; Letter to Mae and Martin Duggan from Blum, September 2, 1965; both in box 19, Duggan 1958–1972 folder, Blum Papers; *Committee for Public Education and Religious Liberty v. Nyquist,* 413 U.S. 756 (1973); Duggan telephone interview.

24. *Fair Share News,* May 1960, p.4, box 26, Fair Share News 1959–1962 folder, Blum Papers; Letter from Blum to Professor Chester Antieau, Georgetown University Law Center, June 14, 1963, box 1, September 1962–August 1963 A folder, Blum Papers; Letter from Blum to Roger Freeman, Hoover Institution, July 27, 1967, box 20, Roger Freeman folder, Blum Papers; Russell Shaw, "CEF: They'd Rather Fight," *The Sign,* November 1965, pp. 13–16, box 31, National Office 1964–1965 folder, Blum Papers; *Everson v. Board of Education* 330 U.S. 1 (1947).

25. Blum to Freeman, July 27, 1967, box 20, Roger Freeman folder; Assembly Substitute Amendment 1 to 1969 Assembly Bill 801; CEF Wisconsin March 6 1969 Meeting Minutes, box 34, CEF Wisconsin 1969 January–May folder, all in

Blum Papers. A similar bill was introduced in the Wisconsin Senate. "Greater Milwaukee Council of Churches Arguments in Opposition to Tuition Bill," box 34, CEF Wisconsin January–May folder; Letter from Blum to James Landry, January 9, 1970, box 35, CEF Wisconsin January–March folder; both in Blum Papers; E. Wentworth, "OEO to Give Vouchers in School Choice Test," *Washington Post,* May 23, 1970, p. A3; Dougherty, *More than One Struggle,* pp. 115–116.

26. See, for example, his essay "Little Catholic Support for Tuition Tax Credits," in Blum, *Quest for Religious Freedom,* p. 225.

27. Worthwhile Films, *Decade of Discontent;* Dahlk, "The Black Educational Reform Movement in Milwaukee"; Stolee, "The Milwaukee Desegregation Case," in Rury and Cassell, eds., *Seeds of Crisis.*

28. *Amos v. Board of School Directors,* 408 F. Fupp. 765 (1976); *Armstrong v. Board of School Directors,* 471 F. Supp. 800 (1979); *Armstrong v. Board of School Directors,* 616 F. 2d 305 (1980); and Bruce Murphy and John Pawasarat, "Why It Failed: School Desegregation Ten Years Later," *Milwaukee Magazine,* September 1986, p. 37.

29. Legislative Fiscal Bureau, "School Integration Aid," pp. 1–16.

30. Fuller, "The Impact of the Milwaukee Public School System's Desegregation Plan"; Harris, "Criteria for Evaluating School Desegregation in Milwaukee," pp. 423–435; Murphy and Pawasarat, "Why It Failed," pp. 34–50; and Legislative Fiscal Bureau, "School Integration Aid."

31. Stolee, "The Milwaukee Desegregation Case," p. 250; Fuller, "The Impact of the Milwaukee Public School System's Desegregation Plan," pp. 233–235.

32. Joanna Richardson, "The Unexpected Superintendent," *Education Week,* May 25, 1994, p. 22; Fuller, "The Impact of the Milwaukee Public School System's Desegregation Plan," pp. 236–239; Murphy and Pawasarat, "Why It Failed," p. 45.

33. Mikel Holt, "School District Proponents Take City to Task, Cite Errors," *Milwaukee Community Journal,* October 7, 1987, pp. 1, 6; Derrick Bell, "Harvard Professor Says Proposed District Plan on Sound Legal Footing," *Milwaukee Community Journal,* October 14, 1987, pp. 2, 6. Professor Bell later highlighted the Milwaukee proposal in an appendix to *And We Are Not Saved,* pp. 262–264. See also Bell, "The Case for a Separate Black School System," pp. 136–145.

34. Taki Raton, "Proposed School District Gets Shot in the Arm, Hundreds Express Support," *Milwaukee Community Journal,* October 21, 1987, pp. 1, 6.

35. Sharon Gibson, "Fuller: MPS Failing, Now Community's Turn," *Milwaukee Community Journal,* November 18, 1987, pp. 1, 5; Bell, "The Case for a Separate Black School System," pp. 141–145; Peter Murrell, Jr., "North Division Plan: 'Our Children Deserve Better,'" *Rethinking Schools* 2, no. 2, December–January 1988, pp. 1, 4, 15.

36. Raton, "Proposed School District Gets Shot in the Arm," pp. 1, 6; Mikel Holt, "Ministers Reject North Division Proposal," *Milwaukee Community Journal,* March 2, 1988, pp. 1, 9; Holt, "School District Proponents Take City to Task," pp. 1, 6; Fonfara Interview.

37. "Action on District Proposal Sends a Message to MPS," *Milwaukee Community Journal,* April 6, 1988, p. 2.

38. Commission on the Quality of Education in the Metropolitan Milwaukee Public Schools, *Better Public Schools,* 1986; Fonfara Interview.

39. Mikel Holt, "Governor Supports Williams' Bill," *Milwaukee Community Journal,* November 1, 1989, pp. 1, 7; Wisconsin Department of Public Instruction, *DPI Bulletin,* November 1990 and August 1991.

40. Rauch, "The Changing Status of Urban Catholic Parochial Schools," pp. 52–54. The five schools were located in a predominantly black residential area bounded by the Menomonee River to the south, Martin Luther King, Jr., Drive (formerly 3rd Street) to the east, Locust Street to the north, and 27th Street to the west.

41. Dahlk, "The Black Education Reform Movement in Milwaukee"; Flood Telephone Interview.

42. Dahlk, "Black Education Reform," p. 166. Participant Patrick Flood put things differently: the Archdiocese urged the subsidized schools to seek alternative means of funding or face closing. Flood Telephone Interview.

43. Dahlk, "Black Education Reform," p. 167. Moldinski and Zaret, *The Federation of Independent Community Schools,* pp. 15–16.

44. Dahlk, "Black Education Reform," pp. 166–168; Mikel Holt, Editor of the *Milwaukee Community Journal,* Telephone Interview; Flood Telephone Interview; Leslie Darnieder, Assistant Superintendent of Milwaukee Catholic Schools, Telephone Interview; Modlinski and Zaret, *The Federation of Independent Community Schools,* pp. 17–18.

45. Darnieder Telephone Interview.

46. Becker Interview; Flood Telephone Interview.

47. Dahlk, "Black Education Reform," pp. 174–177.

48. Ritsche and Watchke, "List of Bills," pp. 2–4; Flood Telephone Interview.

49. For discussions of conservative responses to civil rights and to the impact of civil rights on urban Catholics, see Perlstein, *Nixonland,* and Sanders, *The Education of an Urban Minority,* p. 223. Blum, "We Need a Martin Luther King," 1968, Writings and Manuscript Series, box 2, "We need a Martin Luther King" Manuscript folder, Blum Papers.

50. Blum, "Inner City Private Elementary Education," circa 1979, box 7, Inner City Private Elementary Education folder, Blum Papers.

51. Ritsche and Watchke, "List of Bills," pp. 2–4.

52. Dougherty, *More Than One Struggle,* p. 116; Holt, *Not Yet "Free at Last,"* pp. 25–26.

53. Holt, *Not Yet "Free at Last,"* p. 27–29; Dougherty, *More Than One Struggle,* p. 116.

54. Becker Interview.

55. Dahlk, "Black Education Reform," p. 177.

56. Holt, *Not Yet "Free at Last,"* pp. 170–179; Robinson, Principal of Harambee Community School, Interview; Holt Telephone Interview; Flood Telephone Interview.

57. Amy Stuart Wells, "Milwaukee Parents Get More Choice on Schools," *New York Times,* March 28, 1990; Morales Telephone Interview, United Community Center Executive Assistant.

58. Wing, Principal of Woodlands School, Telephone Interview; Becker Interview.

59. Robinson Interview; Wing Telephone Interview; Becker Interview; Mikel Holt, "Reps, Private Schools Eye Choice Bill," *Milwaukee Community Journal,* August 23, 1989, pp. 1, 9.

60. Dougherty, *More Than One Struggle,* p. 53; Eisinger, *Patterns of Interracial Politics* p. 118; Wong, *City Choices,* p. 85; Becker Interview; Holt Telephone Interview. In the late 1970s, the legislature reduced the MPS school board from 15 members, all elected at large, to 9 members, the majority of which are elected by district.

61. Dahlk, "Black Education Reform," p. 177; Richardson, "The Unexpected Superintendent," p. 22.

62. Ron Grossman, "Polly's Political Paradox," *Chicago Tribune,* August 20, 1993, p. 1.

63. Wisconsin Advisory Committee to the United States Commission on Civil Rights, "Impact of School Desegregation in Milwaukee," p. 11; Olson, "Choice Plan's Architect" p. 15.

64. "Lawmaker, MCJ Editor Call Choice 'Grass Roots Solution,'" *Milwaukee Community Journal,* pp. 1, 16.

65. Frank Aukofer, "Williams on Ascent with Ideas for Schools," *Milwaukee Journal,* May 13, 1990, p. 20; see also Michael Joyce, "Private Initiative to Expand Choice Follows Best Progressive Tradition," *Milwaukee Journal,* June 21, 1992.

66. Paul A. Gigot, "A Republican Who's Unafraid to Experiment," *Wall Street Journal,* April 26, 1991.

67. Ibid.

68. Debra Viadero, "Wisconsin 'Learnfare' Law Delayed to Ease Expected Enrollment Rush," *Education Week,* November 25, 1987, p. 1; Judith Davidoff, "Is 'Reformer' Thompson Robbing the Poor?" *Isthmus,* July 2–8, 1993, pp. 5–6; Steve Schultze, "Learnfare May Mean Turmoil for Schools," *Milwaukee Journal,* October 5, 1987, pp. A1, 17; Mike Mulvey, "Lawsuit Challenges Learnfare Program, *Milwaukee Sentinel,* November 7, 1989, pp. 1, 8. Learnfare was expensive to administer. The program transferred money from welfare recipients to social workers and administrators employed to monitor the program.

69. Matthew Stelly, "Polly Williams Outlines Goals for Upcoming Term," *Milwaukee Courier,* September 24, 1988, p. 1; Schultze, "Learnfare," p. A17.

70. Neil H. Shively, "WEAC Leader Raps School Choice Plan," *Milwaukee Sentinel,* March 1, 1989.

71. Marcia Coggs, "Coggs, Legislature Face Uphill Battle Against Governor Thompson's Vetoes," *Milwaukee Community Journal,* May 25, 1988, pp. 2, 6; Kenneth Lamke, "No Educational Innovation in this Legislative Session," *Milwaukee Sentinel,* August 11, 1989, p. 20.

72. See, for example, Lagemann, *The Politics of Knowledge.* For a general history of think tanks in the United States, see Smith, *The Idea Brokers. Foundation Reporter* (Washington, D.C.: Taft Group, 1994), pp. 145–157, 433–438, 1031–1034. See Also Internal Revenue Service Form 990, Return for Organization Exempt

from Income Tax, Filed by the Lynde and Harry Bradley Foundation for 1993. Hereafter Bradley IRS Return.

73. Bruce Murphy, "The Right Stuff," *Milwaukee Magazine* 13, no. 12, December 1988, pp. 54–55; 1988 Bradley Foundation IRS Return, p. 3. Another Milwaukee foundation, the Jane and Lloyd Pettit Foundation, established by Bradley heir Jane Pettit, also expanded after the Allen-Bradley sale; Quoted in Barbara Miner, "The Bradley Foundation and Milwaukee," *Rethinking Schools* 8, no. 3, Spring 1994, p. 18.

74. Bradley 1988 IRS Return, pp. 4–5; Quoted in Barbara Miner, "The Power and the Money: Bradley Foundation Bankrolls Conservative Agenda," *Rethinking Schools* 8, no. 3, p. 16; Wisconsin Policy Research Institute, Mission Statement; The following were published as Wisconsin Policy Research Institute Reports: George Mitchell, "The Rising Costs of the 'Chapter 220' Program in Wisconsin," October, 1988, vol. 1, no. 4; John Chubb and Terry Moe, "Educational Choice: Answers to the Most Frequently Asked Questions about Mediocrity in American Education and What Can Be Done About It," March, 1989, vol. 2, no. 3; George Mitchell, "An Evaluation of State-financed School Integration in Metropolitan Milwaukee," June, 1989, vol. 2, no. 5; Richard Bringham and John Heywood, "Evaluating Wisconsin's Teachers: it can be done," December, 1989, vol. 2, no. 9; Michael Fischer, "Fiscal Accountability in Milwaukee: Where does the Money Go?," September, 1990, vol. 3, no. 4; James Cibulka, "Restructuring Wisconsin's Educational System: How effective is the Department of Public Instruction?," September, 1991, vol. 4, no. 4; George Mitchell, "The Milwaukee Parental Choice Program," March, 1992, vol. 5, no. 5; Susan Mitchell, "Why MPS Doesn't Work: Barriers to Reform in the Milwaukee Public Schools," January, 1994, vol. 7, no. 1.

75. Gordon S. Black, "The Lack of Confidence in Public Education"pp. 1–27; Chubb and Moe, *Politics, Markets, and America's Schools.*

76. Bradley IRS 1988 Return; Clune and Witte, *Choice and Control in American Education,* vol. 2. The authors acknowledge that the original idea for the conference came from Michael Joyce and Robert Haveman, director of the La Follette Institute. The Joyce Foundation and the Spencer Foundation also contributed; Mikel Holt, "Black Parents, Activists Endorse Voucher Plan," *Milwaukee Community Journal,* March 9, 1988, pp. 1, 5, 12; "Parental Choice Idea is Worthy of Passage," *Milwaukee Community Journal,* March 9, 1988, p. 2.

77. See Bradley IRS Returns, 1990, 1992; Commission on Schools for the 21st Century, "A New Design for Education in Wisconsin," State of Wisconsin, December 1990, p. 45.

78. Harwell, Policy Director, Rep. Williams' Office, Interview, August 25, 1993.

79. Bradley IRS returns, 1988–1992. In 1988, Bradley granted $275,000 to the United Community Center, which took Bruce Guadelupe over in 1990; Bradley Foundation IRS Return, 1990. Bruce Guadelupe received $2,000 from the Bradley Foundation in 1990. DPI had not publicized the choice program to parents in Milwaukee. Jane Pettit received $600 million from the sale of Allen Bradley. Gurda, *The Bradley Legacy,* p. 152; Jane and Lloyd Pettit Foundation IRS Returns, 1988–1992.

80. Polly Williams discussed public support for Milwaukee's community schools with other legislators prior to 1988. Lobbyists for private schools, particularly the Wisconsin Association of Non-public Schools (a coalition of Catholic, Lutheran, Christian, and non-sectarian private schools), proposed vouchers and tuition tax credits for several years. Wisconsin Association of Non-Public Schools, Madison Wisconsin, Mimeographed; Harwell Interview; Richard Bradee, "Thompson Shift Causes Disappointment," *Milwaukee Sentinel,* January 11, 1989, pp. 1, 11; "Parental Choice Idea Worthy of Passage," *Milwaukee Community Journal,* March 9, 1988, p. 2.

81. Jeff Cole, "Governor to Revive Voucher Plan," *Milwaukee Sentinel,* May 3, 1988, pp. 1, 9; Mikel Holt, "Farrell Calls 'Parental Choice' Plan a Step in the Right Direction," *Milwaukee Community Journal,* April 19, 1989, pp. 1, 11; John Kole, Steve Schultze, and Patrick Jasperse, "Thompson would let Parents Choose Schools," *Milwaukee Journal,* January 10, 1989, p. 1; Grover, State School Superintendent, Interview.

82. Alves and Willie, "Choice, Decentralization and Desegregation: The Boston 'Controlled Choice' Plan," p. 21. Essentially, Controlled Choice is a public school, intra-district open-enrollment policy that also guarantees equal racial access to all district schools and programs.

83. Mikel Holt, "Group Eyes Third Black Board Member," *Milwaukee Community Journal,* November 2, 1988, p. 2; Bradee, "Thompson Shift Causes Disappointment," pp. 1, 11; Mikel Holt, "Williams Unveils New Region Plan," *Milwaukee Community Journal,* January 18, 1989, pp. 1, 12.

84. Kole, Schultze, and Jasperse, "Thompson would let Parents Choose Schools," p. 1; Minnesota was something of a pioneer in school choice reforms Among them: the state passed a private school tuition tax credit for parents in 1971. In the 1980s, Minnesota passed the nation's first state-wide open enroll-ment program and an options program for high school students to take university courses. Less than one percent of Minnesota students transferred between school districts. Mazzoni, "The Changing Politics of State Educational Policymaking."

85. Bradee, "Thompson Shift Causes Disappointment," pp. 1, 11.

86. Ibid; Holt, "Williams Unveils New Region Plan," pp. 1, 12; Thomas Mitchell, Jr., "Plan to Reorganize School District Detailed at Forum," *Milwaukee Community Journal,* April 19, 1989, p. 1.

87. Haselow, MPS Government Relations Coordinator, Telephone Interview; Bradee, "Thompson Shift," pp. 1, 11.

88. Neil Shively, "WEAC Leader Raps School Choice Plan," *Milwaukee Sentinel,* March 1, 1989, p. 1; Steve Schultze, "Thompson Proposal Slashed," *Milwaukee Journal,* April 19, 1989, pp. A1, 12; *Milwaukee Sentinel,* June 8, 1989.

89. Priscilla Ahlgren, "Bill Would Aid Private School Option," *Milwaukee Journal,* June 27, 1989; Mitchell, "Plan to Reorganize School District Detailed at Forum," p. 1.

90. Harwell Interview; Thomas Mitchell and Mikel Holt, "'Black Ribbon' Panel to Develop Busing Plan," *Milwaukee Community Journal,* June 12, 1989, pp. 1, 10.

91. Robinson Interview; Farrell, "School Choice and the Educational Oppor-tunities of African American Children," p. 533.

92. Lamke, "No Educational Innovation," p. 20; Priscilla Ahlgren, "Union Key in Defeating 'Choice' Plan," *Milwaukee Journal,* July 6, 1989, p. B1, 9; Mikel Holt, "Democrats Kill Parental Choice Legislation, *Milwaukee Community Journal,* July 5, 1989, pp. 1, 13.

93. Holt, "Democrats Kill Parental Choice Legislation," pp. 1, 13.

94. Mikel Holt, "Reps, Private Schools Eye Choice Bill, *Milwaukee Community Journal,* August 23, 1989, pp. 1, 9; William Snider, "Voucher System for 1000 Pupils Adopted in Wis.," *Education Week,* March 28, 1990, pp. 1, 14; Harwell Interview.

95. Mikel Holt, "MPS Hopes to Counter Williams' Parental Choice," *Milwaukee Community Journal,* October 18, 1989, pp. 1, 7; Kenneth Lamke, "Thompson Predicts Passage," *Milwaukee Sentinel,* October 27, 1989; "Governor Supports Williams' Choice Bill," *Milwaukee Community Journal,* November 1, 1989, pp. 1, 7.

96. Mikel Holt, "Hearing, Confab Could Pave Way for Education Options," *Milwaukee Community Journal,* January 17, 1990, pp. 1, 16; Mikel Holt, "Battlelines Being Drawn Over Choice Controversy," *Milwaukee Community Journal,* November 15, 1989, pp. 1, 9; Robert Peterkin, Letter to the Editor, *Milwaukee Community Journal,* November 8, 1989, p. 2; Haselow Telephone Interview.

97. Grover Interview; Steve Dold, DPI's Bureau of Policy and Budget Director, Interview; Steve Schultze, "State to be 1st to Offer School-Choice Program," *Milwaukee Journal,* March 23, 1990.

98. Harwell Interview; Fuller Interview; Gary George and Walter Farrell, "School Choice and African American Students: A Legislative View," *Journal of Negro Education* 59, no. 4, 1990, p. 524; Lynn Olson, "Milwaukee's Choice Program Enlists 391 Volunteers," *Education Week,* September 12, 1990, p. 15; Robinson Interview.

99. Mikel Holt, "Lawmakers bombarded with Support for Choice Proposal," *Milwaukee Community Journal,* February 28, 1990, pp. 1, 14.

100. Legislative history of Assembly Bill 601, p. 166. Not all Republicans and conservative Democrats supported the bill, however.

101. George and Farrell, "A Legislative View," p. 524; Bulletin of the Proceedings of the Wisconsin Legislature, 1989–1990 Session, at 1–141; Legislative history of Assembly Bill 601; 1989 Senate Bill 542, p. 68; Hawkins Hearning, "Field Hearing on Parental Choice," November 16, 1990, Serial No. 101–131, p. 7; William Snider, "Voucher System for 1000 Pupils Adopted in Wis.," *Education Week,* March 28, 1990, p. 1; Mikel Holt, "Board Director, Senator Endorse Choice Bill," *Milwaukee Community Journal,* February 21, 1990, pp. 1, 6.

102. David Umhoefer, "Council Can't Decide about School Choice Bill," *Milwaukee Journal,* March 21, 1990; "School Choice Plan to Effect [*sic*] 1000 Poor Children in City," *Milwaukee Sentinel,* March 23, 1990; Tommy G. Thompson, press release, April 27, 1990; Mikel Holt, "Federal, State officials Laud Choice Initiative at Community Celebration," *Milwaukee Community Journal,* May 16, 1990, pp. 1, 18; Kenneth Lamke, "Bush Appearance Works for Thompson," *Milwaukee Sentinel,* June 8, 1990, pp. 1, 13.

103. Priscilla Ahlgren, "School Choice Plan Transcends Roots," *Milwaukee Journal,* June 10, 1990, p. 20.

104. Matthew Stelly, "Rep. Williams' Persistence Pays Off!: Thompson Signs Parental Choice Bill," *Milwaukee Courier,* May 5, 1990, p. 1.

105. Marable, *Race, Reform, and Rebellion,* p. 98; Mikel Holt, "GOP Landslide Leaves Black Voters in Mud?," *Milwaukee Community Journal,* November 9, 1994, pp. 1, 12.

CHAPTER 5: THE CHURCH IN THE CITY

1. Anthony M. Pilla, Remarks at the State Legislative Breakfast, Columbus, Ohio, March 20, 1995, in Catholic Diocese—box 42, series 1.2, Bishop Pilla folder, George V. Voinovich Papers, Robert E. and Jean R. Mahn Center for Archives and Special Collections, Alden Library, Ohio University, Athens, Ohio (hereafter Voinovich Papers).

2. Bryk, Lee, and Holland, *Catholic Schools and the Common Good,* quotes on pp. 304, 305, and 341.

3. Coleman et al., *Equality of Educational Opportunity;* Jencks et al., *Inequality,* pp. 188–190; Carl, "Harold Washington and Chicago's Schools," p. 323.

4. Gabel, *Public Funds for Church and Private Schools,* p. 660; McAfee, *Religion, Race, and Reconstruction,* p. 177; Fraser, *Between Church and State,* p. 107; Gutowski, "Politics and Public Schools in Archbishop John Purcell's Ohio," pp. 170–179.

5. Leahy, "The Insurmountable Wall," p. 8; Letter from Bishop J. H. Albers to Virgil Blum, November 4, 1957, box 1, Sept. 1957-August 1958 A—L folder, Blum Papers; Gabel, *Public Funds,* pp. 670–671; Curtin, *Ohio Politics Almanac* 2nd ed., p. 70.

6. Gabel, *Public Funds,* pp. 672–673; Leahy, "The Insurmountable Wall," p. 139.

7. Russell Shaw, "CEF: They'd Rather Fight," *The Sign,* November 1965, p. 14; Letter from Archbishop Karl Alter to Blum, October 8, 1968, box 6, Sept. 1968 A–D folder, Blum Papers.

8. Caliguire, "A History of Cooperation between the Cleveland Public Schools and the Cleveland Catholic Diocesan Schools"; *Wolman v. Essex,* 342 F. Supp. 399 (1972); *Wolman v. Kosydar,* 353 F. Supp. 744 (1972); *Lemon v. Kurtzman,* 430 U.S. 602 (1971); Ohio Department of Education, "Funding for Non-public Schools."

9. Ohio Rev. Code Ann. § 3317.063; Ohio Rev. Code Ann. § 3317.06.

10. Peace, "Labor-Management Cooperation"; Barbara Byrd-Bennett Interview.

11. Tal Barak, "Cleveland Board Slashes $100 Million from Schools," *Education Week* 23, no. 41, June 23, 2004, p. 4; Catherine Gewitz, "Cleveland Budget Cuts Hurt Gains, Departing Schools Chief Laments," *Education Week* 25, no. 1, August 31, 2005, p. 10.

12. I use this term for the public schools. In 1997 the name changed to "The Cleveland Municipal School District," and in 2006 it changed again, to "The Cleveland Metropolitan School District." Beth Reinhard, "Cleveland: A Study in Crisis," *Education Week* 17, no. 17, January 8, 1998, p. 26; Tyack, *The One Best System,* p. 220.

13. Miggins, "Cleveland Public Schools," in Van Tassel and Grabowski, eds., *The Encyclopedia of Cleveland History,* p. 280; "Cleveland: A Study in Crisis," *Education Week,* January 8, 1998, pp. 26–28, 31; Office on School Monitoring and Community Relations Fact Sheet, n.d., mimeographed.

14. Phillip Richards, "Leaving the Folk: The Journey Out of a Cleveland Childhood," *Harper's Magazine,* October 1995, pp. 76–86; Cleveland Initiative for Education, "Redirecting Resources Through Changes in Building Utilization," 1994, p. 6, in Chris Carmody Education Series, box 54, untitled folder, Michael R. White Mayoral Papers; Ohio Legislative Service Commission, "Historical Revenues and Expenditures."

15. Cleveland Public Schools, *Vision 21,* pp. 11–16; Henderson, "Demography and Desegregation in the Cleveland Public Schools," p. 520.

16. Statistics from 2000 Census and *Reed v. Rhodes* 422 F. Supp. 708 (1976); Keating, *The Suburban Racial Dilemma.*

17. Phillips, *AlabamaNorth,* p. 159; *Mixon v. State of Ohio* 193 F.3d 389 (6th Cir. 1999); *Reed v. Rhodes* 422 F. Supp. 708; Moore, *Carl B. Stokes,* p. 29.

18. Moore, *Carl B. Stokes,* pp. 28–38; X, "The Ballot or the Bullet"; Robinson, *The Making of a Man,* pp. 70–79; Bellman, "Testimony of Mr. Richard Bellman, Attorney, U.S. Commission on Civil Rights," Hearing Before the United States Commission on Civil Rights, Hearing held in Cleveland, OH. Supt. of Documents, U.S. Government Printing Office, Washington, D.C., 1966, pp. 274–279; Green, *And They Called It Public School Education;* Campbell, "Cleveland: The Struggle for Stability," in Bernard, ed., *Snowbelt Cities,* pp. 109–136.

19. Office of School Monitoring and Community Relations, *Fact Sheet,* (Cleveland, 1985, in Author's possession); *Reed v. Rhodes* 455 F. Supp. 546 (1978); "Cleveland School Officials Jailed," *Education Week* 7, no. 7, September 7, 1981, p. 5; Saatcioglu and Carl, "The Discursive Turn in School Desegregation."

20. Cleveland Public Schools, *Vision 21;* Evelyn Theiss, "School Summit Meets," *Plain Dealer,* May 2, 1993, p. 11B; Evelyn Theiss, "District Seeks to Reduce Bussing," *Plain Dealer,* June 8, 1993, p. 1B.

21. C. Sheridan, "Reformers Forget the Classroom," *Plain Dealer,* February 23, 1997; P. M. Jones, "City Schools' 'Vision 21' Reform Plan Gets C Grade," *Plain Dealer,* February 1, 1995; Evelyn Theiss, "School Board Repeats Failed Reform Pattern," *Plain Dealer,* August 27, 1995; Saatcioglu, "Latent Conflict and Institutional Change."

22. Notably, in the 1980s desegregation was the principal policy innovation for the Cleveland Public Schools; there were no other reforms competing with school desegregation. In May 1978, the Court established the Office on School Monitoring & Community Relations, which tracked student outcomes by collecting reports from the School Board and by producing several of its own reviews. All reports were compiled into a "comprehensive report" in 1991. In addition, the Board kept yearly student records, containing demographic and academic data. Office on School Monitoring and Community Relations Report Pursuant to Order of July 10, 1990 in *Reed v. Rhodes.* Cleveland, OH: United States District Court, 1991. Northern District of Ohio, Eastern Division. Case No. C73–1300.

23. Boardman and Field, "Spatial mismatch and race differentials"; Wang and Minor, "Where the Jobs Are"; Chilton and Datesman, "Gender, Race, and Crime"; Chow and Coulton, "Was There a Social Transformation of Urban Neighborhoods in the 1980s?"

24. Wilson, *When Work Disappears;* Miggins, "Between Spires and Stacks," in Krumholz, Keating, and Perry, eds., *Cleveland: a Metropolitan Reader;* Astone and McLanahan, "Family Structure, Parental Practices and High School Completion"; McLoyd, Jayaratne, Ceballo, and Borquez, "Unemployment and Work Interruption."

25. G. Segall, "Speaking against Transfer: Residents Oppose Busing Needed for Cranwood Switch," *Plain Dealer* April 18, 1989, p. 4A; Bell, *Silent Covenants;* R. Rutti, "Students Need More Support, Tolliver Says," *Plain Dealer,* February 27, 1990 p. 4B.

26. *Reed v. Rhodes,* 869 F. Supp. 1274 (N.D. Ohio 1994); *Plain Dealer,* November 17, 1994, p. 1A; *Plain Dealer,* November 18, 1994, p. 1A; *Reed v. Rhodes* 934 F. Supp. 1533 (N.D. Ohio 1996); Krupansky, N.D. Ohio, March 3, 1995 Order; Rich and Chambers, "Cleveland: Takeovers and Makeovers Are Not the Same," in Henig and Rich, eds., *Mayors in the Middle.*

27. *Reed v. Rhodes* 934 F. Supp. 1533 (N.D. Ohio 1996); Cleveland Municipal School District News and Information, "Desegregation and Governance."

28. Mary Beth Lane and T. C. Brown, "Court Hears Pros, Cons of School Financing," *Plain Dealer,* September 11, 1996, pp. 1A, 10A; Ohio School Funding, "Background Information."

29. Gunther, *Inside U.S.A.;* Odenkirk, *Frank J. Lausche.*

30. HB 1242, *Bulletin,* 109th General Assembly of the State of Ohio, 1971–1972; HB 1466, *Bulletin,* 11th General Assembly of the State of Ohio, 1973–1974; HB 41, *Bulletin,* 111th General Assembly of the State of Ohio, 1975–1976; HB 825, *Bulletin,* 119th General Assembly of the State of Ohio, 1991–1992.

31. Wye, "At the Leading Edge," in Van Tassel and Graboswki, eds., *Cleveland: A Tradition of Reform,* p. 131; Campbell, "Cleveland," p. 117; Moore, *Carl B. Stokes,* pp. 38–39.

32. Nelson, "Cleveland: Evolution of Black Political Power," in Keating, Krumholz, and Perry, eds., *Cleveland: A Metropolitan Reader,* pp. 283–299; Stephen Koff, "Voinovich: Sometime Rebel and Full-time Policy Wonk," *Plain Dealer,* November 29, 2010, p. A6; Milton Coleman, "Blacks Help Elect Republicans in New Jersey, Cleveland," *Washington Post,* November 19, 1985, in Container 54, National Media Articles Folder, Voinovich Mayoral Papers.

33. Nelson, "Cleveland," pp. 283–299; Patrice M. Jones, "White Says It's Time for Change in Schools," *Plain Dealer,* November 13, 1994.

34. Remarks by George V. Voinovich on Education, Jerusalem, Israel, container 93, April 1980 folder, Voinovich Mayoral Papers; Joe Hallett, "'Education Governor' Under Fire," *Plain Dealer,* September 8, 1996, p. 4B; Letter to Voinovich from Robert Shanks, Director of National Association for Neighborhood Schools, March 6, 1980, container 2, NANS folder; Voinovich remarks to Greater Cleveland Roundtable, March 23, 1989, container 9, GCGA speeches folder; all in Voinovich Mayoral Papers.

35. Letter from Voinovich to Supt. of Public Instruction Franklin Webster, March 1, 1989, container 5, Bd. Of Education—Perk, Ralph Jr. folder; Remarks at Central Middle School, Sept. 12, 1988, container 93, Sept. 1988 folder; George Voinovich Knights of Columbus Speech, June 10, 1989, container 95, June 1989 Folder; all in Voinovich Mayoral Papers.

36. "Ohio Governor Mulls Plan for Cleveland Takeover," *Education Week* 10, no. 39, June 19, 1991, p. 25; Peter Schmidt, "Cleveland Elections Are Seen as Pivotal for Schools' Future," *Education Week* 11, no. 8, pp. 1, 18; Peter Schmidt, "Atlanta Incumbents Hold On; Mayor's Slate Wins in Cleveland," *Education Week* 13, no. 10, November 10, 1993, p. 5; Alison Grant, "White Tells City Club Teachers Must Agree to Change Work Rules," *Plain Dealer*, August 22, 1996, p. 1A.

37. Chris Carmody to White, March 2, 1992, box 54, Weekly Reports folder; Letter from White to Richard Boyd, February 1, 1996, box 1X, Cleveland City Schools folder, Governor Voinovich Papers; Triad Research Group, "A Survey of Voter Attitudes Towards an Operating Levy for the Cleveland Public Schools," Cleveland, August 1996, in box 191, Cleveland Studies on Governance folder; both in Education Series, White Mayoral Papers; Alison Grant, "White Open to School Takeover," *Plain Dealer*, September 12, 1995, pp. 1B, 10B.

38. Laura Lee, "Parents Should Choose Schools, Legislator Says," *Plain Dealer*, November 13, 1991; Jones, "White Says It's Time for Change in Schools," *Plain Dealer*, November 13, 1994.

39. Fannie Lewis Interview; Peter Zicari, "Outspoken, Revered Councilwoman Fannie Lewis Dies," *Plain Dealer*, August 11, 2008.

40. Lewis Interview; "Issue of School Choice," *Call and Post*, December 5, 1991, p. 4A; "The Voucher Experiment," *Call and Post*, July 13, 1995, p. 4A.

41. Lewis Interview; Scott Stephens, "Lewis Will Push for School Vouchers," *Plain Dealer*, December 14, 1994; Laura Lee, "Parents Should Choose Schools, Legislator Says," *Plain Dealer*, November 13, 1991; Scott Stephens, "Storming the Statehouse," *Plain Dealer*, February 1, 1995. Indeed, reporting in the *Plain Dealer* (the major daily) and the *Call and Post* (an African American weekly) in 1994 and 1995 implied that Lewis, rather than Voinovich, spearheaded the voucher program for Cleveland. Whether Lewis's convoy of Cleveland parents and children helped persuade state lawmakers to vote for vouchers is debatable. According to one insider, state representatives and senators are rarely persuaded by lobbying from the grass roots. Boas Interview (legislative aide to State Rep. C. J. Prentiss).

42. Bositis, "The Politics of School Choice," in Salisbury and Lartigue, Eds., *Educational Freedom in Urban America*, p. 190; Sweeney Interview.

43. Sweeney Interview; H. B. No. 182, 110th General Assembly, Regular Session, 1973–1974; H. B. No. 635, 119th General Assembly, Regular Session, 1991–1992.

44. Bodwell, "Grassroots, Inc.," pp. 48–54.

45. Pilla, "The Church in the City," pp. 2–4; Patrick Hyland, "Bishop Pilla Seeking Renewed Commitment to Needs of Cities," *Catholic Universe Bulletin*, December 3, 1993, p. 2.

46. Pilla, "The Church in the City," p. 4; The Church in the City Task Force, "A Brief Summary of the Implementation Plan," mimeographed, n.d.; Jennifer A.

Webb, "Bishop Praises State for Extending Voucher Program," *Catholic Universe Bulletin,* July 11, 1997, p. 1.

47. Barbara Ballenger, "Hopes Fading for Quick Answer on Ohio's Education Voucher Proposal," *Catholic Universe Bulletin,* December 3, 1993, p. 2; Letter from Voinovich to Pilla, May 23, 1995, box 42, Bishop Pilla folder, Governor Voinovich Papers.

48. Letter from Voinovich to Pilla, April 18, 1991; Letter from Pilla to Voinovich, April 29, 1991, box 42, Bishop Pilla folder, both in Governor Voinovich Papers; Patrick Hyland, "Catholic Schools Score Well on Proficiency Test," *Catholic Universe Bulletin,* June 2, 1995, p. 1; "Letters," *Catholic Universe Bulletin,* January 14, 1 994, p. 4.

49. The Catholic Diocese of Cleveland, "Examples of Church in the City," n.d., in handouts from The Church in the City National Symposium, The Temple, University Circle, April 20, 1998; Letter from Donald Grace, Director of Development, Diocese of Cleveland, to Voinovich, December 11, 1992, enclosures, box 47, Education—Choice Committee folder; Letter from Paul Schloemer (Director of Inner-City School Fund and CEO of Parker Hannifin) to George Voinovich, January 7, 1992, box 46, Education folder, Governor Voinovich Papers.

50. "Ohio Governor Mulls Plan for Cleveland Takeover," *Education Week* 10, no. 39, June 19, 1991, p. 25.

51. Letter from Mike DeWine to Voinovich, January 23, 1992, box 46, Education folder,; Governor's Address to Great Lakes Regional Conference on Education, July 26, 1991, box 46, Education folder, Governor Voinovich Papers.

52. "Fact Sheet," Governor's Education Management Council; National Governor's Association, "Business Involvement in Ohio (In Brief)," August 1993; Memo from Jean Droste to Tim Cosgrove, March 14, 1991; all in box 1P, GEM Council folder; "Governor Voinovich's Thoughts Regarding What the Ohio Education Improvement Steering Committee Should Be Doing," October 27, 1993, box 46, Education folder; all in Governor Voinovich Papers; Banham, "Building a Stronger Partnership," p. 5.

53. Governor's Talking Points, GEM Council Meeting, August 12, 1993; State of Ohio, "Education for Results Reform Package," n.d., box 1P, GEM Council folder; Memo from Voinovich to Sanders, January 4, 1993, box 46, education folder; all in Governor Voinovich Papers.

54. Memo from Sanders to Joe Gorman and other business leaders, December 24, 1992; Letter from Ron Marec to Voinovich and Sanders, March 12, 1992, box 46, Education folder; "Choice—A Business Roundtable Position," faxed October 18, 1991, Governor Voinovich Papers; Letter from Voinovich to Tom Mooney, President of the Cincinnati Federation of Teachers, March 25, 1992, box 47, Education Choice folder, Governor Voinovich Papers; Memo from Janet Durfee-Hidalgo to Jean Droste, October 18, 1991; Letter from Voinovich to Wehling, March 26, 1992; both in box 1P, Business Roundtable folder, Governor Voinovich Papers.

55. Memo from Voinovich to Droste, April 30, 1992, box 47, Education Choice folder; Letter from Voinovich to Pilarczyk, June 14, 1991, box 42, Catholic—Pilarczyk

folder; Letter from Pilarczyk to Voinovich, July 3, 1991, box 47, Education Choice folder; Letter from Schloemer to Voinovich, March 6, 1992, box 49, Education Reform folder; Letter from Voinovich to Wehling, March 26, 1992, box 47, Education Choice folder, all in Governor Voinovich Papers.

56. Glenn Gamboa, Bob Paynter, and Andrew Zajac, "Big Man in Akron," *Akron Beacon Journal,* March 31, 1996; Glenn Gamboa, Bob Paynter, and Andrew Zajac, "Going Public," *Akron Beacon Journal,* April 1, 1996; Glenn Gamboa, Bob Paynter, and Andrew Zajac, "Shaky Footing on Home Ground," *Akron Beacon Journal,* April 2, 1996; Doug Oplinger and Dennis J. Willard, "Voinovich Distances Himself from Any Deal," *Akron Beacon Journal,* December 13, 1999.

57. Brennan Interview; Gamboa, Paynter, and Zajac, "Going Public."

58. Brennan Interview; Gamboa, Paynter, and Zajac, "Going Public"; Brennan, *Victory for Kids,* p. 51; Jerry Pockar, "School Choice Tops Brennan's List," *Catholic Universe Bulletin,* February 28, 1992, p. 9.

59. Letter from Brennan to Droste, September 8, 1992, box 47, Education Choice folder, Governor Voinovich Papers; see also Saltman, *The Edison Schools.*

60. Gamboa, Paynter, and Zajac, "Shaky Footing on Home Ground," April 2, 1996, *Akron Beacon Journal;* Brennan Interview.

61. *Mueller v. Allen,* 463 U.S., 388 (1983); L. Nusbaum, "Review of Ohio Citizen Attitudes Toward Tuition Tax Credits as an Education Reform," Division of Research and Communications, Ohio Department of Education, December 10, 1991; Memo from Sanders to Voinovich, December 11, 1991; both in box 49, Education Reform folder, Governor Voinovich Papers.

62. Memo from Voinovich to Droste, April 30, 1992, box 47, Education Choice folder, Governor Voinovich Papers; Center for Choice in Education, U.S. Department of Education, July 8, 1992, box 47, Education—GEM Council folder, Governor Voinovich Papers; Brennan, *Victory for Kids,* p. 148; A Bill to amend section 3301.0711 and to enact sections 3313.974 to 3313.9710 of the Revised Code to establish a local option private school scholarship program in public school districts, January 3, 1993, box 47, Education Choice folder, Governor Voinovich Papers.

63. Fred McGunagle, "Schools 'Choice'—a Hot Potato," *Chronicle Telegram,* January 11, 1993, box 47, Education Choice folder, Governor Voinovich Papers; Brennan, *Victory for Kids,* p. 33; Letter from Pilarczyk to Voinovich, March 17, 1993, box 42, Bishop Pilarczyk folder, Governor Voinovich Papers. In 1995, the Summit County Board of Education, in Brennan's home county, passed a resolution in favor of vouchers, the only school board in Ohio to do so.

64. Letter from Pilarczyk to Voinovich, March 21, 1994; Memo from Greg Browning, Budget Director, to Voinovich, November 15, 1994; Letter from Timothy Luckhaupt to Thomas Needles, December 29, 1994; all in box 1KK, Non-public—Catholic Conference folder, Governor Voinovich Papers. See also Doug Oplinger and Dennis Willard, "Voucher System Falls Far Short of Goals," *Akron Beacon Journal,* December 14, 1999.

65. "Republican Contract with America," 1994; Brennan, *Victory for Kids,* p. 73; Gamboa, Baynter, Zajac, "Shaky Footing on Home Ground."

66. Fox Interview; Fox, "Education Reform that Makes a Difference for Children"; John Kiesewetter, "Embattled Fox's Foes Want to See Him Hit the Highway," *Cincinnati Enquirer,* June 14, 2004.

67. Fox Interview; Peter Schmidt, "Cleveland Eyes Layoffs, Reform-Plan Cuts to Balance Budget," *Education Week* 13, no. 37, June 8, 1994, p. 3.

68. Fox Interview; Letters from Luckhaupt to Pastors and Principals, February 2, 1995, in box 1KK, Non-public—Catholic Conference folder, Governor Voinovich Papers.

69. Brennan, *Victory for Kids,* p. 22; Fox Interview; Janet O'Donnell, "Ohio's School Voucher Debate Alive Despite Opposition," *Catholic Universe,* June 2, 1995, pp. 1–4; Drew Lindsay, "Wisconsin, Ohio Back Vouchers for Religious Schools," *Education Week* 14, no. 40, July 12, 1995.

70. Ohio Revised Code, Sections 3313.974–3313.979; Am. Sub. H. B. No. 117, section 45.05, p. 872. See also the pamphlet, "The Cleveland Scholarship and Tutoring Program: A Chance to Choose Your Child's School," Ohio Department of Education, November 1995, in Author's possession.

71. Letter from Pilarczyk, Pilla, and others to Voinovich, June 26, 1995; Thomas Suddes, "Few Merits to Choice Plan," *Plain Dealer,* July 18, 1995; George V. Voinovich, "Scholarship Plan Is Working in Ohio," Letter to the Editor, *Toledo Blade,* September 29, 1996.

72. George V. Voinovich, "State of the State Address," February 13, 1996, p. 13, box 65, State of the State folder, Governor Voinovich Papers.

73. Memo from Goff to Voinovich, July 20, 1995, box 94, Cleveland Scholarship Program folder, Governor Voinovich Papers; Brennan, *Victory for Kids,* pp. 89–91; Schiller, "Cleveland School Vouchers: Where the Students Come From."

74. Brennan, *Victory for Kids,* p. 94; Hanauer, "Cleveland School Vouchers: Where the Students Go."

75. Owen Interview; Urban Community School 2003–2004 Annual Report, in Author's possession.

CHAPTER 6: FIXING SCHOOL VOUCHERS

1. Darcia Harris Bowman, "Voucher Advocates Want Court to Rehear Case," *Education Week,* October 10, 2001, pp. 3–5; Richard A. DeColibus, Letter to the Editor, *Cleveland Plain Dealer,* January 26, 1996; *Davis v. Grover,* 480 N.W.2d (1992), p. 477, quoted in Bolick, *Voucher Wars,* p. 42. The first three quotes are taken from Judge James Ryan's dissent in *Simmons-Harris v. Zelman* 2000.

2. "State School Chief Hoping for Lawsuit over 'Choice' Issue," *Lacrosse Tribune,* May 8, 1990; Rogers Worthington, "Public Funding for Private Schools Faces Legal Test," *Chicago Tribune,* July 22, 1990, pp. 1, 8; "Where We Stand on Milwaukee Parental Choice," *The Professional,* September 1990; Grover Interview. The law designated the Department of Public Instruction with authority to oversee the program.

3. Herbert J. Grover, Superintendent of Public Instruction, Notice of School's Intent to Participate in the Milwaukee Parental Choice Program, May 29, 1990;

"Schools Hold Their Ground on Choice Plan," *Milwaukee Journal,* June 18, 1990; "Parents Sue Grover on 'Choice' Plan," *Milwaukee Sentinel,* June 26, 1990, p. 5; Larry Harwell Interview; Bolick, *Voucher Wars.* The Bradley foundation donated $350,000 to Landmark 1990–1992.

4. Steven Walters and Debby Lynn Davis, "Supreme Court Dismisses 'Choice' Plan Suit," *Milwaukee Sentinel,* June 27, 1990; Neil Shively and Amy Rinard, "Grover Seeks Halt to Choice Program," *Milwaukee Sentinel,* June 11, 1990, pp. 1, 9; Julie Underwood Interview. A University of Wisconsin law professor, Underwood helped prepare Grover's Amicus brief.

5. Wisconsin Constitution, article IV, Section 18; Wisconsin Constitution, Article X, Section 3; Underwood Interview, Steve Dold Interview. Dold was Policy and Budget Director, Wisconsin Department of Public Instruction.

6. "Blocking the Schoolhouse Door," *Wall Street Journal,* June 27, 1994; "Quayle Praises Choice Plan, Raps 'Socialized' Schooling," *Milwaukee Sentinel,* September 19, 1990; Priscilla Ahlgren, "Cavazos Takes a Look at Choice," *Milwaukee Journal,* September 24, 1990; Steven Walters and Gloria Howe, "Grover Raps Thompson, Bush for Backing Choice," *Milwaukee Sentinel,* August 8, 1990, pp. 1, 7; Pamela Cotant, "Grover Defends Opposition to School Choice," *Capital Times,* June 28, 1990, pp. 1, 11.

7. Steingass Ruling, Dane County Circuit Court, State of Wisconsin, August 6, 1990, p. 2; "Choice Plan Opponents File Appeal," *Milwaukee Journal,* August 11, 1990, p. A7; Wisconsin Court of Appeals, District IV, November 13, 1990, p. 4; Bolick, "The Wisconsin Supreme Court's Decision," p. 25; *Davis v. Grover,* 166 Wis. 2d 501 (1992) at 533.

8. 1993 Wisconsin Act 16.

9. Thomas Grogan, "In the Matter of the Eligibility of Messmer High School for Participation in the Milwaukee Parental Choice Program, State of Wisconsin, 1993," pp. 28–29; Bradley IRS Return, 1992.

10. Bolick, *Voucher Wars,* pp. 67–68; Witte, *The Market Approach to Education,* p. 168; 1995 Wisconsin Act 27, §§ 4002–4009.

11. Witte, *The Market Approach to Education,* pp. 168, 178; Ritsche, "Milwaukee School Choice Voucher Program," p. 2.

12. Witte, *The Market Approach to Education,* p. 178; Bob Davis, "Class Warfare: Dueling Professors Have Milwaukee Dazed over School Vouchers—Studies on Private Education Result in a Public Spat About Varied Conclusions—Candidates Debate the Point," *Wall Street Journal,* October 11, 1996, p. A1, quoted in Henig, *Spin Cycle,* p. 62; Bolick, *Voucher Wars,* p. 101; Kava, "Milwaukee Parental Choice Program," p. 9; *Jackson v. Benson,* 570 N.W.2d 407 (Ct.App.1997).

13. *Jackson v. Benson,* 578 N.W.2d 602 (Wis. 1998), at 611, 619; "A Timeline of the Milwaukee Parental Choice Program," SchoolChoiceWI.org; *Lemon v. Kurtzman* 403 U.S. 602 (1971).

14. *Gatton v. Goff* Complaint, Case No. 96CVH-01–193, January 10, 1996; *Simmons-Harris v. Goff* Complaint, Case No. 96CVH-01–721, January 31, 1996; *Gatton v. Goff* Decision, Case No. 96CVH-01–193, July 31, 1996; Bodwell, "Grassroots, Inc.," p. 105, Bolick, *Voucher Wars,* p. 91.

15. *Gatton v. Goff,* July 31, 1996, pp. 27, 29, 33, 36, 38.

16. *Simmons-Harris v. Goff,* Case No. 96APE08–982, May 1, 1997, pp. 11–12, 15, 18, 28; Bolick, *Voucher Wars,* p. 115.

17. Ohio Department of Education, "2009–2010 Ohio Community Schools Annual Report"; Brennan, *Victory for Kids,* p. 115; Ohio Department of Education, "Table of School Options in Ohio"; Hanauer, "Cleveland School Vouchers." In 2009 Ohio had 324 charter schools that enrolled 87,824 students, compared to 39 participating voucher schools enrolling 5,388 students.

18. *Simmons-Harris v. Goff* 711 N.E.2d 203 (Ohio 1999) at 208; *Agostini v. Felton* 521 US 203 (1997) at 230; Bolick, *Voucher Wars,* p. 138. The Wisconsin Supreme Court also emphasized *Agostini* in its 1997 decision upholding MPCP.

19. Bolick, *Voucher Wars,* p. 140–143; Bodwell, "Grassroots, Inc.," p. 139; *Simmons-Harris v. Zelman,* 54 F. Supp. 2d 725 (N.D. Ohio 1999). Ohio State Superintendent of Public Instruction Susan Tave Zelman succeeded John Goff.

20. Bodwell, "Grassroots, Inc.," p. 150; Memo from Tom Needles to Governor Voinovich, January 21, 1998, in *Zelman v. Simmons-Harris,* in Lodging by Amicus Curiae, Ohio Association for Public Education and Religious Liberty, in Support of Affirmance for Respondents, Nos. 00–001777, 00–1779.

21. *Simmons-Harris v. Zelman* 234 F. 3d 945 (2000) at 953, 959, 964, 973; Bolick, *Voucher Wars,* p. 158.

22. Bolick, *Voucher Wars,* p. 159; Toobin, *The Nine,* p. 272; Bodwell, "Grassroots, Inc.," pp. 251–252, 305–308. Interestingly, Toobin did not cover the *Zelman* decision in his otherwise comprehensive expose of the Supreme Court.

23. *Zelman v. Simmons-Harris* 536 U.S. 639 (2002), at 648, 652, 655, 657, and 661.

24. *Zelman v. Simmons-Harris* 536 U.S. 639 (2002), at 671, 673, and 694. See also *Everson v. Board of Ed. of Ewing* 330 U.S. 1 (1947).

25. Harvey, *The New Imperialism,* p. 115, quoted in Arrighi, *Adam Smith in Beijing,* p. 216.

26. Gerstle, *American Crucible.*

27. Micklethwait and Wooldridge, *The Right Nation,* p. 14.

28. For examples of voucher programs in the United States, see National School Boards Association, "Voucher Strategy Center" (the National School Boards Association opposes vouchers) and Foundation for Educational Choice, "School Choice Programs" (Founded by Milton and Rose Friedman, this organization favors school vouchers).

29. Conway, Goodell, and Carl, "Educational Reform in the USA," Griffin, ed., *Education in Transition;* Center for Education Reform, "National Charter School and Enrollment Statistics, 2010"; Wisconsin Department of Public Instruction, "MPCP Facts and Figures for 2010–2011"; Ohio Department of Education, "Table of Ohio's School Options."

30. See, for example, Rothstein, *Class and Schools.*

BIBLIOGRAPHY

MANUSCRIPT COLLECTIONS

Blum, Reverend Virgil C.S.J. Papers. Department of Special Collections and University Archives, Marquette University, Milwaukee, Wisconsin.

Louisiana Collection, New Orleans Public Library. New Orleans, Louisiana.

Morrison, De Lesseps S. Collection. New Orleans Public Library. New Orleans, Louisiana.

NAACP Orleans Branch Collection. Earl K. Long Library, University of New Orleans, New Orleans, Louisiana.

National Catholic Welfare Conference Papers, American Catholic History Research Center, Washington, D.C.

New Hampshire Education Voucher Project Records. New Hampshire State Records and Archives, Concord, New Hampshire.

New Hampshire Department of Education Records. Concord, New Hampshire.

Office of Economic Opportunity Records, Lyndon Baines Johnson Library and Museum, Austin, Texas.

Orleans Parish School Board Collection. Earl K. Long Library, University of New Orleans.

Perez, Leander H. Papers. Louisiana Collection. New Orleans Public Library. New Orleans, Louisiana.

Rainach, William. Papers. Archives and Special Collections. Noel Memorial Library, Louisiana State University-Shreveport.

Rogers-Stevens Oral History Collection. Amistad Research Center. Tulane University, New Orleans, Louisiana.

Save Our Schools Collection. Amistad Research Center, Tulane University, New Orleans, Louisiana.

Thomson, Governor Meldrim. Papers. NH State Records and Archives, Concord, New Hampshire.

Tureaud, Alexander Pierre. Papers. Amistad Research Center, New Orleans, Louisiana.

Voinovich, George V. Papers. Robert E. and Jean R. Mahn Center for Archives and Special Collections. Alden Library, Ohio University. Athens, Ohio.

Voinovich, George V. Mayoral Papers. Western Reserve Historical Society. Cleveland, Ohio.

White, Michael R. Mayoral Papers, Western Reserve Historical Society, Cleveland, Ohio.

INTERVIEWS BY THE AUTHOR

Becker, Dismas. Madison, Wisconsin. March 15, 1995.

Boas, George. Columbus, Ohio. March 7, 2003.

Brennan, David. Interview with Author and Gerald Read. Akron, Ohio. October 27, 1997.

Byrd-Bennett, Barbara. Cleveland, Ohio. December 3, 2002.

Darnieder, Leslie. Telephone Interview. November 2, 1994.

Dold, Steve. Madison, Wisconsin. July 13, 1993.

Doyle, Denis P. Telephone Interview. August 11, 2006.

Duggan, Mae. Telephone Interview. August 10, 2010.

Flood, Patrick. Telephone Interview. March 2, 1995.

Fonfara, Tom. Madison, Wisconsin. July 27, 1993.

Fox, Michael A. Fairfield, Ohio, November 10, 2005.

Friedman, Milton. Telephone Interview. December 2, 2005.

Fuller, Howard. Milwaukee, Wisconsin. June 7, 1994.

Grover, Herbert. Madison, Wisconsin. August 9, 1993.

Harwell, Larry. Milwaukee, Wisconsin. August 25, 1993.

Haselow, Douglas. Telephone Interview. May 29, 1994.

Holt, Mikel. Telephone Interview. April 22, 1994.

Jencks, Christopher. Telephone Interview. February 12, 2007.

Lewis, Fannie. Cleveland, Ohio. December 6, 2005.

Morales, Sara. Telephone Interview. November 14, 1994.

Owen, Sr. Martha. Cleveland, Ohio. October 7, 2005.

Phillips, Howard. Telephone Interview. May 1, 2007.

Robinson, Sr. Callista, Milwaukee, Wisconsin. May 16, 1995.

Sweeney, Patrick. Cleveland, Ohio. October 31, 2005.

Underwood, Julie. Madison, Wisconsin, July 6, 1993.

Wing, Susan. Telephone Interview. October 14, 1994.

OTHER INTERVIEWS

Kane, Pearl Rock. *An Interview with Milton Friedman on Education.* Occasional Paper No. 67. National Center for the Study of Privatization in Education. Teachers College, Columbia University, New York, November, 2002.

Perez, Leander Interview on Working Press, WYES, June 13, 1961, Save Our Schools Papers.

Rainach, William, in Humphreys, Hubert. Interviews. Louisiana State University Oral History Collection. Noel Memorial Library, Louisiana State University-Shreveport.

Singlemann, George, Interview by Glen Jeansonne, March 15, 1973, Leander Perez Collection, Earl K. Long Library, Louisiana State University-Shreveport.

Singlemann, George, and Cullen Vetter, November 15, 1978, Rogers-Stevens Oral History Collection, Amistad Research Center.

Wisdom, Betty, November 17, 1978, Rogers-Stevens Oral History Collection, Amistad Research Center.

NEWSPAPERS AND MAGAZINES

Akron Beacon Journal
Call and Post
Capital Times
Catholic Universe Bulletin
Chicago Tribune
Chronicle Telegram
Cincinnati Enquirer
Concord Monitor
Education Week
Harper's Magazine
Isthmus
Lacrosse Tribune
Manchester Union Leader
Milwaukee Community Journal
Milwaukee Journal
Milwaukee Magazine
Milwaukee Sentinel
New York Times
Plain Dealer
The Professional
The Sign
Southern School News
States-Item
Times-Picayune
Toledo Blade
U.S. News and World Report
Wall Street Journal
Washington Post

COURT CASES

Aaron v. Cook, Civ. Act.3923 (N.D. Ga. May 16, 1956).
Agostini v. Felton, 521 US 203 (1997).

Americans United for Separation of Church and State v. Paire, 359 F. Supp. 505 (1973).

Amos v. Board of School Directors, 408 F. Fupp. 765 (1976).

Armstrong v. Board of School Directors, 471 F. Supp. 800 (1979).

Armstrong v. Board of School Directors, 616 F. 2d 305 (1980).

Bush v. Orleans Parish School Board, 138 F. Supp. (1956).

Committee for Public Education and Religious Liberty v. Nyquist, 413 U.S. 756 (1973).

Davis v. Grover, 166 Wis. 2d 501 (1992) at 533.

Davis v. Grover, 480 N.W.2d (1992).

Davis v. Grover. Decision and Order, Case No. 90 CV 2576, Circuit Court Branch 8, Dane Country, Wisconsin, August 6, 1990.

Davis v. Grover. Wisconsin Court of Appeals. District IV. November 13, 1990.

DeRolph v. State, 91 Ohio St. 3d 1274 (2001).

Everson v. Board of Education, 330 U.S. 1 (1947).

Gatton v. Goff Complaint, Case No. 96CVH-01–193 (January 10, 1996).

Gatton v. Goff Decision, Case No. 96CVH-01–193 (July 31, 1996.)

Green v. School Board of New Kent County, 391 U.S. 430 (1968).

Jackson v. Benson, 570 N.W.2d 407 (Ct.App.1997).

Lemon v. Kurtzman, 403 U.S. 602 (1971).

Mixon v. State of Ohio, 193 F.3d 389 (6th Cir. 1999).

Mueller v. Allen, 463 U.S., 388 (1983).

Orleans Parish School Board v. Bush, 365 U.S. 569 (1961).

Poindexter v. Louisiana Financial Assistance Commission, 275 F. Supp. 833 (1967).

Poindexter v. Louisiana Financial Assistance Commission, 296 F. Supp. 686 (1968).

Reed v. Rhodes, 422 F. Supp. 708 (1976).

Reed v. Rhodes, 455 F. Supp. 546 (1978).

Reed v. Rhodes, 869 F. Supp. 1274 (N.D. Ohio 1994).

Reed v. Rhodes, 934 F. Supp. 1533 (N.D. Ohio 1996).

Reed v. Rhodes. Cleveland, OH: United States District Court, 1991. Northern District of Ohio, Eastern Division. Case No. C73–1300.

Sloan v. Lemon 413 U.S. 825 (1973).

Simmons-Harris v. Goff, Complaint. Case No. 96CVH-01–721 (January 31, 1996).

Simmons-Harris v. Goff, Case No. 96APE08–982 (May 1, 1997).

Simmons-Harris v. Goff, 711 N.E.2d 203 (Ohio 1999).

Simmons-Harris v. Zelman, 54 F. Supp. 2d 725 (N. D. Ohio 1999).

Simmons-Harris v. Zelman, 234 F. 3d 945 (2000).

Wolman v. Essex, 342 F. Supp. 399 (1972).

Wolman v. Kosydar, 353 F. Supp. 744 (1972).

Zelman v. Simmons-Harris, 536 U.S. 639 (2002).

GOVERNMENT DOCUMENTS

1989 Senate Bill 542. State of Wisconsin.

1993 Wisconsin Act 16.

1995 Wisconsin Act 27, §§ 4002–4009.

Bellman, Richard. "Testimony of Mr. Richard Bellman, Attorney, U.S. Commission on Civil Rights." Hearing Before the United States Commission on Civil Rights, Hearing held in Cleveland, OH. Supt. of Documents. U.S. Government Printing Office, Washington, D.C., 1966.

Census of the Population, 1970. General Population Characteristics, New Hampshire.

Commission on Schools for the 21st Century. "A New Design for Education in Wisconsin." State of Wisconsin, December 1990.

Commission on the Quality of Education in the Metropolitan Milwaukee Public Schools. *Better Public Schools.* Final Report. Madison: State of Wisconsin, 1986.

Constitution of the State of Ohio, art. 6, sec. 2, 1851.

Constitution of the State of Louisiana, art. 8, sec. 1, 1974.

Constitution of the State of New Hampshire, art. 83, 1783.

Grogan, Thomas. "In the Matter of the Eligibility of Messmer High School for Participation in the Milwaukee Parental Choice Program." Madison: State of Wisconsin, 1993.

Grover, Herbert J. Superintendent of Public Instruction. Notice of School's Intent to Participate in the Milwaukee Parental Choice Program. State of Wisconsin, May 29, 1990.

Hawkings Hearings. Field Hearing on Parental Choice, Subcommittee on Elementary, Secondary, and Vocational Education of the Committee on Education and Labor, House of Representatives, 101st Congress, Second Session, Hearing held in Milwaukee, Wisconsin, November 16, 1990.

HB 1242, *Bulletin.* 109th General Assembly of the State of Ohio, 1971–72.

HB 1466, *Bulletin.* 110th General Assembly of the State of Ohio, 1973–74.

HB 41, *Bulletin.* 111th General Assembly of the State of Ohio, 1975–76.

HB 825, *Bulletin.* 119th General Assembly of the State of Ohio, 1991–92.

Jane and Lloyd Pettit Foundation. IRS Returns, 1988–1992.

Kava, Russ. "Informational Paper 29: Milwaukee Parental Choice Program." Madison: Wisconsin Legislative Fiscal Bureau, January 2007.

Legislative History of Assembly Bill 601. State of Wisconsin.

Legislative Fiscal Bureau. "School Integration (Chapter 220) Aid." State of Wisconsin, Madison, 1993.

Lynde and Harry Bradley Foundation. IRS Returns, 1988–1993.

Needles, Tom. Memo to Governor Voinovich. January 21, 1998. In *Zelman v. Simmons-Harris,* in Lodging by Amicus Curiae, Ohio Association for Public Education and Religious Liberty, in Support of Affirmance for Respondents, Nos. 00–001777, 00–1779.

Nusbaum, L. "Review of 'Ohio Citizen Attitudes Toward Tuition Tax Credits as an Education Reform.'" Division of Research and Communications. Ohio Department of Education, December 10, 1991.

Office of School Monitoring and Community Relations. *Fact Sheet.* In Author's possession. Cleveland, 1985.

Ohio Department of Education. "2009–2010 Ohio Community Schools Annual Report." Columbus: Author, 2010.

Ohio Rev. Code Ann. § 3317.06

Ohio Rev. Code Ann. § 3317.063

President's Panel on Nonpublic Education. *Nonpublic Education and the Public Good.* Washington, D.C.: Author, 1972.

Ritsche, Dan and Gary Watchke. "List of Bills Related to Providing State Financial Aid to nonpublic schools in Wisconsin." Legislative Reference Bureau, 1993.

Ritsche, Dan. "Milwaukee School Choice Voucher Program: An Update." Madison: Legislative Reference Bureau, Revised December 10, 1998.

State of Louisiana. *Acts of the Legislature.* Baton Rouge: Author, 1958.

The Cleveland Scholarship and Tutoring Program: A Chance to Choose Your Child's School." Ohio Department of Education, November 1995.

Thompson, Tommy G. Press release. April 27, 1990.

United States Senate Subcommittee on Education and Early Childhood Development, New Orleans, Louisiana. July 14, 2006.

Wisconsin Advisory Committee to the United States Commission on Civil Rights. "Impact of School Desegregation in Milwaukee Public Schools on Quality Education for Minorities: 15 Years Later." August 1992.

Wisconsin Constitution, Article IV, Section 18.

Wisconsin Constitution, Article X, Section 3.

Wisconsin Department of Public Instruction. *DPI Bulletin.* November, 1990 and August, 1991.

ELECTRONIC SOURCES

"About Claiborne Academy." http://claiborneacademy.org.

The American Presidency Project. *Public Papers of U.S. Presidents. Lyndon B. Johnson, 1963–4.* University of California, Santa Barbara. http://www.presidency.ucsb.edu/ws/.

Bolick, Clint. "Vouching for Children: Grinches are an Obstacle to Constructive Education Aid." *National Review Online,* October 4, 2005. http://www.nationalreview.com/articles/215596/vouching-children/clint-bolick.

Center for Education Reform. "National Charter School and Enrollment Statistics, 2010." http://www.edreform.com/_upload/CER_charter_numbers.pdf.

"Decade of Discontent: 1960–1970," Worthwhile Films; a Project Self Help and Awareness Production. Created, written and produced by Charles Taylor. Madison: Praxis Publications Inc., 1995. http://www.youtube.com/watch?v=EOE3G1ci-Rw.

"Desegregation and Governance." Cleveland Municipal School District News and Information. http://cmsdnet.net/community/desegregation.htm.

Foundation for Educational Choice. "School Choice Programs." http://www.edchoice.org/School-Choice.

Knabb, Richard D., Jamie R. Rhome, and Daniel P. Brown. "Tropical Cyclone Report, Hurricane Katrina: 23–30 August 2005." *National Hurricane Center.*

Last modified: August 10, 2006. http://www.nhc.noaa.gov/pdf/TCR-AL1 22005_Katrina.pdf.

Legislative Service Commission (Ohio), "Revenue History." http://www.lsc.state. oh.us/fiscal/revenuehistory/staterevenue128.htm.

Morris, Roger. "The Undertaker's Tally: Sharp Elbow's (Part 1): Sharp elbows." *Tomdispatch.com,* 2006. http://www.tomdispatch.com/index.mhtml?pid= 165669.

National School Boards Association, "Voucher Strategy Center." http://www.nsba. org/MainMenu/Advocacy/FederalLaws/SchoolVouchers.

Newman Since 1903, Isadore Newman School, http://www.newmanschool.org/.

Nixon, Richard M. "Second Inaugural Address of Richard Milhous Nixon." January 20, 1973. The Avalon Project, Yale Law School, Lillian Goldman Law Library. http://avalon.law.yale.edu/20th_century/nixon2.asp.

Ohio Department of Education. "Funding for Non-public Schools." www.ode. state.oh.us/GD/Templates/Pages/ODE/ODEPrimary.aspx?Page=2&TopicI D=990&TopicRelationID=1193.

Ohio Department of Education. "Table of School Options in Ohio." http://www. ode.state.oh.us.

Ohio School Funding, "Background Information." http://ohioschoolfunding.org.

"Republican Contract with America." 1994.

http://www.house.gov/house/Contract/CONTRACT.html.

SchoolChoiceWI.org. "A Timeline of the Milwaukee Parental Choice Program." http://www.schoolchoicewi.org/data/k12/timeline3.pdf.

U.S. Department of Education. "New Support for Families and Areas Affected by Hurricane Katrina." September 16, 2005. http://hurricanehelpforschools. gov/0916-factsheet.doc.

Walter J. Brown Media Archives and Peabody Awards Collection. Clip wsbn 44811, December 1960. http://crdl.usg.edu.

Wisconsin Department of Public Instruction. "MPCP Facts and Figures for 2010–2011." http://dpi.state.wi.us/sms/choice.html.

X, Malcolm. "The Ballot or the Bullet." Cleveland Ohio, April 3, 1964. http://www. edchange.org/multicultural/speeches/malcolm_x_ballot.html.

DISSERTATIONS AND UNPUBLISHED MANUSCRIPTS

Bodwell, Gregory B. "Grassroots, Inc.: A Sociopolitical History of the Cleveland School Voucher Battle, 1992–2002." PhD diss., Case Western Reserve University, 2006.

Caliguire, Arthur J. "A History of Cooperation between the Cleveland Public Schools and the Cleveland Catholic Diocesan Schools, 1966–1976." PhD diss., University of Akron, 1980.

Dahlk, William. "The Black Educational Reform Movement in Milwaukee, 1963–1975." Masters' thesis, University of Wisconsin-Milwaukee, 1990.

Fillion, Paul. "The State System of School Finance in New Hampshire, 1919–1982." Ph.D. dissertation, Vanderbilt University, 1983.

Fox, Michael A. "Education Reform that Makes a Difference for Children." Unpublished Manuscript. August 1, 1997.

Friedman, Milton. Letter to the Author, in Author's possession. November 21, 2005.

Friedman, Milton. Letter to Henry Levin. October 24, 1968.

Fuller, Howard. "The Impact of the Milwaukee Public School System's Desegregation Plan on Black Students and the Black Community (1976–1982)." Ph.D. dissertation, Marquette University, 1985.

Gutowski, James A. "Politics and Public Schools in Archbishop John Purcell's Ohio." Ph.D. dissertation, Cleveland State University, 2009.

Hodges, Mary Ann Wolf. "Moral Persuasion and Episcopal Fiat: The Racial Integration of Catholic Schools in the Archdiocese of St. Louis: 1944–1948. Ph.D. dissertation, St. Louis University, 2002.

Leahy, John H. "The Insurmountable Wall: A Study of the Attempts to Secure State Aid for Private School Tuition in Ohio in the 1930s. Ph.D. dissertation, Case Western Reserve University, 1988.

Mazzoni, Tim. "The Changing Politics of State Educational Policymaking: A Twenty-Year Perspective." Presentation, 1992 AERA Annual Meeting, San Francisco, California.

McCarrick, Earleen Mary. "Louisiana's Official Resistance to Desegregation." Ph.D. dissertation, Vanderbilt University, 1964.

Rauch, Dolores. "The Changing Status of Urban Catholic Parochial Schools: An Explanatory Model Illustrating Demand for Catholic Elementary Education in Milwaukee County." Ph.D. dissertation, University of Wisconsin-Milwaukee, 1971.

Saatcioglu, Argun. "Latent Conflict and Institutional Change: Silent Domination in the Rise of Discriminatory Organizational Forms in Public Education." Ph.D. dissertation, Case Western Reserve University, 2007.

BOOKS AND ARTICLES

Adams, Thomas. "NHEA Position on Vouchers Clarified." *New Hampshire Educator* 53 (October, 1973): 1–2.

Alves, Michael and Charles Willie. "Choice, Decentralization and Desegregation: The Boston 'Controlled Choice' Plan." *Choice and Control in American Education* 2. London: Falmer Press, 1990.

Ambrose, Stephen E. *Nixon: Volume Three, Ruin and Recovery, 1973–1990.* New York: Simon and Schuster, 1991.

Areen, Judith and Christopher Jencks. "Education Vouchers: A Proposal for Diversity and Choice." *Teachers College Record* 72 (February 1971): 327–335.

Armstrong, Philip, Andrew Glyn, and John Harrison. *Capitalism Since World War II.* London: Fontana Paperbacks, 1984.

Arrighi, Giovanni. *Adam Smith in Beijing: Lineages of the Twenty-First Century.* New York: Verso, 2007.

Astone, Nan M. and S. S. McLanahan. "Family Structure, Parental Practices and High School Completion." *American Sociological Review* 56 (1991): 309–320.

Bailey, Beth. "The Army and the Marketplace: Recruiting an All-volunteer Force." *Journal of American History* 94 (June 2007): 47–74.

Baker, George E. *The Life of William H. Seward with Selections from His Works.* New York: Redfield, 1855.

Banham, John. "Building a Stronger Partnership Between Business and Secondary Education." *British Journal of Educational Studies* 37, no. 1 (February 1989): 5–16.

Beadie, Nancy. "Education and the Creation of Capital; or, What I Have Learned From Following the Money." *History of Education Quarterly* 48 (February 2008): 1–29.

Beadie, Nancy. *Education and the Creation of Capital in the Early American Republic.* Cambridge, MA: Cambridge University Press, 2010.

Bell, Derrick. "The Case for a Separate Black School System." *Urban League Review* 11, no. 1&2 (1987–1988): 136–145.

Bell, Derrick. *Silent Covenants: Brown v. Board of Education and the Unfulfilled Hopes for Racial Reform.* New York Oxford University Press, 2004.

Benveniste, Luis, Martin Carnoy and Richard Rothstein. *All Else Equal: Are Public and Private Schools Different?* New York and London: RoutledgeFalmer, 2003.

Black, Gordon S. "The Lack of Confidence in Public Education in Wisconsin: A Survey of How 3,000 Wisconsin Residents View Public Education in Wisconsin." *Wisconsin Policy Institute Reports* 2, no. 4 (April 1989): 1–27.

Blum, Virgil C. *Freedom of Choice in Education.* New York: MacMillan, 1958.

Blum, Virgil C. *Quest for Religious Freedom.* Milwaukee: Catholic League for Religious and Civil Rights, 1984.

Brady, Tom P. *Black Monday.* Address to the Greenwood Chapter of the Sons of the American Revolution, Brookhaven, Mississippi, July 23, 1954.

Brennan, David L. *Victory for Kids: The Cleveland School Voucher Case.* Beverley Hills, CA: New Millennium Press, 2002.

Bringham, Richard and John Heywood. "Evaluating Wisconsin's Teachers: It can be done." *Wisconsin Policy Research Institute Reports* 2, no. 9 (December 1989).

Boardman J. D. and Samuel H. Field. "Spatial Mismatch and Race Differentials: Cleveland and Milwaukee, 1990." *Sociological Quarterly* 43 (2002): 237–255.

Bolick, Clint. "The Wisconsin Supreme Court's Decision on Educational Choice: A First-of-Its-Kind Victory for Children and Families." *Black Issues in Higher Education,* July 30, 1992, pp. 20, 25.

Bolick, Clint. *Voucher Wars: Waging the Legal Battle over School Choice.* Washington, D.C.: Cato Institute, 2003.

Bositis, David A. "The Politics of School Choice: African-Americans and Vouchers." In *Educational Freedom in Urban America: Brown v. Board after Half a*

Century, edited by David Salisbury and Casey Lartigue, Jr., pp. 177–204. Washington, D.C.: Cato Institute, 2004.

Brighouse, Harry. *School Choice and Social Justice.* Oxford: Oxford University Press, 2000.

Brinkley, Alan. *The End of Reform: New Deal Liberalism in Recession and War.* New York: Vintage Books, 1996.

Brinkley, Alan. "The New Deal and the Idea of the State." In *The Rise and Fall of the New Deal Order,* edited by Steve Fraser and Gary Gerstle, pp. 85–121. Princeton: Princeton University Press, 1989.

Brinkley, Alan. "The Problem of American Conservatism." *American Historical Review* (April 1994): 409–429.

Bryk, Anthony S., Valerie E. Lee and Peter B. Holland. *Catholic Schools and the Common Good.* Cambridge, MA: Harvard University Press, 1993.

Campbell, Thomas F. "Cleveland: The Struggle for Stability." In *Snowbelt Cities,* edited by Richard M Bernard, pp. 109–136. Bloomington: Indiana University Press, 1990.

Carl, Jim. "Free Marketeers, Policy Wonks, and Yankee Democracy: School Vouchers in New Hampshire, 1973–1976." *Harvard Educational Review* 78, no. 4 (Winter 2008): 589–614.

Carl, Jim. "Harold Washington and Chicago's Schools Between Civil Rights and the Decline of the New Deal Consensus, 1955–1987." *History of Education Quarterly* 41, no. 3 (Fall 2001): 311–343.

Carl, Jim. "Unusual Allies: Elite and Grassroots Origins of Parental Choice in Milwaukee." *Teachers College Record* 98 (Winter 1996): pp. 266–285.

Carnoy, Martin. *Faded Dreams: The Politics and Economics of Race in America.* Cambridge: Cambridge University Press, 1994.

Center for the Study of Public Policy. *Education Vouchers: A Report on Financing Elementary Education by Grants to Parents.* Cambridge, MA: Author, 1970.

Chilton, R. and S. K. Datesman. "Gender, Race, and Crime: An Analysis of Urban Trends, 1960–1980." *Gender and Society* 1 (1987): 152–71.

Chow, J. and C. Coulton. "Was There a Social Transformation of Urban Neighborhoods in the 1980s? A Decade of Worsening Social Conditions in Cleveland, OH." *Urban Studies* 35 (1998): 1359–1375

Chubb, John and Terry Moe. "Educational Choice: Answers to the Most Frequently Asked Questions about Mediocrity in American Education and What Can Be Done about It." *Wisconsin Policy Research Institute Reports* 2, no. 3 (March 1989).

Chubb, John and Terry Moe. *Politics, Markets, and America's Schools.* Washington, D.C.: Brookings Institution, 1990.

Cibulka, James. "Restructuring Wisconsin's Educational System: How Effective is the Department of Public Instruction?" *Wisconsin Policy Research Institute Reports* 4, no. 4 (September 1991).

Clark, Kenneth B. "Alternative Public School Systems." In *Education Vouchers: From Theory to Alum Rock,* edited by James A. Mecklenburger and Richard W. Hostrop, pp. 10–23. Homewood, IL: ETC Publications, 1972.Cleveland Public Schools. *Vision 21: An Action Plan for the 21st Century.* Cleveland: Author, 1993.

Clotfelter, Charles T. *After* Brown: *The Rise and Retreat of School Desegregation.* Princeton: Princeton University Press, 2004.

Clune, William and John Witte. *Choice and Control in American Education.* Vol. 2. New York: Falmer Press, 1990.

Coleman, James S. et al. *Equality of Educational Opportunity.* Washington, D.C.: Department of Health, Education and Welfare, 1966.

Conant, James B. *Slums and Suburbs: A Commentary on Schools in Metropolitan Areas.* New York: McGraw-Hill, 1961.

Conway, Paul F., Joanne E. Goodell and Jim Carl. "Educational Reform in the USA: Politics, Purposes, and Processes." In *Education in Transition: International Perspectives on the Politics and Processes of Change,* edited by Rosarii Griffin, pp. 83–109. Oxford: Symposium Books, 2002.

Coons, John and Stephen Sugarman. "Family Choice in Education: A Model State System for Vouchers." *California Law Review* 321 (1971): 321–438.

Crain, Robert and Morton Inger. "School Desegregation in New Orleans: A Comparative Study of the Failure of Social Control." Chicago: National Opinion Research Center, 1966.

Curtin, Michael F. *Ohio Politics Almanac.* 2nd ed. Kent, OH: Kent State University Press, 2006.

Devore, Donald and Joseph Logsdon. *Crescent City Schools: Public Education in New Orleans, 1841–1991.* Lafayette: University of Southwestern Louisiana Press, 1991.

Didion, Joan. "Cheney: The Fatal Touch." *New York Review of Books,* October 5, 2006.

Donaldson, Gordon. *Education Vouchers in New Hampshire: An Attempt at Free Market Educational Reform.* Newton, MA: C. M. Leinwand, 1977.

Dougherty, Jack. *More Than One Struggle: The Evolution of Black School Reform in Milwaukee.* Chapel Hill: University of North Carolina Press, 2004.

Dudziak, Mary L. *Cold War Civil Rights: Race and the Image of American Democracy.* Princeton: Princeton University Press, 2002.

Ebenstein, Lanny. *Milton Friedman: A Biography.* New York: Palgrave MacMillan, 2007.

Ehrlichman, John. *Witness to Power.* New York: Simon and Schuster, 1982.

Eisinger, Peter. *Patterns of Interracial Politics.* New York: Academic Press, 1976.

Fairclough, Adam. *Race and Democracy: The Civil Rights Struggle in Louisiana, 1915–1972.* Athens: University of Georgia Press, 1997.

Feinberg, Lawrence. "Tax Credit on Tuition Is Favored by Shriver." *Washington Post,* September 7, 1972.

Fischer, Michael. "Fiscal Accountability in Milwaukee: Where does the Money Go?" *Wisconsin Policy Research Institute Reports* 3, no. 4 (September 1990).

Floden Robert E., ed. "Policy Tools for Improving Education." *Review of Research in Education* 27. Washington, D.C.: American Educational Research Association, 2003.

Foundation Reporter. Washington, D.C.: Taft Group, 1994.

Fraser, James W. *Between Church and State: Religion and Public Education in a Multicultural America.* New York: St. Martin's Griffin, 1999.

Fraser, Steve. *Every Man a Speculator: A History of Wall Street in American Life.* New York: HarperCollins, 2005.

Friedman, Milton. *Bright Promises Dismal Performance.* Edited by William R. Allen. Sun Lakes, AZ: Thomas Horton and Daughters, 1983.

Friedman, Milton. *Capitalism and Freedom.* Chicago: University of Chicago Press, 1962.

Friedman, Milton. *Free to Choose.* New York: Harcourt Brace Jovanovich, 1979.

Friedman, Milton. "The Role of Government in Education." In *Economics and the Public Interest,* edited by Robert A. Solo, pp. 123–144. New Brunswick: Rutgers University Press, 1955.

Friedman, Milton. "Why Not a Volunteer Army?" In *The Draft: A Handbook of Facts and Alternatives,* edited by Sol Tax, pp. 200–207.Chicago: University of Chicago Press, 1967.

Friedman, Milton and Rose D. Friedman. *Two Lucky People: Memoirs.* Chicago: University of Chicago Press, 1998.

Gabel, Richard J. *Public Funds for Church and Private Schools.* Washington, D.C.: The Catholic University of America, 1937.

George, Gary and Walter Farrell. "School Choice and African American Students: A Legislative View." *Journal of Negro Education* 59, no. 4 (1990): 521–525.

Gerstle, Gary. *American Crucible: Race and Nation in the Twentieth Century.* Princeton: Princeton University Press, 2001.

Gilbert, James. *A Cycle of Outrage: America's Reaction to the Juvenile Delinquent in the 1950s.* New York: Oxford University Press, 1988.

Goldfield, Michael. *The Color of Politics: Race and the Mainsprings of American Politics.* New York: New Press, 1997.

Goldin, Claudia and Lawrence F. Katz. *The Race Between Education and Technology.* Cambridge, MA: Belknap Press of Harvard University Press, 2008.

Goldwater, Barry. *The Conscience of a Conservative.* New York: MacFadden-Bartell, 1961.

Green, Wanda Jean. *And They Called It Public School Education: The Cleveland Public Schools.* Cleveland: Academy for a Competitive Edge, 2000.

Gurda, John. *The Bradley Legacy: Lynde and Harry Bradley; Their Company, and Their Foundation.* Milwaukee: Bradley Foundation, 1992.

Gunther, John. *Inside U.S.A.* New York: Harper and Row, 1951.

Hanauer, Amy. "Cleveland School Vouchers: Where the Students Go." Cleveland: Policy Matters Ohio, January 2002.

Haraven, Tamara and Randolph Langenback. *Amoskeag: Life and Work in an American Factory City.* New York: Pantheon Books, 1978.

Harris, Ian. "Criteria for Evaluating School Desegregation in Milwaukee." *Journal of Negro Education* 52 (1983):423–435.

Harvey, David. *The New Imperialism.* New York: Oxford University Press, 2003.

Havinghurst, Robert J. "The Unknown Good: Education Vouchers." In *Education Vouchers: From Theory to Alum Rock,* edited by James A. Mecklenburger and Richard W. Hostrop, pp. 48–50. Homewood, IL: ETC Publications, 1972.

Hayek, Friedrich. *The Road to Serfdom.* Chicago: University of Chicago Press, 1944.

Henderson, William. "Demography and Desegregation in the Cleveland Public Schools: Toward a Comprehensive Theory of Educational Failure and Success." *Review of Law & Social Change* 26, no. 4 (February 2002): 457–568.

Henig, Jeffrey R. *Spin Cycle: How Research is Used in Policy Debates: The Case of Charter Schools.* New York: Russell Sage Foundation, 2008.

Herberg, Will. *Protestant-Catholic-Jew.* New York: Doubleday, 1955.

Herrington, Carolyn and Frances Fowler. "Rethinking the Role of States and Educational Governance." In *American Educational Governance on Trial: Change and Challenges,* edited by William Lowe Boyd and Deborah Miretzky, pp. 271–290. Chicago: University of Chicago Press, 2003.

Hirschman, Albert O. *Exit, Voice, and Loyalty: Responses to Decline in Firms, Organizations, and States.* Cambridge: Harvard University Press, 1970.

Hochschild, Jennifer and Nathan Scovronick. *The American Dream and the Public Schools.* Oxford: Oxford University Press, 2003.

Ignatiev, Noel. *How the Irish Became White.* New York: Routledge, 1995.

Inger, Morton. *Politics and Reality in an American City: The New Orleans School Crisis of 1960.* New York: Center for Urban Education, 1969.

Jacoway, Elizabeth. *Turn Away Thy Son: Little Rock, the Crisis that Shocked the Nation.* New York: Free Press, 2007.

Jeansonne, Glen. "Segregation Forever." Edited by Charles Vincent. *The Louisiana Purchase Bicentennial Series in Louisiana History V. XI, The African American Experience in Louisiana Part C: From Jim Crow to Civil Rights.* Baton Rouge: Louisiana State University Press, 2000.

Jeansonne, Glen. *Leander Perez: Boss of the Delta.* Baton Rouge: Louisiana State University Press, 1977.

Jefferson, Thomas. "Notes on the State of Virginia." In *Thomas Jefferson: Writings,* edited by Merrill D. Peterson, pp. 123–326. New York: Library of America, 1984 [1787].

Jencks, Christopher. "Is the Public School Obsolete?" *The Public Interest* 2 (1966): 18–27.

Jencks, Christopher. "Who Should Control Public Education?" *Dissent* 13 (1966): 161–162.

Jencks, Christopher et al. *Inequality: A Reassessment of the Effect of Family and Schooling in America.* New York: Harper Colophon Books, 1973.

Jenkins, Evan. "Stand by for Vouchers." *Compact 7* (November/December 1973): 7–9.

Jones, Patrick D. *The Selma of the North: The Civil Rights Insurgency in Milwaukee.* Cambridge: Harvard University Press, 2009.

Judt, Tony. *Ill Fares the Land.* New York: Penguin Press, 2010.

Justice, Benjamin. *The War That Wasn't: Religious Conflict and Compromise in the Common Schools of New York State.* Albany: State University of New York Press, 2009.

Justice, Benjamin. "Thomas Nast and the Public Schools of the 1870s." *History of Education Quarterly* 45, no. 2 (Summer 2005): 171–206.

Kaestle, Carl. "Federal Education Policy and the Changing National Polity for Education, 1957–2007." In *To Educate a Nation: Federal and National Strategies of School Reform,* edited by Carl Kaestle and Alyssa Lodewick, pp. 17–40. Lawrence: University Press of Kansas, 2007.

Kahlenberg, Richard D. *Tough Liberal: Albert Shanker and the Battles over Schools, Unions, Race, and Democracy.* New York: Columbia University Press, 2007.

Keating, W. Dennis. *The Suburban Racial Dilemma.* Philadelphia: Temple University Press, 1994.

Kolko, Gabriel. *The Triumph of Conservatism.* New York: Free Press, 1963.

Kozol, Jonathan. *Free Schools.* Boston: Houghton Mifflin, 1972.

Kruse, Kevin M. *White Flight: Atlanta and the Making of Modern Conservatism.* Princeton: Princeton University Press, 2005.

La Noue, George R., ed. *Educational Vouchers: Concepts and Controversies.* New York: Teachers College Press, 1972.

Laats, Adam. "Forging a Fundamentalist 'One Best System': Struggles over Curriculum and Educational Philosophy for Christian Day Schools, 1970–1989." *History of Education Quarterly* 50, no. 1 (February 2010): 55–83.

Labaree, David. *How to Succeed in School without Really Learning: The Credentials Race in American Education.* New Haven: Yale University Press, 1997.

Lagemann, Ellen Condliffe. *The Politics of Knowledge: The Carnegie Corporation, Philanthropy, and Public Policy.* Middleton, CT: Wesleyan University Press, 1989.

Lambert, S., "After All." *Today's Education* 60 (January 1971): 64.

Landphair, Juliette. "'The Forgotten People of New Orleans': Community, Vulnerability, and the Lower Ninth Ward." *Journal of American History* 94, no. 3 (December 2007): 837–845.

Lassiter, Matthew and Andrew Lewis. *The Moderates' Dilemma: Massive Resistance to School Desegregation in Virginia.* Charlottesville: University Press of Virginia, 1998.

Leflar, Robert A. and Wylie H. Davis. "Segregation in the Public Schools—1953." *Harvard Law Review* 67 (1954): 404–407.

Levin, Henry. "The Failure of the Public Schools and the Free Market Remedy." *Urban Review* 2 (June 1968): 32–37.

Levine, Robert. *The Poor Ye Need Not Have With You: Lessons from the War on Poverty.* Cambridge: MIT Press, 1970.

Lukas, J. Anthony. *Night-mare: The Underside of the Nixon Years.* Athens: Ohio University Press, 1999.

Marable, Manning. *Race, Reform, and Rebellion: The Second Reconstruction in Black America.* Jackson: University Press of Mississippi, 1991.

McAndrews, Lawrence. *The Era of Education: The Presidents and the Schools, 1965–2001.* Urbana: University of Illinois Press, 2006.

McAffe, Ward M. *Religion, Race, and Reconstruction: The Public School in the Politics of the 1970s.* Albany: State University of New York Press, 1998.

McLoyd, V. C., T. E. Jayaratne, R. Ceballo and J. Borquez. "Unemployment and Work Interruption among African American Single Mothers: Effects on

Parenting and Adolescent Socioemotional Functioning." *Child Development* 65 (1994): 562–589.

McGirr, Lisa. *Suburban Warriors: The Origins of the New American Right.* Princeton: Princeton University Press, 2001.

McGreevy, John T. *Catholicism and American Freedom: A History.* New York: W. W. Norton, 2003.

McGuinn, Patrick J. *No Child Left Behind and the Transformation of Federal Education Policy, 1965–2005.* Lawrence: University Press of Kansas, 2006.

McIntyre, Thomas J. *The Fear Brokers.* Boston: Beacon Press, 1979.

McMillan, Neil R. *The Citizens' Council: Organized Resistance to the Second Reconstruction, 1954–1964.* Champaign: University of Illinois Press, 1994.

Menge, John. "The Evaluation of the New Hampshire Plan: An Early Voucher System." In *Privatizing Education and Educational Choice: Concepts, Plans, and Experiences,* edited by Simon Hakim, Paul Seidenstat, and Gary W. Bowman, pp. 163–182. Westport, CT: Praeger Press, 1994.

Micklethwait, John and Adrian Wooldridge. *The Right Nation: Conservative Power in America* New York: Penguin Press, 2004.

Miggins, Edward M. "Between Spires and Stacks: The People and Neighborhoods of Cleveland." In *Cleveland: a Metropolitan Reader,* edited by N. Krumholz, W. D. Keating, and D.C. Perry, pp. 179–201. Kent, OH: Kent State University Press, 1995.

Miggins, Edward M. "Cleveland Public Schools." In *The Encyclopedia of Cleveland History,* edited by David Van Tassel and John Grabowski, pp. 278–283. Bloomington: Indiana University Press, 1996.

Mills, John Stuart. *On Liberty.* New York: Longman, 2006 [1859].

Miner, Barbara. "The Bradley Foundation and Milwaukee." *Rethinking Schools* 8, no. 3 (Spring 1994): 18.

Miner, Barbara. "The Power and the Money: Bradley Foundation Bankrolls Conservative Agenda." *Rethinking Schools* 8, no. 3 (Spring 1994): 1, 16–21.

Mitchell, George. "An Evaluation of State-financed School Integration in Metropolitan Milwaukee." *Wisconsin Policy Research Institute Reports* 2, no. 5 (June 1989).

Mitchell, George. "The Milwaukee Parental Choice Program." *Wisconsin Policy Research Institute Reports* 5, no. 5 (March 1992).

Mitchell, George. "The Rising Costs of the 'Chapter 220' Program in Wisconsin." *Wisconsin Policy Research Institute Reports* 1, no. 4 (October 1988).

Mitchell, Susan. "Why MPS Doesn't Work: Barriers to Reform in the Milwaukee Public Schools." *Wisconsin Policy Research Institute Reports* 7, no. 1 (January 1994).

Modlinski, Jules and Esther Zaret. *The Federation of Independent Community Schools: An Alternative Urban School System.* Milwaukee, WI, April 1970.

Monti, Daniel J. *A Semblance of Justice: St Louis School Desegregation and Order in Urban America.* Columbia: University of Missouri Press, 1985.

Moore, Leonard M. *Carl B. Stokes and the Rise of Black Political Power.* Urbana: University of Illinois Press, 2002.

Muller, Mary Lee. "New Orleans Public School Desegregation." In *The African American Experience in Louisiana,* edited by Charles Vincent, pp. 336–351. Lafayette, LA: Center for Louisiana Studies, University of Southwestern Louisiana, 2000.

Murrell, Peter Jr. "North Division Plan: 'Our Children Deserve Better.'" *Rethinking Schools* 2, no. 2 (December–January 1988): 1–2, 4, 15.

Nadeau, Jacklyn T. *Berlin.* Charleston, SC: Arcadia, 2008.

National Commission on Excellence in Education. *A Nation at Risk.* Washington, D.C.: U.S. Government Printing Office, 1983.

National Education Association, *Addresses and Proceedings,* 109, Washington, D.C.: National Education Association Publications, June 26–July 2, 1971.

Nelson, William E. Jr. "Cleveland: Evolution of Black Political Power." In *Cleveland: A Metropolitan Reader,* edited by W. Dennis Keating, Norman Krumholz, and David C. Perry, pp. 283–299. Kent, OH: Kent State University Press, 1995.

Nixon, Richard M. *RN: The Memoirs of Richard Nixon.* New York: Grosset & Dunlap, 1978.

Nord, Warren A. *Religion and American Education: Rethinking a National Dilemma.* Chapel Hill: University of North Carolina Press, 1995.

O'Brien, Molly Townes. "Private School Tuition Vouchers and the Realities of Racial Politics." *Tennessee Law Review* 64 (Winter 1997): 359–407.

Odenkirk, James E. *Frank J. Lausche: Ohio's Great Political Maverick.* Wilmington, OH: Orange Frazer Press, 2005.

Offe, Claus. *Contradictions of the Welfare State.* London: Hutchinson, 1984.

Paine, Thomas. *Rights of Man.* New York: Penguin Books, 1984.

Patterson, James T. *Brown v. Board of Education: A Civil Rights Milestone and Its Troubled* Legacy. Oxford: Oxford University Press, 2001.

Patterson, James T. *Grand Expectations: the United States, 1945–1974.* New York: Oxford University Press, 1996.

Peace, Nancy. "Labor-Management Cooperation on Teaching and Learning in the Cleveland Municipal School District." Cambridge, MA: The Program on Negotiation at the Harvard Law School and the MIT Institute for Work and Employment relations, January 9, 2002.

Perlstein, Rick. *Nixonland: The Rise of a President and the Fracturing of America.* New York: Scribner, 2008.

Phillips-Fein, Kim. *Invisible Hands: The Making of the Conservative Movement from the New Deal to Reagan.* New York: W. W. Norton, 2009.

Phillips, Kimberly L. *AlabamaNorth: African American Migrants, Community, and Working-Class Activism in Cleveland, 1915–1945.* Urbana: University of Illinois Press, 1999.

Pilla, Bishop Anthony M. "The Church in the City." Cleveland: Diocese of Cleveland, 1993.

Pollack, Stephen J. "Parochiad: End of the Line?" *Today's Education* 62 (November–December 1973): 77–79, 96.

Ravitch, Diane. *The Troubled Crusade.* New York: Basic Books, 1983.

Rawls, John. *A Theory of Justice*. Cambridge: Belknap Press of Harvard University Press, 2005 [1971].

Rich, Wilbur and Stephanie Chambers. "Cleveland: Takeovers and Makeovers are Not the Same." In *Mayors in the Middle: Politics, Race, and Mayoral Control of Urban Schools*, edited by Jeffrey Henig and Wilbur Rich, pp. 159–190. Princeton: Princeton University Press, 2004.

Rieder, Jonathan. "The Rise of the 'Silent Majority.'" In *The Rise and Fall of the New Deal Order*, edited by Steve Fraser and Gary Gerstle, pp. 243–268. Princeton: Princeton University Press, 1989.

Robinson, Lewis G. *The Making of a Man: Autobiography*. Cleveland: Green, 1970.

Rosenthal, Jack. "O.E.O. to Test Plan to Aid Education." *New York Times*, May 15, 1970.

Rothstein, Richard. *Class and Schools: Using Social, Economic, and Educational Reform to Close the Black-White Achievement Gap*. New York: Teachers College Press, 2004.

Saatcioglu, Argun and Jim Carl. "The Discursive Turn in School Desegregation— National Patterns and a Case Analysis of Cleveland, 1973–1998." *Social Science History* 35 (Spring 2011): 59–108.

Saltman, Kenneth J. *The Edison Schools: Corporate Schooling and the Assault on Public Education*. New York: Routledge, 2005.

Schiller, Zack. "Cleveland School Vouchers: Where the Students Come From." Cleveland: Policy Matters Ohio, September, 2001.

Sizer, Theodore R. "The Case for a Free Market." In *Education Vouchers: From Theory to Alum Rock*, edited by James A. Mecklenburger and Richard W. Hostrop, pp. 24–32. Homewood, IL: ETC Publications, 1972.

Smith, James. *The Idea Brokers: Think Tanks and the Rise of the New Policy Elite*. New York: Free Press, 1991.

Sokol, Jason. *There Goes My Everything: White Southerners in the Age of Civil Rights, 1945–1975*. New York: Alfred A. Knopf, 2006.

Sowell, Thomas. *Black Education: Myths and Tragedies*. New York: David McKay, 1972.

Stanley, Justin. "President's Page." *American Bar Association Journal* 62 (1976).

Steinbeck, John. *Travels with Charley and Later Novels, 1947–1962*. New York: Library of America, 2007.

Stockman, David A. *The Triumph of Politics: How the Reagan Revolution Failed*. New York: Harper and Row, 1986.

Stolee, Michael. "The Milwaukee Desegregation Case." In *Seeds of Crisis*, edited by John Rury and Frank Cassell, pp. 229–268. Madison: University of Wisconsin Press, 1993.

Street, Sal. "The Annihilation: New Hampshire Teachers Kill State Voucher Plan." *Educator* 54 (June 1974): 1–2.

Thomson, Procter. "Educational News and Editorial Comments." *The School Review* 63 (April 1955): 189–200.

Thurow, Lester C. *The Future of Capitalism: How Today's Economic Forces Shape Tomorrow's World*. New York: William Morrow., 1996.

Toobin, Jeffrey. *The Nine: Inside the Secret World of the Supreme Court*. New York: Doubleday, 2007.

Tyack, David. *Seeking Common Ground: Public Schools in a Diverse Society*. Cambridge: Harvard University Press, 2003.

Tyack, David. *The One Best System: A History of American Urban Education*. Cambridge: Harvard University Press, 1974.

Urban Community School. Annual Report, 2003–2004.

Wang F. and W. W. Minor. "Where the jobs are: Employment access and crime patterns in Cleveland." *Annals of the Association of American Geographers* 92 (2002): 435–450.

Weaver, Richard. *Ideas Have Consequences*. Chicago: University of Chicago Press, 1948.

Welsh, James. "The New Hampshire Voucher Caper." *Educational Researcher* 2 (July 1973).

Weinstein, James. *The Corporate Ideal in the Liberal State*. Boston: Beacon Press, 1968.

Wieder, Alan. *Race and Education: Narrative Essays, Oral Histories, and Documentary Evidence*. New York: Peter Lang, 1997.

Wieder, Alan. "The New Orleans School Crisis of 1960: Causes and Consequences." *Pylon* 48, no. 2 (1987): 124.

Wilentz, Sean. *The Age of Reagan: A History, 1974–2008*. New York: Harper, 2008.

Wilson, William Julius. *When Work Disappears: The World of the New Urban Poor*. New York: Vintage Books, 1996.

Witte, John F. *The Market Approach to Education: An Analysis of America's First Voucher System*. Princeton: Princeton University Press, 2000.

Witte, John F. "The Milwaukee Voucher Experiment." In *Urban Education in the United States: A Historical Reader*, edited by John L. Rury, pp. 309–331. New York: Palgrave Macmillan, 2005.

Wong, Kenneth. *City Choices: Education and Housing*. Albany: SUNY Press, 1990.

Wye, Christopher. "At the Leading Edge: The Movement for Black Civil Rights in Cleveland, 1830–1969." In *Cleveland: A Tradition of Reform*, edited by David Van Tassel and John Graboswki, pp. 113–135. Kent, OH: Kent State University Press, 1996.

Zimmerman, Jonathan. *Whose America? Culture Wars in the Public Schools*. Cambridge: Harvard University Press, 2002.

INDEX

About the Author

JIM CARL is an associate professor of foundations of education at Cleveland State University, where he chairs the Department of Curriculum and Foundations.